Frederick Soddy

WEALTH, VIRTUAL WEALTH and DEBT

THE SOLUTION OF THE ECONOMIC PARADOX

Frederick Soddy
(1877–1956)

English chemist and recipient
of the 1921 Nobel Prize for Chemistry

Wealth, Virtual Wealth and Debt

the solution of the economic paradox

First edition, London: George Allen & Unwin, 1926.

ISBN: 978-1-913890-53-7

Published by
Omnia Veritas Ltd

www.omnia-veritas.com

DEDICATED TO ARTHUR KITSON

The British Pioneer of the New Economics,
To Whose Writings the Author Owes
His Initial Interest in the Fascinating
Problems of Wealth
and Currency

“That which seems to be wealth may in verity
be only the gilded index of far-reaching ruin; a
wrecker’s handful of coin gleaned from the beach
to which he has beguiled an argosy; a camp-follower’s
bundle of rags unwrapped from the
breasts of goodly soldiers dead; the purchase-pieces
of potter’s fields, wherein shall be buried
together the citizen and the stranger.”

JOHN RUSKIN, *Unto this Last*, 1862.

Foreword to the American nation

The second edition of this book owes its appearance to the American nation and to the interest they have taken in Technocracy. The author expresses his grateful thanks to them in general, and to the American publishers of the first edition in particular, for having brought his work so opportunely to notice at the present crisis of the world's affairs. Had Thorstein Veblen lived but a little longer he also would no doubt have felt the joy of living in this present age. For in what earlier period of history would truths so upsetting and so contrary to the established order have had a chance of impartial examination until those originating and those offended by them were all 'safely dead'?

Since the British edition appeared the financial system has undergone in America another of those periodic collapses which are the inevitable as they are now the most conspicuous feature of modern so-called banking. The choice is now actually before the American nation whether to make this kind of "banking" safe for the banker, according to the strictest canons of British, Continental and International systems, or safe for the American nation.

The two things are not the same thing, as is so easily assumed by the banking interests, but are in fact exact opposites. The only way banking to-day can be made safe both for the banker and the nation is for the nation to be the banker. The state of Europe at the present time, and of its once proud nations reduced severally to internal chaos and many to despair, is eloquent of the rule of the banker. Here, what is dangerous to the banker is considered altogether too dangerous for the nation to be allowed even to discuss, and the public are most carefully and elaborately shielded from any real knowledge of the preposterous humbug which it was one of the objects of this book to elucidate.

America, almost alone among the nations now, has any freedom of choice of its rulers and the world looks to her as its last hope of destroying what has become easily the most powerful tyranny and the most universal conspiracy against the economic freedom of individuals and the autonomy of nations the world has yet known.

We are always being told, and the Technocrats have already been told, that plain speaking is calculated to destroy the public's confidence which is so necessary to the banking system 'just when it is beginning to be restored.' It may be doubted whether any amount of plain speaking could effect more in this direction than the banking system has already done for itself. Admittedly a private banking and money-minting system cannot function without the public's gullibility. Even in that it has now surely "touched bottom with a bump and the only direction it can go is up." Let us hope it will "go up" for good. As for the public's confidence, what better calculated to restore it than to put behind a national system the whole wealth and credit of the nation. What a change that would be from the *reputation* for integrity and bottomless affluence which is the private banker's whole stock-in-trade. The rest he derives from the public without even requiring the bark of a mulberry tree as Kubla Khan did.

Modern science can unravel secrets vastly more intricate and well concealed than that of a modern money system, and when unravelled they do not need more than ordinary common-sense to see through. The simple question which the scientist asks about the mysterious appearances and disappearances of anything–"Where does it come from and where does it go to?" – suffice whether we deal with matter, energy or money. However voluminous the writings of those who have essayed to teach the public the mysteries of money, these are the questions that are *not* asked and the inference is that the orthodox money experts either cannot or dare not answer them.

The public, however, need not feel any alarm that a scientific money system in place of the present relic of barbarism would occasion them any interference in their business and domestic affairs. It would mean that they then would have the system most of them now believe they now have. Just as the general public do not know or believe now that irresponsible private mints are now creating and destroying money arbitrarily at the rate of thousands of millions of dollars many times a year, they would not be at all inconvenienced in any legitimate social activity if the quantity of money and the price-level stayed put. But they would be saved a vast toll of secret and unsuspected pocket-picking. And anti-social speculation with their money without their knowledge.

All the difficulties and objections which those living on the private issue of money raise to a national system are in fact those that would disappear with the present system. The industrialist and agriculturalist are its dupes not its beneficiaries. The only defence ever urged in public of this secret minting of money which is called banking, is that it enables new men and enterprises to be financed, existing businesses to be expanded and agriculture to be tided over a period of bad years at the expense of and without the knowledge of the community, and that this would not be possible except for the private banking system. The defence is utterly absurd. In fact under a national system this would be the natural and normal result without social injustice rather than an unauthorised private tax on the body of citizens for the immediate benefit and ultimate ruin of a specially favoured few.

For it must be remembered that the new men so financed, the existing businesses so expanded and the hard hit agriculturalists so "assisted" *do now actually pay interest for the loans they are supposed to receive*, just as though they were real loans instead of a new creation of money at the expense of the rest of the community. There is not the slightest reason why they should not get what they are supposed to pay for. There may have been a difficulty in byegone times when the only money was real gold and silver. But it stands to reason that if the nation issued all the money required just as fast as it could be issued without increasing the price-level, – and that is just as fast as there were goods and services to exchange for it, – there would be an abundance of money instead of a scarcity, to lend and borrow as well as to spend and invest. This is the natural consequence of a scientific age in which there never would be any fear of shortage of wealth to distribute, if the money system did its proper part in distributing it. That is the only real issue – Are people artificially to be kept poor by the money system or allowed naturally to prosper?

Thorstein Veblen, whose 1921 book "The Engineers and the Price System" has only become known to the author since the appearance of the second British edition of this book, adumbrated a Soviet of Technicians, which is believed to be one of the sources of the doctrines of the Technocrats. Its irony, to-day at least, needs no accentuation. It is a satire for all time on this age, great only in its science and science the hired-man!

But as in his other, and hitherto more widely known, works (and the criticism might equally well be applied to all the "red" sociological and political literature of Socialism, Communism and Marxism) he never probed into the physical underlying reasons for the inversion which has overtaken Capitalism – starting out to rebuild the world with the inanimate power, of which human "sweat of the brow" is merely an insignificant bye-product, and ending his turning that power to the destruction of what it has created. His "Vested Interests," the growing sabotage of competitive industry by "Captains of Industry and Finance," and "Elder Statesmen" are personified expressions of deep underlying ignorance of physical necessities his analysis stops short of. One has in this book, as in the rest of the revolutionary literature, simply to take it for granted that capitalists, big-business men and financiers, – down logically to the humblest individual of the investing public trying to "save" in a world in which wealth rots, – are all inhuman devils by nature and of necessity, and then everything else follows from that as the night the day.

This criticism may seem odd coming from the author as he has been himself accused – and by no less a person than by Mr. H. G. Wells – of assuming the same about the banking hierarchy. In any case, looked at either way, it is a delightful example of the *argumentum ad hominen* which has been translated as "No case! Abuse the plaintiff's attorney!" However a word more in explanation of the apparent inhumanity of scientific criticism may not be out of place.

The scientific attitude with regard to these questions differs entirely from the sociological, as it is not in the least concerned with motives, intentions or protestations but only with consequences. Reform to-day literally has to hack its way through an interminable jungle of wordy and irrelevant controversies before it can come out into the daylight.

Those who want to understand how a conjurer performs his tricks should take the advice of one conjurer to another, and watch *the other hand*, not the one to which the attention of the audience is being so volubly and persuasively directed. But as regards the scientifically trained mind, it is mercifully deaf. It is not so much that it disbelieves in all the interminable protestations of high-minded and altruistic social motives and intentions of Scotsmen, Quakers, Jews, Christians and who not, as that it simply does not hear them, so intent is it on how the mechanism *works*.

The mechanism of Nature has us all still in its grip, as it has had from the days of the first man though it has taken humanity a very long time to disentangle the mechanism from the highly picturesque and melodramatic personifications man has invented in explanation of his plight. The upholders and detractors of Capitalism alike are still envisaging it in the thoroughly old-fashioned human guise of god and demon, but in this book angels and devils give place to the underlying mechanism. The one and only way to control a mechanism is, not by edicts and legislation, but by understanding it. Science has started civilisation on a new road in which the old economic terms of wealth and debt, capital, labour, money and the like have assumed new meanings, and before we start political and sociological controversies it is as well to know that we are all speaking the same language.

FREDERICK SODDY.

Oxford.

March 11th 1933.

Preface to the second edition

The almost instantaneous rise to world prominence of the new American doctrine of social and industrial salvation known as Technocracy has resulted in this book, which first appeared in 1926, going suddenly out of print. A new edition has been peremptorily demanded, and to meet it as expeditiously as possible, the original has been reproduced intact, save for minor proof-corrections, with a prefatory addition, explaining its relation to Technocracy, as the author understands it, and to other cognate schools of thought. The opportunity has also been taken of developing further some points and features, for the benefit both of the new reader and of those who have already read the first edition, in accordance with experience gained from numerous lectures and discussions on the subject. One particular question dealt with last, the relation of the author's Virtual Wealth Theory of Money to the older Quantity Theory of Money, with which it has a superficial resemblance, has also been dealt with in this way. But the reader of the work for the first time will naturally hardly be in a position fully to follow this until he has made himself acquainted with the newer theory as expounded in the original work.

It looks as though the times were ripe for a great intellectual renascence synthesising all the partial and scattered contributions into an established body of doctrine, based on "the still almost unknown science of national economics and as far removed from disinterested controversy as the propositions of geometry." This book emphasises rather a flaw in the monetary system, than "a flaw in the price system" which Technocracy affirms. Both still await impartial examination and judgment. It has been the author's belief, strengthened and matured with the passage of the years, that to a slip in accountancy – a mistake which when pointed out is as obvious as an arithmetical blunder – is to be traced the whole hell's brew which the scientific civilisation' has become. In that unexpected quarter, I think, will be found "the fatal destiny which makes human misery eternal." But whether it is the whole solution or not, its instant correction would seem to be a necessary first step to a saner world.

Oxford, *February 1933.*

Preface to the first edition

The introductory chapter of this book describes how it came to be written, and the summary at the end sets forth the chief positive conclusions arrived at. Although it is not a novel, but rather, a serious treatise upon what is sometimes called "The Dismal Science," the habit of glancing at the end before starting the book is by no means to be deprecated. Intended for all sorts of readers sincerely anxious to understand the causes of modern unrest in the political and economic sphere, the summary will explain better than a brief preface the goal to which the book is directed. It is as well to take a look at the wood before plunging in among the trees, or the view may be dismal indeed.

It is an attempt, rarely made nowadays, by a specialist in one field of knowledge to solve the problems in another. In science, we recognise that the border-land between related subjects is usually the most fruitful field for new discoveries, and also that it is not unknown for entirely new subjects to start from and be based upon more or less minor advances in subjects apparently unrelated to them.

This inquiry commenced with the attempt to obtain a physical conception of wealth that would obey the physical laws of conservation and be incapable of imitating the capricious behaviour of the subject-matter of psychical research. During the progress of the investigation, a new theory of money gradually took shape, and in time constituted itself the corner-stone of the whole superstructure. Just because this theory, unlike others, did not pretend to correlate price with the state of trade or quantity of goods being produced, it was recognised that the problems of stimulating production and abolishing poverty and unemployment were distinct from the purely monetary problem. One could "stabilise stagnation." The solution was in due course arrived at, and the general conditions were worked out for the progressive economic expansion of a community, without change in the value of money or alternating fits of boom and depression. As was to be expected, the solution, when found, proved to be most ordinary incontrovertible common sense, requiring nothing more than that to prove it.

Every accession to the quantity of wealth immobilised in a productive system must be paid for by abstinence from consumption. The owners, the time being, of money contribute a part – usually a small part – unwittingly. The rest must be met by genuine permanent surrender of rights to consume. These conditions observed, the revenue of wealth can be permanently expanded, in a scientific era, to an almost indefinite extent. It is because the genuine initial abstinence is burked that the existing system is what it is. This, in brief, is the solution of the economic paradox.

Acknowledgments are due to a larger number of authors, for material help in the understanding of these problems, than it has been possible to refer to specifically in the text, as well as to numerous correspondents and friends who have discussed the writer's conclusions and drawn his attention to many of the pregnant passages in the literature quoted, of which otherwise he might have remained in ignorance.

FREDERICK SODDY.

January 1926.

Addition to the second edition

Dedicated to the Law Officers of The Crown of The British Empire

TECHNOCRACY AND THE NEW ECONOMICS

Technocracy claims that by the use of the inanimate energy of Nature and by means of machines and mass production, man has become independent of his own physical exertions for his maintenance, the so-called 'iron law of scarcity,' upon which the older economics was founded, has been abolished, that poverty *and* unemployment at one and the same time is now a horrible anachronism, that the average income and expenditure of the whole American nation could easily be multiplied many times with less hours of labour and more of leisure, and that the banker is out of date as the ruler of a scientific and technological civilisation.

In this it is similar to the thesis developed in the present books save, possibly, that I was and am more conservative both with regard to the extent and the rapidity with which the average scale of living can be augmented. It is the doctrine which in Great Britain calls itself the New Economics. Ever since the War there has been developing a school of thought, more or less independently on both sides of the Atlantic, believing in a new economics of abundance rather than in the old economics of want. In Great Britain, Major Douglas, who initiated the Social Credit Reform movement – which is criticised rather than expounded in this book – is the pioneer as regards the total change of outlook which the new view demands. But all new economists regard Arthur Kitson, to whom this book was dedicated, as the doyen of the movement through his reiterated attacks during the last forty years on the fallacies of modern monetary systems. The influence of the American efficiency engineers, who have given Technocracy its distinctive statistical foundation, as well as those of Thorstein Veblen, now described as the "Father of Technocracy," has been felt, but rather as echoes and reflections than directly, the latter through the confused medium of warring political and sociological antipathies.

But whereas in Great Britain the new economists, with the possible exception of the Douglas School, have been rather like isolated voices crying in the wilderness, in America they have now the ear of the nation. The spectacle of want and despair, with 13 million unemployed, in the richest of the nations, so familiar to us in the Old World, has there, as we have always hoped and expected it would, brought instantly into the forefront the broad issue whether the machine is to be allowed to enslave or liberate humanity. We are so much nearer the "iron law," and the traditions of resignation, subordination and sacrifice it enforced, that the people here still see no remedy for what has been (and therefore must always be!) the traditional lot of a large part of humanity. Even in America, probably, there are still hardy believers in the doctrine "Blessed is he who expecteth little, for he will not be disappointed."

POINTS OF UNANIMITY

All new economists, including in the term the Technocrats, are quite agreed on the complete possibility of immense improvement in the standard of living at the cost of much less expenditure of time and "diligence" or "watchfulness" (not to use the misleading, because obsolescent, term "labour") and at a gain of the corresponding hours of "leisure." Some of us think that term also obsolescent if it is to connote nothing better for the majority of people than it does to-day. Even here probably wide divergence might be discovered as to exactly how much "leisure" would remain if the majority of people flung themselves as whole-heartedly into developing their intellectual and cultural aptitudes (with all the attendant paraphernalia of universities, academies and the like which that involves) as they now do, in their relatively limited time, into amusement. We are all, again, in complete agreement as to the necessity of there being an equitable redistribution of this "leisure," for example, as between those who build and teach in universities and those who are to have the "leisure" to "work" there. The system of an overworked middle with voluntary and involuntary leisure at the two ends, has got to end, and the sooner the better. But I am still probably alone in the belief that this would automatically look after itself if the monetary system were honest and incapable of being tampered with, and I therefore escape the most insoluble part of the problem as to how this just redistribution is to be secured. It is not that I burke the issue so much as that I feel the problem is insoluble until this first step is taken, and then it can be dealt with if and as it is necessary.

On what might be termed the diagnosis of the trouble, again, new economists are in general agreement that undoubtedly the source is to be located in the very nature of the modern monetary systems, as they have become. We all scorn as an intellectual absurdity the facile slogan of "Machine *versus* Man" and the theory it implies that men live to work rather than work to live. For us in one way or another it is "Money *versus* Man." It is sinister that what was the original slogan of the ignorant and desperate Luddite rioters should be becoming more and more adopted by supposedly highly educated and intelligent people. If, by lightening the labours of living, science increases production beyond the capacity of the distributive mechanism, it is the distributive mechanism that must be overhauled or scrapped, not the productive mechanism, and the distributive mechanism of a monetary civilisation – in contradistinction to the earlier patriarchal, serf, clan, feudal forms of communism – *is* money.

POINTS OF DIFFERENCE

On the question whether the money system should (1) be scrapped, (2) greatly amplified and extended, or (3) simply corrected to subserve what it was invented to do, that is distribute what there is to consume and use, irrespective of quantity, the widest differences of opinion are revealed. It would seem, in fact, that the time were now ripe for the authoritative exponents of the various systems to explain them and to answer all relevant questions arising to a *disinterested* and *trained* jury of eminent thinkers, accustomed to dealing with abstract and scientific thought, and to leave it with them to advise which of the ways should first be tried out. They should be regarded as alternatives, not complementary but mutually exclusive, and any attempt to compromise and combine parts of them would almost certainly result in disaster. It is notorious in these questions that those who have formed definite conclusions and promulgated concrete schemes cannot rightly appreciate other and mutually destructive proposals. At the same time the proposer of each scheme should have the right to challenge any individual member of the jury as being not disinterested in, or sufficiently familiar with, the general habits of thought necessary to understand the implications of his proposals. It would be as absurd to try the case before a packed jury of those whose conduct was under revision and whom it might be necessary to dispense with, as of people accustomed only to word-spinning and with no knowledge of realities.

Of the three classes above distinguished the Technocrats (though the writer has only second-hand knowledge of the proposal, and does not understand it) would appear to put themselves in the first by their attack on the "price-system," and their proposal to do away with money and to use "energy-certificates." The outside world, at least, still awaits precise information as to what exactly is proposed, and how the products of industry and agriculture are to be distributed to individuals under this system, and it would be idle at the present time to anticipate this by any premature criticism.

THE DOUGLAS SCHOOL

The Douglas School in England, through its proposal to sell goods below cost and to make up the difference to the manufacturer and vendor by an issue of "Social Credit" (which, so far as I understand it, is new money), appears at first to be closely allied to the Technocrats. But, so far as I understand the proposals that have been put forward, they seem rather to fall in the second class – namely, a great amplification and extension of the system of creating money as credits, but to the consumer rather than the producer.

Up to a point the remedy is easy to understand. The great over-production of capital, though what already exists is largely lying idle, is obviously to some extent traceable to the existing system, whereby producers, by depositing collateral security and paying interest, can have money created temporarily to enable them to produce at the expense of the whole community. But in modern monetary systems there is no money created, or even no regular machinery for creating money, for distribution.

Every student of the subject now knows that it is just as necessary to supply money to consumers to enable them to consume as it is to producers to enable them to produce, and the putting of the new money always into the producer's side of the system is one undeniable factor in causing production to outrun distribution.

But this is not the real spear-head of either doctrine, which has penetrated, at least for the moment, the very citadel of "Capitalism." In the words of the one, owing to fewer and fewer workers producing ever and ever larger quantities of goods "the purchasing power distributed by industry is becoming increasingly insufficient to distribute the products of industry." Or, as the other claims, with the technical development of production, the traditional method of distribution by wages, etc., has broken down, and it is a pure illusion to suppose it can ever be restored. Not one-half the unemployed in America would be re-absorbed by a return to the earlier maximum peak of prosperity, and we are rapidly approaching the time when the majority will be out of work. Both condemn the existing wage-system or price-system as already impracticable and as ultimately absurd. In this I am the cause of sorrow, if not of anger, among my brother new-economists as here my position is much nearer that of the older economics than the new.

My own objection to the Douglas scheme in part is one of degree, as to how much new money is needed, having in mind the impossibility of withdrawing again money *given*, in contrast to the possibility when it is only *lent*. But a deeper division exists, arising out of the theme expounded in this book – the energy theory of wealth, and the real nature of Capital that follows from it as communal debt rather than wealth. Hence the necessity of writing off from the possible output of distributable wealth all capital produced as dead loss. It is a subtraction from rather than an addition to the flow. The much-discussed A+B theorem of the Douglas School seems to regard Capital conventionally as wealth rather than debt, and if so it reduces the practical proposal to issue Social Credit (or new money) on anything like the scale apparently contemplated to one of simple inflation. Of such schemes I am told a Berlin organisation studying the problem has collected about two thousand.

In this second category also are to be classed all schemes of banking reform, retaining as now the power over the creation and destruction of money in private hands but altering the methods of doing it and the ostensible objective, or, alternatively, to nationalise the banks and leave them to continue much as now, as I would put it, to wreck socialism as they have nearly wrecked individualism. Clearly it would be even more idle for me to attempt to expound them than the Douglas proposals.

THE AUTHOR'S SCHEME

The third method of correcting the monetary system to make it distribute, in effect re-creating a distributive mechanism, since the *raison d'être* of all money systems is now absent from ours, is the method I have from the first advocated in this and other books.[1] It cannot claim to be supported yet by any "school", though it has its individual converts. Broadly, it takes its stand on the conclusion that the whole of the benefits supposed to be conferred on the community by the monetary system, whatever they may have been once, are now an illusion and as dishonest as tampering with weights and weighing machines. With the growing distinction between the *acquisition* of wealth and the creation of it – between Demosthenes and Bishop Berkeley – all this monkeying with the quantity of money by pretending to lend it and creating it, by pretending to be repaid it and destroying it, appears in the first place as of no real physical significance whatever from the national standpoint. It results merely in some people acquiring at the expense of and without the knowledge of others. In the second place, it makes the distribution of wealth at a constant price-level, or indeed at any price-level, an impossibility. The supposed advantages it once had – stimulation of production as distinct from consumption – are now a disadvantage, but it may seriously be doubted whether any consequence not, on the balance, evil has come from it from the standpoint of the nation as a whole. If there are famines and vast natural or human cataclysms, such as wars and pestilence, it is better to face them *without* the additional and equally devastating catastrophe of a variable money unit, which merely gives short weight to one set of people and overweight to another – the last straw, surely, in the way of "assistance."

It would revert to the purpose for which money was invented and to the axiom with regard to its issue in all monetary civilisations precedent to this one. It would destroy utterly, without leaving a single loophole, the power of private people to create and destroy money at will. It would substitute a scientific national monetary system, leaving everything else as it is, and it claims that the recovery of the patient would be swift and complete. As in the case of the last Czarevitch, it is the doctors called in who cause the disease in anticipation of the call, and the disease itself can be best described as the secret administration of a drug which leaves its victim unaware of what has undone him.

---

[1] Compare, *Money versus Man* (Mathews and Marrot, London, 1931).

WEALTH, CAPITAL AND MONEY

Though, in this book, the positive contribution to the subject from the standpoint of immediate practical politics is contained in the suggestion to revert to a monetary system for the distribution of all that science and human diligence is able to make out of the raw energy and materials of the globe, the reader may be warned early that the analysis of the impasse depends on conceptions of Wealth, Capital and Money, utterly different from those held or avowed before either by economists, sociologists, business men or politicians or from those at the basis of the conflicting stale controversies between Capitalism, Socialism and Communism. It is, personally, extremely interesting and flattering that the viewpoint with regard to Wealth and Capital appears to have been adopted by—or, at least, to have been of some influence in—the independent work of the Technocrats, but as regards Money, though time is working wonders, I think I can still call it my own.

The reader will find in the opening chapters an energy theory of wealth developed which calls here for no extra elaboration. But he must bear in mind the nature of Capital (*Agents of production* as defined) following from this, of already consumed wealth, and – since wealth, no more than fuel, can really be consumed twice in the normal way – Capital is an irrecoverable loss and communal debt rather than communal wealth. A very apt illustration is the position of the Railways in Great Britain to-day which are not yet bought or paid for from the descendants who have inherited claims derived from whoever abstained from consuming in order to let those who produced them consume. Controversial as the question of the identity of the original individuals who did the abstaining may be, there is no real controversy about the abstinence. Contrast with these the motor highways, paid for as built by an excessive tax on motorists, four times as high as in any other country in the world. This makes one believe that Great Britain, as the oldest sufferer from the delusion that capital was communal wealth rather than debt, still leads the world, in its intuitive beliefs at least if not in its avowed attitudes. It is therefore very significant that the same ideas have also now taken firm root in America, judging at least from the accounts of Technocracy and its principles that have come through, illustrated as they are by many striking illustrations of the fecundity of *debt* rather than of wealth.

CAPITAL AS ALREADY CONSUMED WEALTH

As regards the more eminent orthodox economists (all orthodox economists are necessarily eminent, as otherwise they would be incredible), they seem to be still in the unhappy position of knowing all about the impossibility of consuming cake twice, at least intuitively, but still believing in the dizzy virtues of compound interest. It is now rather among new economists (in the Douglas proposals, and the A+B theorem) that these misconceptions seem to linger in the sphere of national economics. Because new wealth may be obtained for capital, by getting some other individual who wants it to take it in exchange, this must not blind us to the fact that a nation cannot turn its capital wealth back into consumable wealth again, or eat its ploughs if it is short of bread.

A reviewer of the first edition of this book, with far-sighted humour, quoting from the preface that the solution of the economic paradox was "the most ordinary incontrovertible commonsense requiring nothing more than that to prove it," prophesied that it would be rejected by every student of economics. He himself, however, supplied the clue. He said that Marshall, who "in his great work defined economics as how a man gets his income and how he uses it", characterised the distinction between "consumers' goods" and "producers' goods" (in this work distinguished as wealth for consumption and use and Capital, or as Wealth I and Wealth II) as "vague and perhaps of not much practical use"—a distinction without a difference, in fact, just as J. Stuart Mill dealt with the same question. Quite so, when we consider how an individual gets his income, but not when we consider how a nation does. Once this fundamental point is appreciated the turmoil of present-day political and social controversy about Capital appears almost devoid of meaning.

"WEALTH IN THE PIPES"

Arising, however, from this difference of viewpoint, the orthodox economists seem to have committed a definite error of accounting which vitiates their whole effort to account for the monetary system, and why it is behaving so erratically and spasmodically. When one passes from the conception of wealth as a "realised amount" to the more elegant conception of it as a "periodical receipt" or flow – and on the energy theory also one is, of course, really dealing with flows – we must not omit to account correctly for what may be termed the wealth in the pipes, meaning the total amount of partially produced wealth in existence corresponding with any given rate of delivery or revenue ("volume of trade"). Thus the great American oil industry [2] uses 100,000 miles of pipe-lines, which permanently hold three-quarters of an American billion (1,000 million) gallons of oil. The *quantity* of three-quarters of a billion gallons of oil has to be put in, but does not come out, though the oil does. We may say this quantity of oil is not burnable, though the oil is – that, though the oil is always passing through from production to combustion, three-quarters of a billion gallons are *as good as wasted so long as the supply is maintained.*

A certain rate of flow of wealth from production to consumption demands a certain quantity "in the pipes" in the semi-manufactured or partly grown condition, and if we are to increase the flow we must increase this lost quantity in proportion.

Because the rate of production, unlike that convenient fiction "the velocity of circulation of money," about to be dealt with, depends on such things as seed-time and harvest and their industrial equivalents rather than on bankers pretending to lend money.

If this quantity is not honestly accounted for by someone abstaining from consumption to an equivalent extent, it accounts for itself dishonestly, by the something-for-nothing money trick, and lowers the value of every one's money by changing the value of each unit. Omission to do so renders it perfectly idle to try to keep the index number constant. The sufficient proof in these days of disbelief in physical miracles is that *there is nowhere else it can come from.*

The banker, as he has become, affects to treat the quantity of consumable wealth which is not consumable, and which is necessary to fill the pipes, as consumable wealth, just because it can be drained out to repay him, thus dislocating the whole service. But that is not quite good enough.

The point may appear a trivial one, but it is the key of the whole problem of how to keep a value of money constant while increasing the rate of flow to the maximum extent possible of the state of civilisation. Its consideration in Cap. XI, prior to the fuller treatment of the real nature of Capital Accumulation in Cap. XII, to which identical

---

[2] *Nature*, April 19th, 1930, p. 589.

considerations as regards irrepayable abstinence apply, may cause the reader, if not put on his guard, unnecessary difficulty.

MONETARY CIVILISATIONS

Monetary civilisations arose out of and displaced the earlier communisms because they allowed a greater degree of individual economic freedom to men, though not to women. Monetary civilisations are, at least as so far developed, essentially male civilisations. They may fail or need revision on the latter count, but they only need to be practised to secure the former without reverting to communism.

What we know has fallen, or is in danger of falling, with a reversion to the former type, simply because modern money does not play the game.[3] The essential rule is that whoever, in the way of business, receives wealth for money – itself now intrinsically valueless – must give up the equivalent, and this is simply enough secured by his having in the preceding transaction given up for the intrinsically worthless money the equivalent of wealth. But it is not *and cannot be* observed with credit-money, falsely so called, in the first issue of new money, and as a direct result the whole scientific civilisation has been brought about as near ruin as it is possible for it to go.

It is *only* in regard to its *first* issue (and final destruction, if it is ever destroyed) that modern money is in the least difficult to see through. In the *first* exchange of new money for wealth, the issuer, whoever he is, gets something for nothing, *and cannot help getting something for nothing,* unless the community has to go to all the wasted effort of incorporating something valuable, such as gold, in the money token. With regard to bank-notes there may once have been some plausibility in the belief that it was the credit of the bank that caused them to circulate, but to-day one can hardly imagine a State so corrupt that its credit is not vastly superior to that of any corporation. But when it comes to the money created to lend and destroyed when the money is

[3] These points are excellently brought out in a recent book by D. W. Maxwell, *The Principal Cause of Unemployment* (Williams and Norgate, 1932).

repaid, the users of it neither know who created it nor how it was created. It differs from all the rest *only* in the *first* transaction in which it exchanges for wealth, and the *last* in which it is decreated, and, indeed, what does "all the rest" now amount to?

KINGSHIP

Modern money is a game with counters that cannot be started until each individual pays real wealth for the counters into a common pool, and *there is no common national authority in charge of the pool.* In the days of absolute rulers this indispensable functionary was typified by the ruler's effigy on each token to indicate it was "genuine". Indeed, in times of peace at least, the main justification for the central authority was just this necessity of protecting the nation's medium of exchange from those who would multiply it by spurious imitations and to maintain faith between debtors and creditors by keeping the value of the money up to the standard. In America they may still have no use for kings, but, equally with countries that have them, they are in just as dire need of somebody responsible to take charge of the pool. Much as some of the early English kings may have betrayed this trust, in Great Britain for a century Royalty has a uniform record of conscientious devotion to the public service, and the Royal Family works probably harder in the public interest than most of the citizens. It would seem natural here to re-enforce the prerogative of the Crown over the issue of money, which the cheque system has rendered a dead-letter.

A NATIONAL MINT

Almost all the proposals that have been made in this field are for the extension of the practice of issuing and destroying money to municipal banks, mutual aid societies and the like, or to nationalise the banks without in the least altering the existing flaw in the money system, but rather exaggerating and multiplying it to an absurdity. The proposal in this book is to re-establish the National Mint as having control over the issue or destruction of all money, i.e. legal tender, and, if necessary, proceeding against all substitutes by specifically illegalising them. The rate of new issues would be controlled by a panel of statisticians, presided over by the Supreme Head of the Realm, who would have status similar to the judicature and functions analogous to the official testing institutions which standardise the national weights and measures. In Great Britain the average rate at which new money is issued (that is the excess of "loans" over "repayments") has been £1,000 an hour, every hour of the day and night, for the past 226 years. The present average rate is probably at least three times this. It would be the duty of the statistical authority to say at what rate the new issues should be made to preserve the index of prices unchanged. Nowadays, the tendency would be uniformly in the one direction, the fall of prices through production outrunning distribution.

The past issues in Great Britain are of the order of two thousand million pounds.

It would require the wealth of two thousand millionaires to repay the citizens what they have given up to the pool for money counters, which I termed first in this book the Virtual Wealth of the nation. But, alas! the "wealth" of the millionaires turns out on examination to be virtual, if not Virtual, and to consist mostly of claims to wealth like those of the citizens themselves. What business any individuals or corporations have to assume entire responsibility for a nation's currency, or what they can do but harm, is difficult to imagine, least of all in such a civilisation as ours has become. In fact, the historian will probably trace as one of the most important reasons for the stranglehold on industry, and the economic development of the nations which we are experiencing, the total inadequacy of any such individuals or banks, however "wealthy" or trustworthy, to undertake liability for the national currency. It is like trying to finance a national central electricity scheme from a penny savings bank, and getting instead nothing better than we now have.

DEMOCRACY AND THE ISSUE OF MONEY

Yet as President Wilson learned too late in 1916: "A great industrial nation is controlled by its system of credit – our system of credit is concentrated. The growth of the nation and all our activities are in the hands of a *few men ... who can chill and check and destroy our economic freedom*."

If he had called a spade a spade, and instead of talking of a "system of credit" had revealed what the term conceals, and said the "creation and destruction of our money," even a bright child with no more than a school knowledge of history could have understood him.

So ends Democracy in an absolute stranglehold by a few unknown men! At least we have a right to know who our rulers really are, even if it means their unearthing again as much of their re-buried gold as will make them crowns. To seek them out is to find no one in the least resembling the sort of person a great scientific empire or republic would have voluntarily chosen to throttle them, but a number of pettifogging relics and penny bankers mopping and mowing about gold! Away with them! Let the great nations get on with their job.

THE LAW!

But how? A revolution would not leave us any nearer to but much farther from our goal. It is now in the absolute power of the citizens to put an end to these nefarious practices in the simplest and most unexpected way – namely, by invoking the law! It only remains for a sufficient number of substantial people to get together and refuse to pay their taxes on the ground that owing to the private issues of money on a colossal scale, a large fraction of the whole tax is bogus, to make a clean sweep of all the webs woven to entangle humanity by the magicians who have discovered how to get something out of nothing and, moreover, to make it bear perennial interest. The Law Officers of the Crown cannot proceed indefinitely against the wretched counterfeiter of a false note for high treason rather than for theft and wink at the defraudation of the taxpayer by the same means to an annual extent of over a hundred million pounds. But Anglo-Saxon law being what it is, it is highly undesirable that any individual should attempt to do this, without at least very full and adequate financial backing, or a premature defeat might establish a precedent which would settle the legal aspect of the question to the end of time.

HOW THE SYSTEM WOULD WORK

Assuming the necessary first step safely accomplished – and it is, as with all monetary problems, the first step that counts – there would then be the interest of some thousands of millions a year for the relief of taxation, plus the yearly increment in the quantity of money, amounting now to many tens of millions a year, and the added advantage that the payment in perpetuity of the interest on these yearly increments would also be avoided.

After the prolonged period of deflation we have been passing through, it would be natural to put these new issues into the system at the consumer's side, so that the first exchange – the only one that counts – takes out some of the gluts of wealth in the system.

Like the passage of oxygen to the blood in the lungs, in which each cell gets its due share, the new money would thus confer new purchasing power on every individual member of the community in proportion to his holding in the pool, and no scheme could possibly be juster or more equitable than that. The very term used by orthodox exponents of monetary science – *monetary policy* – is sufficient to condemn them. For whoever would talk of a *weights and measures policy*, or think it fair to say "that poor fellow is a deserving case, give him twenty ounces to his pound, and that rascal need only have twelve to make it square."

Later on, if appetites outrun supply, and it became necessary to stimulate production, they would more naturally be put in at the producer's side, as, for example, by redeeming permanent national debt and so liberating new wealth for expenditure in new capital production, not forgetting the "wealth in the pipes" already considered. This also is as just as before, as the citizens are saved for ever after paying further interest on the debt destroyed. The nation is, in fact, "saving" to pay for the cost of new capital, a necessity which the application of individual economics to nations has formerly neither provided for nor even allowed.

CAPITAL REDEMPTION

The first step taken, the second, the gradual redemption of the communal capital debt, explained in Cap. XIII, calls for no further comment, except to say that in my belief (having regard to the conservative estimate, relatively to the technocrats, which I take of the possible rate of useful technological expansion), I think these two steps would suffice for a long time to come. But it is perhaps well to state a little more fully the reasons for this.

The redemption scheme in effect makes all securities terminable after a definite term, and with the return of a total sum definitely greater than that invested according to the rate of tax, as can be worked out by anybody from the Tables given. Once one grasps clearly that capital is wealth already consumed and is, at best, only of limited life, the real problem is to unburden from the shoulders of the nation the dead debt, not to discourage but rather to encourage the sinking of wealth in the production of fresh capital. True, if somebody likes to erect a rayon silk factory capable, almost without any one working it (which seems an impossibility even from the standpoint of the new economics), of supplying more artificial silk than the world wants, that is their affair. The index number standard, under which goods not wanted fall in value *relatively* to those that are wanted as now, is all that is needed to stop such folly. But if leisure is to be other than mere sloth and idleness, in my opinion even the scientific production system will have its work cut out to supply its infinitely diverse requirements. Some of the technocrats' figures seem germane.

> "As our society is constituted in America, but 7 per cent of the energy output is devoted to the direct provision of sustenance. Ninety-three per cent is used to keep our social scheme going."[4]

This, then, is the author's scheme for the salvation and regeneration, not to say rejuvenation, of the scientific civilisation, and those who read the book ought not to find much difficulty in understanding its theoretical basis. Of course, it can be decked out and embroidered to suit the fancy of any section of the public without in the least affecting its potency, so long as the decorators and embroiderers understand that it has a basic principle that it is not possible to compromise upon. That is the principle of money itself – that no one shall receive it in the way of business without giving up the equivalent of wealth for it. Let us give up our belief in conjuring tricks, if not at Christmas parties, at least in the world of business and economics, and the attempt there really to get something for nothing. Play the money game with an open pool and a responsible croupier, if not a real king.

NATIONAL OLD-AGE LEGISLATION

With the truer realisation of the precise nature of wealth and of capital accumulation which the energy theory of wealth gives, their capacity for harm largely disappears. There arises the hope that it may even neutralise that "principle of death" which Trotter has recognised

---

[4] *The A.B.C. of Technocracy*, Frank Arkright, 1933. Hamish Hamilton, London.

as hitherto inherent in the very nature of civilisation, here diagnosed as the conflict of inborn instincts of acquisition (rather for future security than for either miserly or ostentatious reasons) with the physical impossibility of accumulating wealth.

It remains also to add little as to the international aspect beyond that already said. If each nation faces and solves these problems internally, the international and external problem would disappear also. But the mere union of the autonomous States under the world rule of the banker can at most stave it off for a moment and threatens an eclipse of economic freedom not in one State but in all. As before, neither the whole world nor even the whole universe is capable of "assuaging an infinite thirst." The mathematical artifice which the Hindu mathematicians invented for the facilitation of reckoning has sent civilisation off the rails just as the square root of that artifice is now sending physics and astronomy on the endless pursuit of absurdity. We may be thankful for the engineer that there, at least, we must still keep at least one foot on the ground. But we must keep both feet there, if nations are to have an economy that enables them to grow to old age and yet live.

THE QUANTITY THEORY OF MONEY CONTRASTED WITH THE VIRTUAL WEALTH THEORY

It is as invidious for an author of one theory of money to criticise a rival theory destructively as for one manufacturer to decry another's goods. It is psychologically more subtle, if less informative, to proclaim what one's own will not do, as in the case of the celebrated soap that "won't wash clothes." But the odium has to be faced for the sake of clearness.

The Quantity Theory of Money[5] attempts to establish a relation between the purchasing power of money, that is, the amount of goods the unit of money will buy, or *its reciprocal, price,* that is the amount of money that has to be paid for a unit quantity of goods, and three other

---

[5] *Vide* Irving Theory, *The Purchasing Power of Money* (p. 18) (Macmillan and Co., New York, 1922).

magnitudes – namely, the quantity of money in circulation, the velocity of circulation and the quantity of goods exchanged, or "volume of trade." The relation is that prices must vary proportionately with the quantity of money in circulation, and with the velocity of circulation, and inversely as the quantities of goods exchanged.

Actually in practice price means the index number of price-level.[6] The quantity of money in circulation is a vague expression, as the only definite quantity is that in existence, in the ownership of somebody, not, of course, reckoning quantities in joint ownership as more than one quantity.

The velocity of circulation is vaguer. It is defined as the number of times "the quantity in circulation" is exchanged for goods in a year. But by multiplying the last two quantities together, the vaguenesses neutralise and we get the quite definite quantity of goods exchanged for money in a year or the volume of trade. This and the price-index and the quantity of money in existence are definite, though the latter to-day could scarcely be said to be independently ascertainable.

The so-called equation of exchange, "The sum of the products of quantities of goods exchanged multiplied by their respective prices," equals "total money changed for goods," or "volume of trade" equals "product of quantity of money in circulation multiplied by velocity of circulation" seems to be what the mathematician would call an identity like "twice two" equals "four," since the assumptions made in considering how much of the money is in circulation must of necessity affect in the inverse manner the velocity of circulation. So that only the first equation is real – that the sum of all the goods bought multiplied by their respective prices equals the total money changed for goods.

If this is correct, it is not remarkable that statistical studies have confirmed the quantity theory to a very high degree of accuracy, as anything else would be an impossibility. True, if the quantity of money available to buy a certain quantity of goods is altered, price as the quotient of the money by the goods bought with it, must alter with the quantity of money. Though all the painful implications of this are not usually understood until after long and bitter experience, it is merely a definition of price as determined by index number. Since it is physically

---

[6] References are to this book.

impossible to increase the quantity of goods in existence by increasing the quantity of money available to buy them, any increase in the goods available necessarily lagging behind by at least the minimum time to produce them, the above must be true on *any* theory of money.

PRICE

Price is essentially a relation between two quantities, the one a quantity of money and the other a quantity of wealth. On my theory the dual relation which brings in the psychological as well as the physical factor is got by considering the price not only as how much money is required to buy goods, but also as how much goods the owners (for the moment) of the money are prepared to do without or give up solely of their own volition (without interest or other inducement except their own convenience and necessities).

The quantity theory merely tries to get over the difficulty that every theory in this field encounters, of relating a total *quantity* of existing money with a *rate* of distribution of wealth (volume of trade), much as in earlier attempts, I think, by taking into account the time required for the money to circulate. But the so-called 'velocity of circulation,' defined as the average number of times the money changes hands in a given period, is more of a will-of-the-wisp even than the old time of circulation.

VELOCITY OF CIRCULATION

As developed in Chap. XI, from the standpoint of national economics, the economics cycle proper boils down to two *interlocked* operations, payments by producers to their employees and themselves for producing new wealth, and then the payment of the same money by the same people and other consumers to get the wealth out of the production system *after* it is made. All simple exchanges of finished property are only of individual importance. It really does not matter whether A or B, C, D … owns the racehorse, the estate, the factory, the stocks and shares, or what-not. The velocity of circulation of money can be enormously affected by people on a stock exchange rushing about buying and selling shares and buying them back again *ad infinitum* without any direct effect on the periods of seed-time and harvest and their industrial equivalents, or upon the rate at which new wealth can be made for distribution, which determines the fate of nations.

These spectacular and, nationally, profoundly regrettable speculative activities merely effect the distribution of *money* and *capital* between individuals, not the new creation of wealth except on the rebound. How much of so-called trade and commerce, especially in the foreign and international market, is in a similar category, having little to do with genuine production and distribution and arising out of mere change of speculative owners, is a very important enquiry.[7] So many of the existing difficulties arise from the facilities which speculators and *entrepreneurs* now possess for getting money created for them and destroyed again when they have done with it, that it would be waste of time to take them into account in a system postulated to be worked by genuine permanent national money of constant value in goods, and in which every transaction in which it changed hands would connote a corresponding exchange of equivalent wealth.

This is indeed the key-note of the treatment of money in this work. The objective is to find the conditions under which a monetary system will distribute all there is to use and consume without boom or slump and at a constant debtor-creditor standard of money. It is not to follow the vagaries of the present system which are of as little scientific interest as the behaviour of an instrument in which some one was always tampering with the calibration to make it read either high or low.

To finish at least with what it will not do, the Virtual Wealth Theory of Money makes no pretence, of itself, to establish a relation between the quantity of money and the "volume of trade." But by the aid of the further principle of conservation (a veritable mariner's compass in dealing with realities) – indeed, by little else than the trite consideration that the mere existence of any quantity of wealth is evidence that some one has produced it (and presumably been paid in consumable wealth for doing so), and that no one as yet has consumed it – it is possible to lay down the conditions that must be observed if the revenue of wealth of a community is to be expanded by scientific advances *without* change of the price-level. The virtual wealth looks after itself. The independently variable quantity of money has to be made to follow and keep in step with it, if the price-level is not to change. If the analysis here given, "depending on incontrovertible

---

[7] Compare *The Principal Cause of Unemployment*, D. W. Maxwell (Williams and Norgate, 1932).

common sense," or what has here been termed "the wealth in the pipes," is correct, it requires nothing more than the powers the State now has of remitting or imposing taxation to issue and destroy money and therefore to keep the index number constant. If its private issue and destruction were prevented, the most important factor causing it to vary now would be eliminated and its regulation would be a relatively easy task. I have yet to be convinced that this is not all that would be necessary for a long time to come.

CHAPTER I

INTRODUCTORY

Science the World Ferment

What has gone wrong with the world? In the throes of the Great War, many discovered for the first time that they were living in a scientific civilisation, and even scientific men themselves realised the difference between the leaven of theory and its practical aspect in a world boiling in ferment. Science then almost emerged from its esoteric seclusion to become a cult – at least, something worth cultivating, for professional ends. So indispensible in wartime, it seemed curiously insignificant among the public services in time of peace. Fortunately for science the danger passed. There are scientific professions, many of them, but science is not a profession. It is a quest. What has gone wrong in the world? Let us follow the quest.

The time is opportune. Much of what has been attributed to our inevitable destiny – superiority of character, unquenchable spirit, invincibility of purpose, and other human qualities – takes on a new valuation with the discovery that we are living in a scientific era. As much might be said of the virtues attributed to democracy and free political institutions; or again, of the capitalist system in its pride of an Empire on which the sun never sets and of the phenomena of class-hatred and slums on which the sun never rises. Science has changed the nature of our economic life, and older systems based on a different mode of living are, on all hands, admitted to be working most dangerously if, indeed, they have not already become impossible. They remain only because there is nothing constructive to replace them, and are conventionally defended for fear of anarchy and chaos following their open repudiation. Everything in the world now is so delicate – which is merely another way of saying that nobody seems to have any real understanding of how the economic system works at all or why it works so dangerously – that the policy of all parties seems to be rather to bear the ills we have than to fly to others which we know not of. The people in this respect have frankly given up real hope that Governments, of whatever complexion, will find any solution even for any of the immediate practical problems of the day, and it is a period of marking time. The Great War itself is seen to be not a separate historical event but more and more as an inevitable consequence of the same ultimate cause. The sudden rise of the Western world to a position of dominating material greatness and power, the dangerous and manifold insoluble social problems that accompanied it, and now threaten our times, and the phenomenon of modern world-shattering war on the scale we have just survived, are all now more generally seen to be due primarily to the changes introduced into the economics of life by the discoveries of a handful of scientific pioneers in possession of a new and fruitful method of gaining natural knowledge, and to the failure of the older humane sciences to cope with the new situation.

On the one hand, a larger class than ever before have attained to a higher standard of life, greater leisure and opportunity for culture, carrying along with them hosts of servants and dependents, who minister to their comforts and luxuries and share, to some extent, their prosperity. But the workers in the more fundamental and essential industries – such as agriculture, mining and manufactures – have been cheapened by competition with rather than benefited by machinery, and, worse, are deprived by it in increasing numbers of their customary livelihood. For the propertyless masses, if there has been any improvement whatever in the average standard of life, it is so small as to be doubtful and – in comparison with the general progress of wealth production – contemptible. The lot of the masses has certainly become more strenuous and insecure, being now never free from the spectre of unemployment and consequent submersion into destitution and degradation. So that, at the other extreme, a larger class than ever before, *because* of the increase of the world's wealth, are existing in conditions of poverty and economic thraldom that would have shocked a poorer age.

By neglecting the changes that have come over the science of production in the past century, it may be possible to argue that the lot of the majority to-day is a little better or at most but little worse than it was. But this is not the real question at issue.

Rather we have to find out how it comes about that science, which, without economic exhaustion, provided the sinews of war for the most colossal and destructive conflict in history, with the man-power of the nations engaged in military service, has not yet abolished poverty and degrading conditions of living from our midst in the piping times of peace. It is impossible for those who profess to understand economics and government to escape the charge of knowing nothing whatever of these subjects so long as poverty and unemployment exist in an age of brilliant scientific achievement. Never tired of attributing economic heresies to others, the state of the whole world is the monumental evidence of their own.

The Glasgow of James Watt and Adam Smith

It is significant to reflect that Glasgow, which produced James Watt, the inventor who brought the steam engine to practical success, was the home of Adam Smith, the father of the system of political economy under which the scientific era has developed. Whilst the former in 1774 was perfecting an engine destined to lift men from the drudgery of animal labour and to establish over the whole world a new mode of livelihood, the latter in 1776 was erecting into a theoretical system the conditions under which, *till then*, men had pursued their economic livelihood. The world might have assimilated either the steam engine or the economics, but it is difficult to understand how it could possibly digest two such mutually incompatible productions simultaneously. Ever since, the world has been attempting to move in two opposite directions at one and the same time – towards a higher standard of life for some and a lower standard for others.

The Glasgow of James Watt and Adam Smith was a city of 28,000 people, hardly less provincial than Kirkcaldy, the birthplace of the author of *The Wealth of Nations*, and the place to which most of his outlook on the subject can be traced.

The Glasgow of James Watt and Adam Smith is, to-day, a city of over a million people, the second largest in the British Empire. It is a monument as much to the work of the one as the other, being, on the one hand, the centre of the great Clydebank marine engineering industry and, on the other, of the social revolution against rent, interest and profit, fostered by unemployment, house-shortage and high cost of living – famous for its ships and street-orators in every corner of the globe.

The Economic Paradox

This book is not concerned with the possibly sensational future progress of science, but is, in origin, rather of the nature of a return to present problems from one such anticipation now a generation old, concerned with the discovery of atomic energy. Though one would hardly guess it in normal times, under the revealing experiences of the Great War many of the consequences which it was natural to anticipate would follow the control of physical powers greater than any we now possess were shown to have come about already with the powers actually available.

Then, for the first time in history, we saw science used without artificial financial restrictions for the purposes of destruction. A degree of liberality and unity of purpose prevailed which is never lavished upon the less spectacular but more necessary tasks of construction. Year after year the industrialised nations produced an ever-mounting tide of munitions of war, with the flower of their man-power withdrawn from production. There seemed no physical limit to the extent which a nation, shaken out of its preconceived habits of economic thought by the imminent peril at its doors, could turn out the material necessities for its existence.

Whereas now we have returned to peace and squalor, to idle factories and farms reverting to grass, we are back as a nation to the pre-war conditions breeding a C3 race, with a million and a quarter workers unemployed, unable to feed and clothe ourselves adequately on a military standard, and unable even to build houses in which to live under the existing economic system. Yet we have the same wealth of natural resources, the same science and inventiveness, with much more settled and favourable conditions for production and an army of unused man-power being demoralised by enforced idleness! The sensationalism of the scientific prophet could hardly imagine anything so sensational as this. A nation dowered with every necessary requisite for an abundant life is too poor to distribute its wealth, and is idle and deteriorates not because it does not need it but because it cannot buy it. This book attempts to give an original analysis into the causes underlying this surprising contradiction.

The Prospect

As often happens in these swiftly changing times, even with pure science, new subjects and fields of discovery are past their most active period of growth before they become accepted as a normal and permanent part of our social inheritance and enter into the ruminations of philosophers or the curricula of universities. As regards the applications of science of most economic importance, the mass production of all kinds of commodities by mechanical power, new modes of transport and communication, and by far the greater part of the inventions by which the physical sciences have been harnessed to the chariot of life to do useful and profitable work, we are merely witnessing now the full fruition of an insight into the laws and processes of Nature obtained quite long ago. Contrary to common belief, such developments are not inexhaustible. A mechanical invention, like a bicycle, after a rapid initial period of everchanging design, reaches its final expression, and so it is in general with the great group of the mechanical applied sciences founded on the perfection of the steam engine in the first instance, and, in general, on the proper understanding of the laws of energy and its transformation, which is the necessary prelude to the control of natural forces. It would appear that in due course something like an end may be reached to major developments. Even in the younger group of electrical sciences the same tendency may already be seen. True, there have been great and sweeping advances in the pure parent sciences of physics and chemistry, but these as yet for the most part are still immeasurably beyond any practical application at all. So that an interregnum, as regards substantial practical progress, is likely to occur. The older fields will be worked out probably before the newer are effectively opened up. The biologists are already claiming that this century will be their innings, as last century admittedly was that of the physical sciences in practical world-revolutionising discoveries, and it is to be hoped that in due course they will implement the promise.

Among the more thoughtful, the profound misgivings as to where such applications of science as we have already made have led and are leading civilisation naturally cloud the outlook as regards the future. They are very different in inception and spirit from those which characterised Butler's *Erewhon*, and other jaundiced satires of the Victorians, but they are of somewhat similar trend. Have we obtained dominion of the major powers of Nature to fall a victim to our own machinery and ultimately to be destroyed by it? Is our civilisation to end in breeding the Robot and the *rentier*, and to go down under class conflicts at home and fratricidal wars abroad? Is there much point in multiplying by a million the powers already conferred by science if the use we make of those we already have are sufficient to endanger the future of civilisation?

There is this difference between the criticism of to-day and the earlier, more interested and professional disparagement to which, in the Victorian era, science was subjected. No one now is disposed to put the blame upon science or the scientific workers for the state of social affairs their discoveries and inventions have produced.

Whoever else may have profited, scientists themselves have not. No one now sees the evil in the greater knowledge of and mastery over the forces of Nature, nor in the material fruits of this knowledge in lightening the labour of living, and in providing material necessities and comforts in abundance. The sourest and most jealous fanatic to-day could hardly maintain that good and nourishing food, sufficient fuel, clothes and houses, efficient and rapid means of locomotion, transport and communication and the multifarious interests of modern life are in themselves evil. The evil is rather that these things, which science makes so prodigally, are not more universally obtainable. The medical man will tell you precisely what is essential for the maintenance and preservation of a healthy body. What the Victorian theology attributed to sin and the devil, medical science to-day would ascribe to poverty and disease.

It is an indication of the backsliding that has occurred from the high standards of the terrible Victorians that an author recently referred to his own great-grandfather, who was responsible for the English Poor-Law, as "not the inhuman devil which his works would imply, but a painfully conscientious, duty-loving Victorian Englishman."[8]

Physical Science and the Humanities

There is always a tendency for complementaries to be treated as opponents. If we start from monistic prepossessions, that Nature is a divine harmony and expresses some single super-law, philosophy is

[8] *Revolution by Reason*, John Strachey, 1925.

presented with the very difficult task of trying to piece-out at least three jig-saw puzzles that have been wilfully mixed up.

Neither mechanical nor biological science, nor the humanities alone, can solve human problems, but each can contribute its quota. In mechanics the basis of the rapid progress made from sweeping generalisations to practical achievement is due to the entire freedom of its problems from the disturbing element of life. It might be thought a policy of despair to seek aid from such a study in problems that have hitherto defied solution by humanists. Nevertheless, life obeys physical laws. Its methods are at the poles from those of the engineer, but it cannot work mechanical miracles.

Physics is complementary to it, and life works according to, not against the principles of the physical sciences.

Indeed, it may be doubted whether, strictly, any other aspect of life has yet come within range of exact scientific inquiry. Life itself is an experience which has yet to find the proper methods of investigation. The biological sciences are almost entirely concerned as yet, because of this, with the physical chemistry of living processes, rather than with life. Biology threatens to give us children without parents by ectogenesis, much as chemistry gives us, by synthesis, indigo innocent of any connection with the indigo plant.[9] But in spite of these imitations there is still something infinitely more interesting and difficult to understand about the natural processes. Still, it is no small thing to be sure that life cooperates with and does not violate natural physical laws, much as the engineer achieves his triumphs by understanding rather than defying the powers he controls. Neither individuals nor communities can escape conforming to the laws of matter and energy, however they may apply them to their own ends.

In this country, especially, there has been a long divorce between natural and human knowledge. The boycott of science and its control by hostile vested interests are still most remarkable features for an age pre-eminently distinguished only by its science. The universities and public schools, in this, set the standard and fashions of popular

---

[9] *Daedalus*, J. B. S. Haldane, 1923.

education, and we shall not escape lightly the penalty of these obscurantist policies.

Their effect on economics, essentially a subject with the closest relations with the world of facts and physical realities, has been singularly disastrous, and the hopeless muddle into which the affairs of the world have been allowed to get is largely to be traced to no clear recognition of the physical principles underlying that subject.

The very first economists in France did have an understanding of the natural knowledge of their time. But though never so necessary as in the scientific era that was to follow, the physical foundations of the subject became more and more neglected, in favour of conventional ideas derived from legal attitudes towards property rights and human interindebtednesses.

But this is merely a single example. Everywhere the idea that the few thousand, at most, active creative workers in science can really be exercising any important influence on the destinies of great nations and that, without these, and the ferment they have introduced, present civilisation would probably not be different from that of previous epochs has yet to receive due political recognition.

As for scientific investigators, they are for the most part too intently preoccupied in their highly specialised and abstruse inquiries to give time to social problems. Their activities regulate more and more automatically the principles that appertain to the normal business of the body politic, but are as completely divorced from the consciousness of society as breathing is from volition. They consider themselves capable of doing better work in the laboratory than in affairs. They recognise that the ability to make the simplest and smallest contribution to the stock of knowledge demands many years of serious preparation and study, many fruitless purely negative results, and that, in the end, the discoveries made are not likely to be those sought for, but the by-products, as it were, of a life of ceaseless quest into the unknown.

They probably more than suspect that something quite analogous applies in any other field of inquiry, and not least to the confusions of politics. This makes them realise that their own political opinions are usually no more original than those of other people and are not in the least likely to be any more helpful.

The Author's Path from Physical Science to Economics.

Some may be interested to know how it was that the author came to stray so far from the confines of his own subject and to lay himself open to the abuse which passes for argument in the matters that affect the pocket rather than the mind or soul.

At least, in defence, he may claim that in consequence he has himself seen things clear and seen things whole which he could not otherwise have done, even though he fails to convey the vision to his readers.

In the closing years of last and the opening years of this century the discovery of radioactivity, and its interpretation in terms of existing knowledge, revealed the existence of stores of potential energy in the atoms of the radioactive elements of the order of a million times greater than any previously known. These stores were and remain impossible to harness to any practical physical purpose, and are given out at very slow rates in a purely natural process of transmutation of the radioactive elements into lead and helium. There is no doubt of their existence in these elements, and the existence of similar stores in other elements has been legitimately inferred, though not as yet experimentally proved. Following the very well-known reasoning that applies in chemistry, it appears certain that any process of artificial transmutation would be able to liberate these stores and to render them available as the energy of coal and fuel now is. Many purely speculative deductions along the same vast lines have since been made from the theory of relativity, and it is to atomic energy, in the first instance, that physicists and astronomers now look to account for the maintenance of the heat of the sun and stars, and in general, the live energy of nature, over cosmical periods of time. It is unnecessary to enter further into this field, as few scientific discoveries have attracted more widespread interest than radioactivity, or have been more fully interpreted for the benefit of the non-scientific public. The names of Becquerel, M. and Mme. Curie, Rutherford, J. J. Thomson, Ramsay, Joly, Bragg and other pioneers in this field are household words.

It was natural to consider what sort of a world it would be if atomic energy ever became available. To compare such a world to that of to-day, it was necessary to contrast the latter with the world before the dawn of history and the art of kindling a fire. Just as the savage died of cold on the site of what now are coal-mines, and perished with hunger on corn-fields now energised with the fertilisers produced at Niagara, so, it seemed, we were leading a pettifogging existence, fighting one another like wild beasts for a share of the supplies of energy somewhat niggardly vouchsafed by Nature, whilst all round us existed the potentialities of a civilisation such as the world had not then even imagined possible.

The Part played by Energy in Human History.

In that way, some conception of the part played by energy in human history began to take shape, and progress in the material sphere appeared not so much as a successive mastery over the materials employed for the making of weapons – as the succession of ages of stone, bronze and iron, honoured by tradition – but rather as a successive mastery over the sources of energy in Nature, and their subjugation to meet the requirements of life. The whole of the achievements of our civilisation – in which it is differentiated from the slow, uncertain progress recorded by history – appeared as due to the mastery over the energy of fire reached with the advent of the steam engine. If, therefore, there is at hand not merely in the remote stars, but at our feet, an unlimited source of energy of the order of a million times more powerful than any known, what tremendous social consequences await the discovery of artificial transmutation!

Yet how far is human society from being safely entrusted with such powers? If the discovery were made to-morrow, there is not a nation that would not throw itself heart and soul into the task of applying it to war, just as they are now doing in the case of the newly developed chemical weapons of poison-gas warfare. In *The World Set Free* Mr. H. G. Wells, just before the outbreak of the Great War in 1914, devoted himself with his customary brilliance and insight to the question, and so vividly depicted the probable consequences that it would be superfluous for anyone of lesser gifts to pursue the topic, at least until the practical realisation of the disturbing dream comes nearer. For this is one of the newer developments of pure science, already referred to as still immeasurably beyond practical application. It may come quickly or again it may never come. At present there is hardly a hint even of how to begin. If it were to come under existing economic conditions, it would mean the *reductio ad absurdum* of our scientific civilisation, a swift annihilation instead of a none too lingering collapse.

“If what you tell us is true,” a scientific colleague, one of the Professors of Engineering, remarked to Rutherford in Montreal as long ago as 1902, "then we ought all, it seems, to be leaving the work we are doing and to concentrate our attention on the solution of this problem." Possibly many have since had the same thought. Yet, in scientific research, nothing is less likely than that the discoverer will discover what he sets out to discover. La Salle set out to discover China by sailing westwards from Europe. Lachine is not in China, but in the middle of the Province of Quebec, a tram ride from Montreal, on the great modern trans-continental route of the C.P.R. to the Orient. But the name still recalls the derision with which La Salle's pioneer attempt was greeted by his contemporaries. Scientific discovery could record episodes as strange. Pasteur studying fermentation discovered the important property of optical isomerism – which has developed almost into a science in itself – in passing on the road to the recognition of the part played by bacteria. But the most important part of his work was neither in brewing nor saccharometry. It revolutionised surgery, and to it countless millions owe their very lives.

Scientific discovery is a growth rather than a journey to plan. The voyage may be west to discover the east, and it is through fog and by dead-reckoning to put places upon, rather than to hit them off from a map. That transmutation may one day be possible and that the Coal and Oil Age will give place to an Atomic Age may be confidently expected, but when, and whether in this civilisation's cycle, none can guess.

The Real Capitalist a Plant

Still one point seemed lacking to account for the phenomenal outburst of activity that followed in the Western world the invention of the steam engine, for it could not be ascribed simply to the substitution of inanimate energy for animal labour. The ancients used the wind in navigation and drew upon water-power in rudimentary ways. The profound change that then occurred seemed to be rather due to the fact that, for the first time in history, men began to tap a large *capital* store of energy and ceased to be entirely dependent on the *revenue* of sunshine. All the requirements of pre-scientific men were met out of the solar energy of their own times. The food they ate, the clothes they wore, and the wood they burnt could be envisaged, as regards the energy content which gives them use-value, as stores of sunlight. But in burning coal one releases a store of sunshine that reached the earth millions of years ago. In so far as it can be used for the purposes of life, the scale of living may be, *to almost any necessary extent*, augmented, devotion to the primitive ideas of the peoples of Kirkcaldy and Judea notwithstanding.

Then came the odd thought about fuel considered as a capital store, out of the *consumption* of which our whole civilisation, in so far as it is modern, has been built.

You cannot burn it and still have it, and once burnt there is no way, thermodynamically, of extracting perennial interest from it. Such mysteries are among the inexorable laws of economics rather than of physics. With the doctrine of evolution, the real Adam turns out to have been an animal, and with the doctrine of energy the real capitalist proves to be a plant. The flamboyant era through which we have been passing is due not to our own merits, but to our having inherited accumulations of solar energy from the carboniferous era, so that life for once has been able to live beyond its income. Had it but known it, it might have been a merrier age! So, if atomic energy is ever tapped, an outburst of human activity would occur such as would make the triumphs of our times seem tawdry, and primitive humanity's struggle for energy as the fantastic memory of some horrid dream.

Is Science Accursed?

But what is gained merely by magnifying a scale? Would an enlarged reproduction of the present age satisfy any human soul? Awkward questions demand an answer. With all this new wealth the poverty of our ancestors has not been abolished, but has come back in a monstrous form. A growing army of unemployed, without proper means of subsistence, haunt a world capable of producing far more than it consumes, so that in a sense, new in history, the poor have become subservient to the rich even for permission to earn their livelihood. Is science accursed? What is the evil genius that perverts even the fulfilment of our sanest hopes and labours, and makes progress more like a nightmare climb among slippery slopes of ever-increasing steepness, than the mass march of humanity along a broad high road, made straight and smooth by increasing knowledge, order and law? It is idle to aspire to a more dangerously exalted civilisation until something of the definiteness and certainty of the economics of a fuel-engine can be extended to the economy of men. So that the crying need becomes not for ever and ever greater accessions of physical power, but the knowledge how to secure the fruits of what we already possess. The strong still plunder the weak, nations and individuals alike, whereas there is that in the growth of knowledge which would make the whole world kin. But that cannot come about until we understand what is wrong, nor whilst we attribute to an economic system mysterious powers which a physicist would laugh at.

Applied Science and Root Science

So as we drop back into the present from, as it were, a telescopic anticipation of a far remote future, the voices of the market-place fall somehow upon ears that hear with a difference. Scientific men are temperamentally unsuited to the tasks of government, but they might make valuable technical contributions in the wider problems of transport, the better utilisation of our natural resources, the more efficient training of labour. The nitrogen of the air might be wedded to the spirit of the waterfall to fertilise our soil in peace-time, so that we may breed more men, and again, to make high explosives in war-time to blow up the surplus, a veritable *sine qua non* of modern civilisation. Or, again, in agriculture, science could assist in breeding better brands of wheat, in making a Burgoyne's Fife that will outcrop the traditional Square Head's Master and stand the climate better. In Empire development, too, with its wealth of tropical possessions uninhabitable by the white man, science alone can hope to cope with the scourge of malaria and allay the ravages of sleeping sickness, and if our civil servants were pathologists, instead of morbid students of the pathology of human nature, much might be achieved. Again, looking on what government is, and on how the actions of the peoples may be swayed by expert appeals to their feelings and enthusiasms, psychology, the youngest of the sciences, might be roped in to lead humanity out of the morass into which it has been tumbled by the too-rapid growth of knowledge. Whilst, like the undertow of life, breaking on the obstructions that bar its flow, a ceaseless warning booms religiously of the scientific spirit and its search after truth for its own sake, without which there can be no hope of regeneration for society.

Science and Government

Are we any nearer the root of the matter? This book deals with none of these things. It does not deny their scope and possibilities in these days of universal education and the growth of intellectual interests, should civilisation last. It is concerned rather with the difference that comes over the familiar viewed from a fresh standpoint. The contribution of a physical scientist from the starting-point of physical science, it has nothing to do with technology or engineering, with psychology or the inculcation of the scientific spirit, but with the problem of government in its highest form! Just as in biology, materialism has proved itself fruitful and vitalism sterile in the winning of new knowledge, not in the least because organisms are merely machines, but because whatever else they may be, they obey the ascertainable laws of physics and chemistry, so in the tasks of government it would seem that a great clarification may result by applying to their elucidation common physical conceptions that are a truism in the inanimate world.

The theme, in various stages of development, has already been the subject of numerous public lectures and discussions and of two pamphlets. [10] The validity of the argument and the deductions therefrom, though sufficiently challenging have never been publicly challenged. But some have desired a fuller and less elliptical treatment.

The attempt to meet this led the author very much further into the subject than he ever hoped or expected to be able to penetrate, and finally, in his own estimation, to the definite solution of the economic paradox of the age. He found himself rather like Saul of Tarsus being converted into St. Paul, setting out to persecute the economists and ending, if not by becoming one – they may not be quite as forgiving a body as the early Christians – hopeful of ultimate reconciliation. At least he now has a more lively respect for the subtle pitfalls with which the subject abounds, and the impossibility of avoiding them all without some such mariner's compass as the physicist's law of conservation. Behind and aloof from the jostling of the individual members of the community, each intent on his own affairs, there exists an almost unknown science of national economics, as far removed from disinterested controversy as the propositions of geometry, and as simple, relatively, as the gas-laws obeyed by all gases in common are in contrast to the infinite complexity of the laws that regulate the

---

[10] *Cartesian Economics: The Bearing of Physical Sciences on State Stewardship*, 1922, and *The Inversion of Science and a Scheme of Scientific Reformation*, 1924. Hendersons.

behaviour of their component molecules. In this vital field at least there should, in this age, be no longer any room for bickering.

Scientific men have been repeatedly urged to co-operate in finding the solution of the problems that threaten our times. This is an unauthorised and individual contribution to a subject which is usually tabooed by them. It must not be taken as representing any but the author's own original studies in the subject. It would be a pity if it were taken as in any way reflecting upon the reputation for vision and nobility of thought which contemporaneous science has inherited as the result of the work of its early pioneers – after they were safely dead.

CHAPTER II

LIFE'S DISCOVERIES

Discovery, Sub-Conscious and Conscious

The keynote of the age is discovery, and life itself is discovery. Once made, countless generations may use it and live by it without conscious apprehension of the nature of it, without further changing their mode of livelihood, and, indeed, deeming it the only possible way to live. Another discovery displaces them, and a new species with new functions arises in the scheme of evolution. As with the origin of species, so it is with the economics of life of modern societies, though the first process is infinitely slow whilst the second is now alarming in its rapidity.

"No one by taking thought can add a cubit to his stature," and the origin of species in the community mirrors the apparently irrational sub-conscious growth of the individual organism. It is inherent and independent of the will. Individuals are born in mystery, develop with sheep-like fidelity into adults, breathe, circulate their blood, digest their food, and secrete the complex enzymes and hormones, the exact nature of which baffles the most skilled chemists, independently of their reasoning faculty and usually in total ignorance of the simplest principles of the sciences of which they are such astonishing examples. The origin of species is equally baffling.

Men grew apparently from the lower orders of the animals utterly unconsciously and only recently informed of the fact.

Whereas, if we consider the successive steps of discovery and invention by which the scientific age has developed from its forerunner, it appears totally different.

The evolution of the steam engine and motor-car from the stage coach, with numberless inventors taking thought over each tiny step and a few succeeding, seems as unlike as it well could be from the way, for example, the amphibians first invaded and brought life up on to the dry land.

Yet, if we take a broader view, more parallel with what, after all, at this distant epoch, must be that of a biologist trying to account for the origin of species, is there really such a vast difference? Did James Watt see himself, as his biographers have seen him, stretching forth his hand to the mighty lever that was to uplift civilisation? Is the average man even dimly conscious of the direction in which he is going? He may be profoundly conscious of *malaise* in the social constitution, possibly as many missing links in the evolution of species felt out of tune with their environment before they disappeared. For a full century after the discoveries which were to change the economic life of the world, the more vocal not only remained almost oblivious but denied that any real change had occurred at all.

The earlier cruder theories of the origin of species – that it was due to the infinitesimal differences that occur among the individuals of a species, under the purely impersonal and external operation of the law of the survival of the fittest leading by a process of natural selection to the origin of new species – are probably no longer held by modern biologists. Clearly, until we have an intelligible theory of normal individual growth, we can hardly hope for one to account for the great and apparently discontinuous departures from the normal which have produced new species. Selection may favour new growths but cannot account for them. Parallel with this earlier view, and the obvious reflection of it, we have the theory that human progress, from the primitive savage to the highly intellectual and powerful races of to-day, has been a sequence of infinitely small steps forced upon the attention of humanity by external necessity, and that it is something like pure chance which among the masses happens to take the step first and so to make the discovery. Such a view of human progress and genius is certainly not true of the scientific discoveries of the present era, it is contrary to the experience of every teacher, it could not be applied to art, literature, or music, and is probably not true of human progress at all.

The discoverer, though he may not know how he makes a discovery, knows that these philosophers know less. He bitterly resents the view of the general public towards discoveries, that they are the normal fruits of progress, whereas progress is, on the contrary, the fruit of discovery, and discovery is not a normal but an exceptional event. Doubtless the nameless discoverers of the arts of smelting bronze and tempering steel felt no better used. Pending a fuller explanation of the origin of species, we may extend our sympathies to the more man-like of the monkeys.

If we keep our attention on the plain facts of the case, rather than upon theories which seem to obliterate the facts, we find both in biological and human history, not continuity but a succession of great discoveries – whether made gradually or slowly, whether by the power of inherent growth or of reason – which, once made, do alter abruptly the whole future trend and mode of existence. Looking backwards through the eyes of historians and economists who have never made a discovery, or of biologists who have as yet not originated a new species, all the steps are slurred over, the dull uneventful interludes fade out, and though the record is of steady continuous progress, the reality was a fitful series of surprises. Looking forwards, discovery partakes much more of the character of a sub-conscious growth akin to that which originated species, and as independent of the consciousness of society as digestion is of the will. Whether Nature jumps or not, life undoubtedly does so.

The Unbroken Flow of Energy from the Inanimate World into Life

Chlorophyll, if not the first discovery of life, must have been a very early one. It is doubtful if any life known to us to-day, and scientifically studied, would survive if that discovery were wiped out. For this green colouring matter of vegetation is the door through which energy enters the living world. The vegetable kingdom still holds the only key to the original source of natural energy, sunshine, and everything living draws the wherewithal to live from the vegetable kingdom through the instrumentality of the dye chlorophyll acting as a transformer of solar energy.

It has been known for nearly a century, but the implications of the knowledge are often forgotten, that, with few and economically unimportant exceptions, the whole of the energy that makes the world a going concern comes from the sun. The internal energy of the living organism is neither created by the organism nor provided by Providence or usury. It gets there through the bodies of plants, and of animals that in turn feed upon plants, from the sun in the form of radiation.

The Internal and External Life-Use of Energy

It is convenient and practical to make a distinction between the internal energy of life, which maintains metabolism, and the external energy which an animal or plant can use in doing work on its environment, the plant in overcoming resistance to the growth of its roots and the spread of its branches, and the animal in locomotion and other movements. With draught-cattle and men, a large proportion of the whole energy of the food consumed may go to the performance of external work. Much of this again may be used merely in overcoming dead resistance, so being transformed into heat, as was first shown by the classic experiments of Count Rumford in 1798, on the continuous boiling of water during the boring of cannon by machinery turned by horses, and as, indeed, was discovered by most primitive peoples, before contact with civilisation, and used to kindle fire. But when the work is done against an active resistance, as in lifting weights against gravity, it may be stored or accumulated as work in potential form, recoverable again, as work, for example, by allowing the weight to fall. Just as a clock must be wound up and provided with a store of available energy before it will go, so a man has to be wound up before he can wind a clock, and the economics of life deals primarily with the ways in which Nature winds up man. The natural tendency of energy to degrade itself at one stage into worthless heat must be circumvented, so that there is something useful at the end to show for it, something, that is, that, at will, can be turned into work again, and used in life.

Now, as regards the internal energy of life, though there are no theoretical barriers to an artificial synthesis of the foodstuffs that furnish it – from such entirely inanimate materials and powers as, say, graphite and water, and the energy of a wind-mill – in practice, it all still comes through the plant. The vast extension of our food supply, which in this country now enables us to feed a population greater by at least five times than in the pre-scientific era, has been *indirectly* effected by the purely inanimate prime-movers used both in transporting the produce of far-distant countries, and in displacing human and animal labour, in the technical sense of physical work, upon the farm. Also, sources of water-power running to waste have been harnessed, and some of their energy stored by chemical processes to give fertilisers which increase the productivity of the soil. Some of these bring to the plant already energised nitrogen, which it cannot itself produce, but for which it is dependent either on bacterial parasites or upon the natural meagre supply from the air produced by the action of lightning flashes and the rays of radium.

Here, as frequently, we are following a single thread, because it is continuous – the flow of energy in nature and how life makes use of it. This does not mean that other factors are unimportant, or negligible, but simply that, if we pursue this unbroken thread, certain physical conclusions emerge which are independent of all other considerations and to which life must always conform. In the present case, for example, a large and increasing share of the credit for an increased food-supply is due to the work of biologists in breeding new varieties of wheat.

Possibly future races of men may feed their internal fires in the same way as we perform external labour, with inanimate energy. But until entirely new discoveries are made, agriculture remains still the key industry of life. All that science has been able to do has been of indirect assistance. Fundamentally it remains unchanged, as the collection of sunlight by the agency of chlorophyll and its transformation into the chemical energy of foodstuffs, either directly or through the intermediate transforming agency of animals. The depression which has overtaken it in this country is of local rather than world significance. It is not in this field, but solely as regards the external energy of life, that science now so largely passes life by and draws directly on purely inanimate energy as it is found in nature, without the necessity of passing it through living bodies. True, men are still necessary, though fewer every year, as routine tasks become more and more automatically performed by machines. But the function has changed. The worker contributes now only an insignificant part of the work required from his own body. He is there rather to contribute intelligence. From a labourer he has become the director of an artificial process, circumventing the natural tendency of energy to go to waste by diligence rather than by strength.

The Origins of Available Energy

The doctrine of energy teaches that although energy is conserved in all processes, and is never either created or destroyed, it has a natural tendency to pass at once into the useless and unavailable form, which is the ultimate end of all kinetic energy – namely, heat of the same temperature as the surroundings. Life is by no means the only process of economic significance by which this tendency is circumvented, but it is by far the most important. In this respect, machines are merely imitations of life, for they all possess some replica of an intelligence to perform an artificial cycle of operations chosen in the first instance by the brain of the designer.

Nowadays, the process of greatest economic importance by means of which the revenue of solar energy is transformed into a useful or "available" form without the intervention of life is that by which water-power originates. A minute fraction of the energy that falls upon the ocean escapes total degradation into useless heat and evaporates the water. By a natural process – very similar, however, to that which is made artificially to occur in the steam engine – the water vapour ascends and suffers "adiabatic cooling and expansion." It so performs useful work upon itself in climbing against gravity. It chills as it ascends, until it is condensed again as rain, collects in rivers, which drive water-wheels and turbines on their course to the ocean. The wind-power, which formerly was of greater economic importance in navigation, and in irrigation and reclamation by means of wind-mills, is in a precisely analogous category.

It is, however, a relatively very insignificant part of the solar income, which escapes the vigilance of life in the first instance that so offers it a second chance. The origin of oil energy is doubtful, and will be referred to again. Tidal power is in the exceptional category of not being derived from radiation. It is furnished from the energy of revolution of the moon round the earth, and of the rotation of the earth on its axis. For this reason, the period of the day and lunar month are increasing slowly over secular periods of time, and in the end the terrestrial day must become the same as the terrestrial year, just as already the lunar day is the same as the lunar month.

The energy of volcanoes and hot springs is derived from the internal heat of the earth, but the origin of this is doubtful in the same sense as the origin of oil energy, and this will be referred to again later.

The Physical Chemistry of Metabolism

Let us now turn to the main sources of energy in nature rendered available for life by the action of life. That part of the solar income which falls on opaque objects goes instantly into heat, and swiftly after that, by conduction, to heat of temperature uniform with the surroundings. In this form it consists of the energy of movement of the ultimate molecules of which matter is made. As kinetic energy, it still exists in undiminished amount, but it is useless. The motions in question are distributed in every direction, or perfectly deco-ordinated, whereas mechanical energy is essentially energy directed in a definite direction of space. It is impossible again to co-ordinate the direction, without performing more work than is gained, though, whilst the heat is of higher temperature than its surroundings, use may be made of its natural tendency to flow into cooler objects, to reconvert a small part of it back into mechanical energy again.

But when the solar energy falls upon the chlorophyll of vegetation it is not turned into heat, but into chemical energy. Few probably of those who have experienced the cool relief from the sunshine on entering a dense forest, realise that it is due to something more than mere shade. The forest is one of the units of Nature's primary transformer house, which in efficiency and scale makes all the works of men seem insignificant. The sunshine is no longer degraded into heat by battling against an opaque resistance, but is, though only to a small extent, transformed into a store of potential energy in the timber, recoverable again when the wood is burned.

In some wholly mysterious, but still purely physical process, the chlorophyll brings together the energy of the waves of light and the material carbon dioxide and moisture of the air, producing from them oxygen and the carbohydrates-formaldehyde, and the many varieties of sugar, dextrin or gums, starch and cellulose, enumerated in order of increasing molecular complexity. As the name "carbohydrate" indicates, they are all made of carbon and water. Of old this would have been considered a chemical synthesis effected by and dependent upon the living organism itself. But now it is known to be due to a process the chemist calls catalysis, in which a reaction that can take place without disobedience to the laws of energy, but nevertheless does not take place, can take place in the presence of a minute quantity of a substance, called a catalyst, which does not itself, apparently, react and which remains unchanged. Buchner, in 1897, found that an extract from yeast, in which all trace of the living yeast cells had been obliterated, still fermented sugar into alcohol like the living plant. The action is due to a catalyst, or enzyme, as it is generally termed in bio-chemistry, *secreted by the organism*, but not itself either organised or alive. Purely mineral substances, such as finely divided platinum and other metals, possess similar powers in inorganic reactions. Though the action of chlorophyll is probably catalytic, i.e. its presence enables other substances to react which do not react in its absence, yet in this case there is the additional feature, which gives the process its outstanding importance, that the chemical reaction cannot go on at all except with the continuous supply of energy furnished by the light. The chlorophyll, in fact, effects the marriage of energy and matter. It is a photo-chemically active catalyst, secreted by the living plant, but itself simply a substance, neither organised nor alive.

When fuel is burned, or food is consumed in metabolism, the reaction which takes place is just the reverse of that produced by chlorophyll in sunlight. The carbohydrates are burnt to carbon dioxide and water by the oxygen of the air, and energy in the form of heat is given out. To unburn the carbon dioxide and water back into carbohydrates and oxygen, the energy given out during the combustion must be refurnished. This is what the plant accomplishes. The energy of the sunshine, in presence of chlorophyll, re-enters the dead products of combustion and metabolism, the oxygen is reliberated into the air, and the compounds of carbon and water formed are stored up in the plant's tissues.

A world originating as ours is supposed to have done, as a planet thrown off from the parent sun, during its evolution from a nebula, may be regarded as having been well "burnt" in the first instance. By the time it was a fit abode for life all the carbon, one must suppose, would exist combined with oxygen. This raises the question of the origin of life from a new angle. How can chlorophyll arise except by life, and how could life maintain itself except by chlorophyll? For chlorophyll is an exceeding complicated carbon compound, provisionally regarded by chemists as compounded out of 55 atoms of carbon, 72 of hydrogen, 4 of nitrogen, 5 of oxygen and one of the metal magnesium. It has not yet been made artificially, and the nature of its molecular structure – which is always a necessary preliminary step in any artificial synthesis – remains in considerable doubt. One can hardly regard this particular compound as coming into existence naturally without life, and yet its existence as we know it is essential to the life-process. Brown varieties of it are known as in the brown algae, which, chemically, are indistinguishable from the green.

We may suppose that life began with simpler photo-chemically active catalysts than chlorophyll, and possibly even used in the first instance purely mineral substances as catalysts. But as far as we have yet traced back the origin of life, it is already making use of an extremely complex and peculiar substance in order to obtain the energy it requires from the sunlight by what is essentially a very remarkable and, indeed, almost unique type of action. The whole range of chemistry and bio-chemistry affords hardly any parallel. Certainly no chemical product is made industrially by any process at all analogous to the natural methods of manufacturing starch and cellulose.

We hear so often of the practical triumphs of chemistry, that it may come as a surprise to the reader that no chemist has as yet the most rudimentary theory of why a chemical change takes place at all. The statement that the products of combustion are unburnt into carbohydrates and oxygen, by the energy of sunlight, in presence of a photo-chemically active catalyst chlorophyll, is a description, not an explanation.

We have, however, got as far as *suspecting* that before *any* chemical change at all can take place, some preliminary process of "activisation," as it is termed, of the reacting molecules must occur, and that radiation, in general, is the agent which transforms the normal chemically inactive molecule into one that will react with another, when it crosses its path. Solar radiation is in the middle of the long gamut of radiation, which extends from the waves used in wireless transmission on the long-side of wave-length, to the X-rays of Röntgen and the *y*-rays of radium on the short-side. We are apt to forget that all known substances are hot, in the sense that a cold body is one without heat-energy at all – which is one at the unattainable absolute zero of temperature, -273° C. All are, like the sun, radiating energy. The amount at ordinary temperature is very small, and the wave-length of the rays is on the long-side of the visible light region. That is, the radiation is of dark-heat rays until we reach the temperature of visible red-heat. But it is always going on, and some modern theories of chemical change appeal to this dark-heat radiation as the activising agent that precedes even the commonest and most spontaneous chemical reactions. If this view proves well-founded, every chemical reaction becomes analogous to that effected by the plant. The whole topic is itself an illustration of how life intuitively arrives at discoveries, which the reason only makes long after and with the utmost difficulty.

Coal and Oil

In earlier years, the geologists tell us, life originated in the sea and, from there, invaded the land. Long before animal evolution had proceeded very far, vegetation flourished in excessive abundance in the form of giant tree-ferns, the fossilised remains of which furnish our coal measures to-day. In this, the carboniferous era, the temperature must have been higher and the amount of carbon-dioxide and water vapour in the air higher than to-day. It was under such conditions that the immense stores of energy upon which, almost entirely, modern civilisation depends, were laid down and accumulated. This accumulation is entirely the work of life. So far as is known, nothing of the kind is happening to-day, and human development, as we know it, is entirely dependent upon a favourable concatenation of biological and geological events untold ages ago.

The origin of mineral oils is uncertain. They consist essentially of compounds of carbon and hydrogen, or hydrocarbons. There are, broadly, two probable origins, both of which may have operated. From the frequent occurrence of traces of marine organisms in natural oil it has been surmised that it may have resulted from the decomposition, and subsequent transformation under heat and pressure, of the remains of fishes, which in earlier times may have inhabited the seas in greater abundance than now. Without specially insisting on its animal origin, it is quite conceivable that vegetable remains, like coal, would meet in the earth favourable conditions for being converted into oil. A modern technical process, still in the experimental stage, known as the "berginisation" of coal, transforms powdered coal, mixed with tar, into oil by heating it with hydrogen under great pressure to a high temperature.

On the other hand, a purely inorganic origin is suggested by the work of Moissan on the metallic carbides, which are produced at the temperature of the electric furnace by heating metals or their oxides with carbon. Thus calcium carbide, obtained by so heating lime and coke, is universally known as the source, when brought into contact with water, of the gaseous hydrocarbon, acetylene. Other metallic carbides give other hydrocarbons in the same way, and from uranium carbide a mixture of liquid hydrocarbons, very similar in character and constitution to natural petroleum, has been obtained. It is almost certain that, deep in the earth's interior, conditions of high temperature and high pressure exist, which would cause the formation of such carbides from their component elements if present. If so, the production of petroleum by the subsequent infiltration of water may be legitimately inferred.

Solar and Atomic Energy

The point is of some interest as, according to the first theory, the origin of the energy of oil is the sunlight, and to the second, the internal heat of the earth. That, again, on the older views was regarded as part of the original legacy of solar heat when the earth was expelled from a still gaseous sun. But on modern views, developed by Joly, the internal heat of the earth is being continuously maintained by the process of radioactivity. If so, oil, on the second theory of its origin, derives its energy from the atom. Its use thus represents an early step in the emancipation of life from entire dependence upon solar supplies. The same is true of small uses of the earth's internal heat that man has probably always practised, much as the Maoris of Whakarewarewa, to-day, use the hot springs for all their domestic needs. The people of Iceland even grow vegetables, which the climate would not otherwise permit, by their aid. The borax industry of Tuscany, where the steam from *suffioni* is used to evaporate the water from hot springs containing borax, is another example.

Indeed, the larger scale utilisation of such energy for power was prospected during the War, owing to the dearness of coal in Italy. It has even been suggested, not entirely chimerically, that if coal failed the internal heat of the earth might be drawn upon on a large scale by boring sufficiently deep wells, and circulating water through them under pressure, so converting it into steam.

As regards the energy of the sun itself, there seems little reason to doubt that it also is due to atomic energy. True, radioactivity and known processes of atomic disintegration are far too special and limited to provide such immense supplies. On the other hand, the theory of relativity has introduced a new conception as to the relation between energy and matter, which though as yet entirely without experimental verification, is regarded as the only likely explanation of the maintenance over cosmical epochs of the prodigal evolution of energy from the sun and stars. This theory blends the laws of conservation of energy and of matter into one, in the sense that matter is only conserved when its energy is unchanged and that energy is only conserved if mass is unchanged. Any loss of energy by a system is accompanied by an actual loss of mass, though infinitesimal and as yet totally unverifiable by experiment. An annihilation of matter, if it could occur, would result in the appearance of energy equal to twice that of the mass lost moving with the speed of light. The loss of mass is too small, in relation to the energy evolved, for it to have been put into evidence, as yet, even in the most energetic changes known. It is supposed that cosmical energy may be the consequence of a slow process of material annihilation.

The evidence of stellar spectroscopy shows that stars begin their incandescent career as hydrogen and helium, and that only later do the heavier elements make their appearance. It is inferred that the heavier elements are formed by condensation from the lighter. If we take one case, from the standpoint of modern views on atomic structure, and suppose the gas hydrogen to be suffering, in the stellar economy, a condensation into helium, so that four atoms of the former coalesce to make one atom of the latter, the process alone would go far to account for the origin of cosmical energy. Because in so condensing into helium, the four hydrogen atoms would experience a loss of mass of about three parts in four hundred, the atomic weight of hydrogen being 1.0075, in terms of that of helium as 4.000. It is to some such source as this that the modern cosmogonist appeals. The *earlier* stages in the evolution of the elements – like the last stage, the breaking up of the most complex elements in radioactivity – may be expected to yield rather than require energy.

Civilisation seeks to control the Flow of Energy from nearer its Source

Having thus briefly dealt with the sources of energy in nature, and with how, in the first instance, they become available for life, the subsequent steps present no novelty. The whole animal kingdom is distinguished from the vegetable by its total inability to use natural inanimate energy in its internal metabolism. This has, first, to be stored in the tissues of plants, upon which the herbivora feed. Carnivora are one similar step farther removed from the original source, and omnivera, like men, have two strings to their bow. From hunting and the chase man more and more developed towards the domestication of animals not only for food, but for wool, leather and the raw materials of clothing. In more settled times, the same tendency led to agriculture and the conscious cultivation of natural plants both for food and raw materials. From the energetic standpoint progress may be regarded as a successive mastery and control over sources of energy ever nearer the original source.

We may attempt to translate the salient facts of this inquiry somewhat as follows.

The diagram depicts the flow of energy in nature from left to right. The line running from solar energy to man is the line life has intuitively developed by the inherent property of its own growth. The lines pointing from right to left indicate the directions in which man has reached out consciously to augment and control the supplies, and the tendency of progress more and more to short-circuit life out of the economic system.

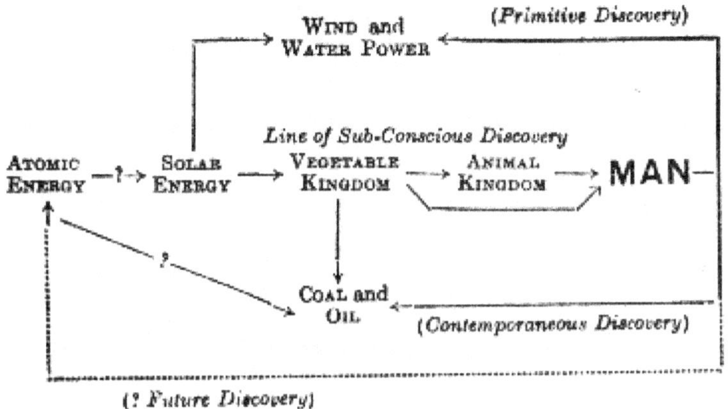

CHAPTER III

THE BASIS OF NATIONAL ECONOMICS

The Struggle for Energy.

Though it was not understood a century ago, and though as yet the applications of the knowledge to the economics of life are not generally realised, life in its physical aspect is fundamentally a struggle for energy, in which discovery after discovery brings life into new relations with the original source. Evolutionary development has been parasitic, higher and higher organisms arising and obtaining the requisite supplies of energy by feeding upon the lower. But with man and the development of conscious reason, that process as regards energy is being reversed. Little by little the scaffolding on which he ascended is being discarded, and he is consciously reaching farther and farther back to the original sources of energy for his life. At the present stage, in the twentieth century, most of the external work of life can be better done by machinery fed with fuel. In this direction there is still a rapid development, though now probably past its most active period. So long as the fuel supplies hold out, there is literally no limit to the production of commodities required for living that can be made in this way, as was alluded to in the first chapter, if financial restrictions were rendered inoperative, as they were during the War. Given a plentiful supply of timber and similar raw materials, this class of manufactured article covers most of the accessories and luxuries required for living, from houses and furniture to motor-cars and wireless sets. It comprises practically all the tools, buildings and plant necessary for production, transport and communication. To such *agents of production* the chameleon-like term *Capital* is confined in the sequel.

As regards food and raw materials of organic origin, the extension of productivity, though practically enormous and hardly less important than in the other categories, is only indirectly favoured by the new step. Food is still essentially produced entirely by the original agricultural process. This is true also of raw materials of vegetable and animal origin, though many of them can be replaced by artificial substitutes of one kind or another, if the natural products are unobtainable.

The Broad Teachings of Thermodynamics

Let us briefly review the great generalisations of the early part of last century with regard to energy, which apply not only to machines but with equal rigour to living beings and the life of communities. They are usually referred to as the First and Second Laws of Thermodynamics, the name recalling their origin. They were, in the first place, recognised for the relations between heat and work, or between thermal and mechanical energy. But the principles are of universal application as between heat and any form of energy. Language only very tardily overtakes ideas, and ideas precede, in point of time, linguistic labels for them. The formal definitions of the laws of thermodynamics would completely fail to convey any idea of their character to those not already possessed of it, whereas descriptive statements lack the precision and universality of the general idea. Those laws are essentially, in the first instance, expressions of experience, tested after their apprehension thoroughly and exhaustively by experiment in new and still untried fields, but they are not such as can yet be simply deduced from first principles.

The Impossibility of Perpetual Motion Machines or Men

The First Law is easy to understand and is nothing else than a statement of the law of conservation of energy. It denies the possibility of a perpetual motion machine, in which any prime mover – machine, molecular system, or man – can continue to furnish work out of nothing, without an equivalent amount of energy being supplied. A motorcar running without petrol or a man living without food would be examples. The forms assumed by physical energy are numerous, but all forms are capable of conversion into, and of measurement as heat energy, much as any account, for the purpose of reckoning, may be transformed into £ sterling, whatever the original currency may be. Thus the scientific unit of heat energy is the Calorie.[11] The Calorie is the amount of heat necessary to raise a kilogram of water 1° Centigrade (or 1 lb. of water 1.023° Fahrenheit). The British unit of work or mechanical energy is the foot-pound, and the metric unit the kilogram-metre. They represent the work done in raising the weight through the distance specified, or the kinetic energy possessed by that weight when it has fallen freely under gravity from that distance. The unit of power, known as the horse-power, is the power required to lift 550 lb. one foot in *one second*, or 1 lb. 550 feet in one second, or 1 lb. one foot in 1/550th of a second. The horse-power-hour is the work done by one horse-power in one hour, and is roughly two million foot-pounds. If the work is done against dead resistance and so converted completely into heat, without any of it being stored up in a potential form, as in the lifting of a weight, 653.6 Calories are produced from one horse-power every hour. Or one horse-power-hour equals 653.6 Calories. In a similar way it is possible to evaluate the energy of the foodstuffs required to maintain the average adult man for a year. It is about a million Calories.

This amount of heat is given out if the food is burnt. Consumed by a man, a small part may be given out as work in labour and locomotion, but most of it always appears as bodily heat. As a working mechanism, a man may be highly efficient from the point of view of the part of the energy value of his food that appears as work.

This sometimes exceeds 30 per cent, and the very best steam engines rarely approach this efficiency.

The First Law, as the law of conservation of energy, is essentially quantitative. It expresses nothing as to the quality or usefulness of the various sorts of energy. In itself it neither affirms nor denies the physical possibility of eating cake and still having it, for in place of the energy of food, when it is eaten, we have an equivalent of heat-energy.

This is the province of the Second Law, which takes into account the natural direction in which energy tends to transform itself, from

---

[11] When spelt with a small *c* a unit a thousand times less is indicated.

food-energy into waste heat-energy by consumption or decay, not from waste heat-energy into food-energy, which would be an unnatural process. An unnatural process in this sense is not necessarily physically impossible, but is always economically impossible as a means of saving work, i.e. of using the same energy twice over, or, more generally, of arriving at a *perpetuum mobile* by employing the same energy over and over again indefinitely.

In its practical significance energy itself is of no importance. It is the flow of energy from one form to another and from one place to another that alone is of importance. This flow always occurs in one natural direction, and it can only be reversed in direction by making more energy flow down stream, so to speak, than flows up. As this analogy suggests, a flow of energy has some of the characteristics of a river, and, indeed, the laws of thermodynamics were originally arrived at on the then prevalent view of heat as an actual fluid. When, later, the kinetic view – that heat is due to the deco-ordinated energy of agitation of the individual molecules of matter – became general, the second law of thermodynamics became less easy rather than more easy to deduce from first principles.

Illustrative Physical Processes

It is easy to imagine a process in which weights, for example, are caused to rise against gravity by the fall of heavier weights. Just about the time when the steam engine came into general use a method of performing human labour was discovered, far more efficient than any other. It was used in building some of the fortifications of Paris, and, but for the steam engine, would probably have by now become very general. The workman works by walking up a flight of steps, and descending by a rope, to which is attached the load he has to lift, and which is only a little less than his own weight. In this way he can do many times as much work as with a wheelbarrow or with any of the older methods.

The ease with which all other forms of energy tend to pass into heat-energy is paralleled by the difficulty of reversing the process. Heat tends to flow from a region of higher temperature to one of lower, just as water tends to flow downhill. To reverse the process is like making water run uphill – an artificial process requiring, *as well as* a mechanical appliance, respectively a pump or a refrigerating plant, *the expenditure of work*. It is easy to see why you have to do work to pump water uphill, because you can get the work back again when the water pumped up is allowed to flow down. But in a modified form the same is true of a flow of heat. A perpetual motion machine of the second sort, as it is termed, would not contravene the First Law of conservation, but would the Second Law of usefulness. Such a machine would be the equivalent of a man eating food and turning it into carbon dioxide, water and heat, and then putting back the heat-energy gained into the carbon dioxide and water and remaking the food. The plant does this, not with spent heat-energy, but with fresh energy of radiation, and radiant heat from a body at high temperature, though similar in name to heat-energy, is a very high quality and a very available form of energy, at the opposite end of the scale to the low temperature heat-energy into which it is naturally degraded.

In the steam engine, the natural tendency for heat to pass from a higher to a lower temperature is used to perform the unnatural process of converting heat into work. Any natural process – whether the flow of water downhill, the flow of heat from a hot body to a cooler one, or the flow of a gas from a higher pressure to a lower one – can, at least in theory, be so directed and performed as to convert a part at least of the flow of energy into mechanical energy or work. But how much of it can be so converted is different for different kinds of energy. Apart from incidental losses, such as are due to the imperfections of any actual mechanism – its friction, resistance, and so on – and which can be reduced indefinitely by better and more "ideal" contrivances, some flows of energy are completely convertible into work and others only partially. An electric motor will – but for the incidental losses referred to – convert the electric energy with which it is supplied completely into mechanical energy, and, even in practice, very high efficiencies, exceeding 90 per cent, are attainable. But a flow of heat can never, even in "ideal" circumstances, be more than partially converted into work. Neglecting, as before, all incidental losses due to practical mechanical imperfections, the maximum proportion of any flow of heat capable of being converted into work is stated by the Second Law in its quantitative form as follows.[12]

[12] Note on the Absolute Temperature Scale: The Real or Absolute Zero of temperature, expressed in the Centigrade scale, is -273 °C. That is to say, at this temperature matter would possess no heat-energy at all. The Absolute Scale of

In the flow of heat from a higher temperature, T1° A., to a lower temperature, T2° A., out of every T1 units of heat T2 units are not convertible, and must remain unchanged as heat whatever process is under consideration; but there is the *opportunity* or *possibility* – never easy, and often practically impossible, to realise – of converting T1 – T2 units at most into mechanical energy by suitable mechanical and other appliances. Thus, in practice, a steam engine, which is supplied with live steam at 200° C. (473° A.) and which rejects the steam to the condenser at 40° C. (313° A.), can – apart from all losses due to frictional and other resistances and imperfections – never convert more than 160/473, or about one-third, of the heat-energy with which it is supplied into work. The internal-combustion engine, in which the heat-energy is supplied by the explosion of gaseous mixtures, at temperatures in the neighbourhood of white heat (2,000° A.), is thermally far more "efficient" than any steam engine.

As an example of a practical process in which the natural flow of energy is reversed – for some special practical purpose – we may take refrigeration, which essentially is the pumping of heat out of a cold body into a hotter body, the latter being usually at the temperature of the surrounding air. In this process it is as necessary to expend work as in pumping water up from a well to ground-level. In practice, refrigeration is effected by first using the work that has to be done, to compress a gas whereby this work is converted into heat (the natural direction of the flow of energy), so that the gas gets hot. The hot compressed gas is cooled to the temperature of the surroundings (again the natural direction of the flow of energy).

Then the compressed gas is allowed to expand and do work, which is the reversal of the first process. The gas is cooled below the temperature of the surroundings by reason of the work which it is made to do being taken from it at the expense of its heat-energy. In this way, paradoxically, work is first converted into heat to gain the opportunity at a later stage of converting heat into work. But unless work is first spent in compressing the gas, against its natural tendency to expand, we

---

Temperature is derived from the Centigrade scale by simply adding 273°. Thus 15° C. is 288° A.

could not later make use of this natural tendency of gases to expand to overcome the natural disinclination of heat to turn into work.

Although heat is not a material fluid, the Second Law is thus much what it would be if it were, and if the temperature of the heat above its surroundings corresponded to the height of the fluid above the level. To raise water from a well requires work, and to refrigerate a substance requires work. The task of converting waste heat-energy of uniform temperature into work is like trying to get water-power from the ocean. The absolute zero of water-level would be the centre of the earth, and the absolute zero of temperature or heat-level would be -273°C. But outlets to the earth's centre and condensers at absolute zero are not possible, and in each case the practical zero level is far above, being the sea-level in the one case and the temperature of the earth in the other.

Wealth as a Form or Product of Energy Its Unlimited Producibility

We thus arrive at the conclusion that any sort of perpetual motion is impossible.

A continuous stream of fresh energy is necessary for the continuous working of any working system, whether animate or inanimate. Life is cyclic as regards the material substances consumed, and the same materials are used over and over again in metabolism. But as regards energy, it is unidirectional, and no continuous cyclic use of energy is even conceivable. If we have available energy, we may maintain life and produce every material requisite necessary. That is why the flow of energy should be the primary concern of economics. In a world which has adequate supplies of energy, scientific knowledge and inventions for utilising it, and the man-power able and willing to perform the necessary duties and services, poverty and destitution are purely artificial institutions, due to ignorance of the principles of government, actively, if not deliberately, fostered for class ends by legal conventions confounding wealth with debt. Under any scientific system of government they would disappear like small-pox and malaria, by means of preventive rather than ameliorative or curative measures.

It is, of course, perfectly well understood by those who have studied the subject, that consumable wealth is not like gold, silver, radium, or other elements that exist only in small quantities in the earth and which cannot yet be artificially made. The attraction of such substances as measures of wealth, upon which to base monetary value, is, of course, in the power over the debtor they put into the hands of the creditor. Money, in fact, becomes a monopoly, and this monopoly is the real government. Wealth, in the sense of the requisites of life, can now be made as required, and has no relation whatever to such ingenious financial devices. Its study has been sadly neglected by the economist.

Although, to everyone except an engineer or a physicist, energy seems to be quite a minor item in the production of wealth, if we concern ourselves with what is used up in the process of creating wealth, it is the largest and most important item.

Thus, in the cost of upkeep of a car the petrol is a minor item. Till lately the tyres cost more. Yet, if we pursue the tyres to their origin, we shall find how much of their cost is due to expenditure of energy. They call for a flow of the solar energy of a particular climate, physical labour in rubber plantations, coal for the railways and ships that transport the raw materials from the tropics, as well as for the factories where it is made into tyres. These railways and ships, again, and all the buildings and equipment necessary for their manufacture, no less than the materials they use – the iron and metals and the coal which have to be mined – are the results of the expenditure of physical energy. The armies of people these industries maintain have to be supplied with food, clothes and houses, and energy under intelligent human direction is the first requisite for the supply of *all* such things.

Poverty and Unemployment
A Monstrous Contradiction

Much of this, of course, if not its implications, is well understood to apply by the specialist, though usually the source of wealth is not quite traced back as far as the physical energy of sunshine. But long ages of penury and subjection, to one form of injurious domination or another, have accustomed people to look upon wealth as something which, like gold, is essentially limited in amount, so that, if some get much, others must go short to make up the balance, rather than a quantity which scientific advances have made capable of almost indefinite expansion. None of the world's real problems centre to-day around the mere provision of wealth. The difficulties arise rather in getting rid of even a small part of what can be made, without fighting for the privilege of either making or selling it. But to people who think of wealth not in terms of energy and human endeavour, but in terms of money-tokens, there seems to be nothing incongruous in the continuance of the acute economic suffering into which Europe has been plunged, nor any evidence of failure in the most elementary function of government in the spectacle of unemployment and poverty *at one and the some time.*

The Change from Labour to Diligence

The elementary discussion of the principles of thermodynamics which has been attempted may not prove entirely superfluous if it directs attention to what is probably the most prevalent confusion in all sociological thought at the present time, between what is here termed work or energy in the purely physical sense and what passes for it in common language. A manual labourer does supply out of his own body the energy of the physical labour he performs. Part of his food goes to produce it. He is a self-contained prime-mover. But a man tending a machine may "work hard" in the ordinary sense without doing any real physical work, to speak of, at all.

His real function has changed. His action is what in physics is known with sufficient expressiveness as "trigger-action." In the action of a trigger an amount of energy is liberated which has no relation to the work of pulling the trigger, and in operating any power-driven appliance it is the same. A woman who complains that a woman's work is never done means that in the domestic operations of cooking, cleansing, and generally providing for the requirements of a household, there is a continuous drain upon her attention and mental activities, and that the multifarious tasks of household management are endless. She is not usually complaining against the actual physical labour and exertion involved in any of these tasks, but of the long and fatiguing round of perpetual vigilance which they exact. Particularly in this field, perhaps, we have still a combination of some physical labour with continuous mental attention, and though labour-saving devices have done much to relieve the drudgery of house management, in the domestic sphere, as also in the transport services and many others, we have good examples of tasks which require both individual care and effort which no growth of science is likely altogether to supplant. Whereas in a factory, engaged in a definitely routine production, only a very small and unimportant part of the actual physical work involved may be contributed by the workers, and this amount is capable of almost indefinite reduction, as machines become more and more automatic. The necessity for unremitting attention to the work in hand remains, though fewer workers are necessary. It is mere boredom to a man who could manage comfortably to attend to a dozen automatic machines to be restricted by trade-union rules to tending only one.

In this connection, as regards industries which are supposed to demand a supply of cheap uneducated labour and the blind-alley occupations which take children from school and do not provide any chance of a reasonable livelihood for an adult, it is a very open question whether they are not the natural result of such labour being plentiful. At least in America, the restriction of immigration was held to threaten the existence of some industries which depended on the continuous supply of cheap, underpaid labour from Europe. But experience showed that when the supply was cut off, it was easy to re-adapt the industries concerned to the new conditions. In general, it may well be doubted whether any occupation, however much it may seem to demand a coarse, animal-like type of worker – or the services of hosts of children and youths, as in delivering newspapers and household supplies – could not to-day be done better if such were entirely eliminated, by proper business organisation and more up-to-date methods.

The function of the worker, since the introduction of mechanical power, has totally changed in many industries, and in none is the change unimportant. More and more he does not work in the physical sense, but is directing an inanimate source of power to do what, left alone, it could not do.

In many industries, as in the mass production of motor-cars, or of any kind of machinery which has gone through its rapid period of evolution and arrived at something like a final and permanent form, the rule will be for greater output with the employment of ever fewer hands, as the processes involved become more and more automatically controlled. Yet there is no chance, even here, of entirely dispensing with the human worker. His task, physically lighter, becomes mentally ever more monotonous and uninteresting. Whilst, if we look round at the multifarious needs of the world, from domestic management and transport of goods and passengers to mining – the source, after all, of the new wealth – there remains a sufficiency of hard work in the sense of continuous diligence, if not in the scientific sense, permanently to occupy a large part of the world's population for some part at least of the day.

Science, more and more displacing human and animal labour, does not displace the labourer, but tends to transform his function. It should give him for an hour's attention what before he got for twelve hours' work.

Mining, building, road-making and maintenance, transport, and, last but not least, agriculture, are unnatural processes in the thermodynamical sense. In thermodynamics the distinction between useless energy and useful turns on the direction and the dissipation of this direction. A useful form is that which has some definite direction in which it tends to flow. A useless form is that in which the direction is internally "higgledy-piggledy," the smallest possible parts moving perpetually, equal numbers in all possible directions, at one and the same time. An unnatural process consists in directing a flow of energy in its natural direction, in such a way that it cannot so flow without performing some useful task and doing some work necessary for living. This is the third essential factor in the creation of wealth, the function which, of old-time, used to be termed "labour," but to-day would be much better termed "diligence." Few are the exceptions in a civilisation worthy of itself in which it would not now be better for mere heavy physical labour to be done by mechanical power.

Curiously, the "agricultural labourer" has always been much more of a diligent tender of the labours of plants and animals than a real labourer in the physical sense.

That his work is far more skilled and irreplaceable than that of many of the operatives employed in the so-called skilled engineering trades was shown during the War. Machine tending could be performed after very little apprenticeship by juvenile and unskilled labour, but only under stress of the direst military necessity were the skilled farm-hands conscripted into the ranks.

Discovery, Natural Energy and Diligence – the Three Ingredients of Wealth

Thus, when we deal with the real factors that underlie the production of wealth – unclouded by questions of property-law, the individual rights of ownership, and the complications introduced by monetary systems – we can sum them up as Discovery, Natural Energy and Human Diligence. The first enters in the form of sudden and more or less spasmodic contributions which, once made, permanently alter the whole future course of history. But the two last must be continuously and unremittingly provided as long as time shall last. Under the term Diligence, used in lieu of Labour, is to be included not merely the services of artisans and labourers, but also those of business men, employers of labour, managers and skilled calculators in so far as they do contribute essentially to the production of wealth and its delivery at the times and places when and where it is required for use. In so far as such "services" go to increase neither the quality nor the quantity of the wealth produced, but merely its sale price, they constitute no addition to the national wealth whatever, for the gains of these individuals are at the expense of the rest of the community. Though it still seems traditional and customary to regard as the producer the masters or employers of labour, and the wage-earners as their hired servants, if not mere chattels of the speculative *entrepreneur*, in this book little distinction is called for between the privates and officers of the economic army. All grades of the whole organisation contributing services by hand or brain essential to the production process, from the manager to the labourer, are equally considered the producers.

Confusions between National and Individual Wealth

It is difficult or impossible to get a physical means of measuring wealth – as, for example, in the units of physical energy and of human life – time expended in its production – which shall be capable of common application to all the numerous varieties of wealth: but this difficulty must not blind us to the palpable absurdities in conventional economics introduced by always measuring wealth by exchange-value or money price. This may easily result in what could only be regarded as a national calamity appearing to increase the national wealth, or what is in every respect a national blessing appearing to reduce it. Unnecessary middlemen and speculators may much increase the prices of commodities without any addition to the national wealth. Combines of producers and trusts for limiting output and raising prices may reduce the national wealth and increase its monetary value, apart altogether from changes of the general price-level and the costs of production. Such "services" as these, which are properly means of acquiring wealth at the expense of the rest of the community rather than producing it, are, of course, not physically necessary ingredients of wealth at all.

The Economic Dilemma

The question is dismissed somewhat superficially by J. S. Mill, in his *Principles of Political Economy*. He draws a distinction between the wealth of an individual and that of a nation, but hardly makes it clear how much of what is considered wealth in conventional economics is at one and the same time a subtraction from as much as an addition to the national wealth. Thus, in his Preliminary Remarks, he raises the question whether, if the atmosphere could be monopolised, there would not result an increase in wealth, and says: "Though air is not wealth, mankind are much richer for obtaining it *gratis*, since the time and labour which would otherwise be required for supplying the most pressing of all wants can be devoted to other purposes." In the event of its being monopolised, he proceeds: "The possession of it, beyond his own wants, would be, to its owner, wealth, and the general wealth of mankind might at first sight appear to be increased by what would be so great a calamity to them. The error would lie in not considering that, however rich the possessor of air might become at the expense of the rest of the community, all persons else would be the poorer by all that they were compelled to pay for what they had before obtained without payment."

One might anticipate from this that he would discuss similarly the cases of rent as the effect of the natural monopoly of land, and of interest and profit – apart from and in excess of payment for the hire of necessary plant and for necessary services rendered in a managerial capacity and the like – but since in these cases the community have always been compelled to pay, the error, if it is one, is apparently justified by tradition.

Again, mankind would also be much richer if it could obtain its food and fuel, like its air, *gratis*, since the time and labour required to supply these most pressing of all wants could then be devoted to other occupations, possibly to leisure to pursue values of little account in the market. Under these circumstances there would be a reduction in the wealth of mankind by what would be so great a boon and a blessing to them. Simple contradictions of this character may serve to show that in attempting to avoid the difficulties of his subject by regarding it merely as a science of market exchanges, the economist has effectually impaled himself upon the horns of a very awkward dilemma. It may justly be asked whether it is a science of wealth, or the want of it, which leads to such curious inversions.

Political Economy and Politic Economics

In these considerations we have the crux of the problem why discoveries and inventions, which are beyond cavil national gains, lead to profound evils in the social and economic organism.

It is only in unsophisticated communities that production is carried on directly for consumption and use. In modern societies the product is not produced for consumption or use, but for exchange or sale. Consumption indeed is regarded as a necessary evil, and the accumulation of wealth by individuals is the driving motive.

But individual wealth, unlike national wealth, may merely be national debt, and indeed this is much easier and safer to accumulate than real wealth.

Out of this exchange, not out of production *per se* claims to individual wealth come into being, and wealth, which in an unsophisticated society must be the actual ownership of existing goods, in modern societies is extended to a generalised claim upon the totality of the community's present and future wealth. Not only do such claims arise from active positive participation in the production process. Purely imaginary services such as the pretence of lending money may be a legal claim to wealth. Also the participation may be negative rather than positive. The claims to wealth of an individual may arise from not preventing production, assisting it in the sense of refraining from hindering it. But since no nation can possibly live whether by imaginary loans, the interest on its debts, nor by refraining from hindering production, so a study which does not at the outset free its conception of national wealth from such confusion is in no proper sense *political* economy. It may be politic economics for those who desire a quiet life and to live on good terms with their neighbours, and if political economy no longer means national economy, it is time its name was changed to politic economics.

The Paralysing Effect of Old Conventions

Never was there an age in history so dowered as ours with all that could have sufficed for a noble and enduring civilisation, whereas it is still to ancient civilisations that we must go if we wish to find evidence of human effort and imagination being squandered on a national scale on something not strictly utilitarian in purpose. The most gigantic powers await our commands to provide us with all that we require, but we lead a harried, driven life, concerned for the most part with the immediate necessity of keeping the wolf from the door, and destroying our *trade* rivals.

At least so far as the immediate present and future are concerned, there is no conceivable requisite that cannot be produced on the earth or dug out of it in accordance with the world's needs. This is a conclusion that goes right against our herd instincts derived from a pre-scientific era and the present illusion of poverty carefully fostered under the rule of the usurer. It cuts the Gordian knot of the social, national and race perils which beset the future. For there is no present political question, however insoluble it may appear to the herd instincts of humanity, which is not fundamentally altered by this discovery. Properly understood and acted upon, the world would gain a breathing space, in which more calmly and scientifically to make the necessary provision and adjustment for the future.

The Growth of Population no Longer a Bugbear

This is not to say that, under every conceivable contingency, the scientific solution of the economic problems of life will bring permanent peace and security to an ever-expanding world population. But our ideas to-day of crowded countries, with populations spilling over the brim, and threatening the immediate future with race conflicts on a gigantic scale, are really derived from conventional standards of the number of people any given country is able to support. Of course, if the expansion of recent times goes on in a geometrical progression unchecked, in time the physical limitations of the planet must make themselves felt. At present there is not more than one individual to every ten or fifteen acres of habitable surface on the average.

This country is estimated[13] to have about twice as many people as it can economically feed according to peace standards and so has to import at least half the food consumed. But ideas of emigration remain much what they were when there were no fast steamships and luxurious floating hotels. Even if the worst came to the worst and the rest of the

---

[13] See before.

world boycotted us and refused to trade with us, the task of transporting half a population is not very formidable. However, there is no great likelihood of the increase of population continuing indefinitely. With the increasing knowledge and practice of birth-control the opposite is more likely. Although racial problems are formidable, it must not be forgotten that, before any other race can challenge the supremacy of the white races, it must adopt science and come under influences the same as those now at work in the Western world, though it is very unlikely to copy all our mistakes.

Again, people are apt to imagine that any great change in the policy of a country is likely to inflict to-day as great hardships upon the workers as were originally caused by the introduction of machinery in the early part of last century. To take an illustration, it might be supposed that, if this country in the future decided to depend on its own resources and less upon its foreign trade, agriculture would boom and the engineering industries would be depressed. This would probably not mean, nowadays, that a vast collection of workers in the towns would be forced back into agriculture and to do unskilled work on the land. What would be much more likely to happen would be that the engineering trades would cater much more for the home farming industries than at present. Agriculture would become more industrialised and, like transport, would probably cease to use animal labour except on a comparatively small scale. Indeed, the tendency in this direction is already most marked.

In all departments of industry the general effect of the scientific advance has been to make men more adaptable and able to turn their hands to a greater variety of occupations than before. In new countries, where the conditions are less stereotyped, people think far less of a total change of trade or occupation than they do at home. As wealth production becomes more and more a finished science, less and less are very special personal qualifications required for its pursuit. The man who before found himself indispensable, for example, by virtue of being able to judge furnace temperatures accurately by eye, is replaced by the even more accurate pyrometer. An inventor, once he has been induced to disclose his invention, becomes an entirely negligible quantity, though, as a business precaution, he would be better chloroformed lest he should invent something taking the place of the first invention. From the general administrative point of view, there would be no great difficulty in changing from one kind of production to another, even if it involves converting one type of worker into another. The problem nowadays is more akin to turning coachmen into motor-drivers, rather than chauffeurs into born whips.

CHAPTER IV

THE FALLACIES OF ORTHODOX ECONOMISTS

Wealth and Debt

Wealth is a positive physical quantity, but debt is a negative quantity. It has no concrete existence, and is to the physicist an imaginary quantity. If we deal with numbers, then we may with great appropriateness give them either sign; but in physics, which deals with real quantities, we can only do so with caution. The positive physical quantity, two pigs, is something anyone may see with their own eyes. It is impossible to see minus two pigs. The least number of pigs that can be physically dealt with is zero. Plus two pigs at least must be taken for granted before we can, even for reckoning, make use of the imaginary quantity, minus two pigs.

Though we may, with the utmost mathematical purism, deduct two from one and have left minus one, we cannot deduct two pigs from one pig and have left minus one pig. Indeed, in pure mathematics, negative quantities were first recognised and justified by the Hindu mathematicians by their analogy to debt.

The economist would probably deny that pigs were necessarily wealth in his sense of the term, for example, if they were running wild and unappropriated.

Assuredly a buyer is not going to give anything to a seller for pigs which the seller *has not get to sell*, and the point seems a meaningless quibble. If the pigs were running wild on a private estate they would be wealth to the owner of the estate, so that we reach the conclusion that it is all a question of private ownership. What is wealth after it is appropriated was not wealth before. So that in a communal as distinct from an individualistic society there would be no wealth in the sense of the economist. This may be a distinction between Wealth and Not-Wealth in the mind of the economist, just as Mill stated, "The distinction between Capital and Not-Capital does not lie in the kind of commodities, but in the mind of the capitalist, in his will to employ them from one purpose rather than another."

But there are other differences of more importance. Pork, for example, has feeding value, which can be measured in calories, irrespective of who owns it, in contradistinction to a machine which has none; and this surely is not an entirely negligible consideration in deciding such matters.

Wealth has proved a quantity too difficult and too involved for analysis by the modern economist. The earlier economists did, according to their lights, attempt to deal with it; but the modern school have more and more taken it and its origin for granted and confined themselves to the study of debt, or, as we shall see, with chrematistics rather than economics. Debts are subject to the laws of mathematics rather than physics. Unlike wealth, which is subject to the laws of thermodynamics, debts do not rot with old age and are not consumed in the process of living. On the contrary, they grow at so much per cent per annum, by the well-known mathematical laws of simple and compound interest. The former applies when the interest is periodically paid, the latter when it is not paid. For sufficient reason, the process of compound interest is physically impossible, though the process of compound decrement is physically common enough. Because the former leads with passage of time ever more and more rapidly to infinity, which, like minus one, is not a physical but a mathematical quantity, whereas the latter leads always more slowly towards zero, which is, as we have seen, the lower limit of physical quantities.

It is this underlying confusion between wealth and debt which has made such a tragedy of the scientific era. It is fundamentally ingrained in the Western mentality and, could it be straightened out, a scientific civilisation might, at long last, yet be put on the right road. The confusion is obvious enough when once pointed out, and in these days of positive knowledge concerning the nature of the material world and the matter-of-fact and common-sense habit of thought it engenders, the task should not present any insuperable difficulty. Historians of the – let us hope – happier future in store for humanity will probably find it difficult to believe that in a scientific age such an error could have exercised the sway over the human mind that it actually does in this the third decade of the twentieth century.

The Origins of the Confusion

The old Greek and Roman jurisprudence was, of course, not concerned with the real nature of wealth, then completely beyond the power of mortals to understand, nor even with its primary object and purpose in the maintenance of life, but with the rights of individuals owning property – which included slaves and their labour – and the duties of individuals owning it. Modern systems of law as affecting property have not kept pace with our knowledge of wealth and are still largely based on ancient codes. They are concerned primarily with the legal titles to wealth, whereby individuals in non-possession of wealth acquire it as wanted through these titles. It is natural for the ordinary man, to whom money or any similar title to wealth is, normally, completely equivalent to real wealth, to consider money as wealth. For the law, which is concerned with government, to remain merely a reflection of earlier and more primitive ways of living is a serious offset against the social value of scientific knowledge.

As for economists, they have made spasmodic efforts to rid their systems of these confusions, it must be admitted with some success, until the rapid developments in modern finance and banking and the changes that have come over the very nature of money in recent years brought back again the demons they had partly exorcised in seven-fold greater force.

The definition of wealth has always been the touch-stone of clear thinking in economic matters, and after centuries of effort that definition still eludes us. Aristotle tried to cut the Gordian knot by defining wealth as all things whose value can be measured in money, and the Roman jurists, in their practical fashion, followed suit in defining wealth as what can be bought and sold.

Money, however, is merely a claim to wealth, and to define wealth as that which can be claimed by claims to wealth, or can be measured by the numerical legal claims to wealth called money, is merely like defining a fluid as that which can fill and be measured by an empty hole, capable of holding the fluid, called a fluid measure.

Such logic has always exerted, and will probably always exert, a powerful attraction to the ruling and legal type of mind, more concerned with the ownership of wealth than the processes which bring it into existence and which it, in turn, brings into existence. To the economist, on the other hand, their fascination was fatal. It solved many little difficulties and apparent inconsistencies regarding the real nature of wealth entirely to ignore it, and to base it, as the Roman jurists did, upon the principle of exchangeability as the sole criterion. That alone is wealth which can be exchanged for money. Still it might have been apparent that a weight, although it is measured by what it will pull up, is nevertheless a pull down. The whole idea of balancing one thing against another in order to measure its quantity involves equating the quantity measured against an equal *and opposite* quantity. Wealth is the positive quantity to be measured and money as the claim to wealth is a debt, a quantity of wealth *owed to but not owned by the owner of the money*. But the ability to measure the exchange-value of wealth by money was deemed the one thing necessary to reduce "economics" to a quantitative science fit to rank with the great mathematico-physical group of exact sciences. Unfortunately, owing to the initial confusion of sign, it reduced it to the utter futility everywhere apparent to-day, whereby Society is administered not by and for those who create wealth and health, but by and for those who create want, and every scientific advance seems to be countered by a retrogression in the science of government.

It is difficult to believe that the ancients were really such fools as they have been made to appear. Indeed, Xpñua, usually translated as "wealth," in the first instance meant *want* or *demand*, and by derivation came to mean anything wanted or demanded. If the ancients were used to logic at all, and it is supposed to have been their strong point, they must have known that although the *thing* wanted may be the same as the *thing* possessed, the *want* of a thing is the opposite of the *possession* of it. Chrematistics, the science of wants and demands and of how they exchange one for another, is quite a distinct study, more plainly termed commerce. But economics, in a national sense, is concerned with wealth as what is produced by human beings to maintain their lives. Again, contrast Demosthenes and Bishop Berkeley. The one said, "Credit is the greatest capital of all to *the acquisition* of wealth," and the other asks "whether power to command the industry of others (i.e. Credit) be not real Wealth."

In the eighteenth century the French school of philosophers, known as the Physiocrats–"the original Economists" – did attempt to base economics upon physical reality. They traced the origin of all wealth to the land, and got as near it as the science of their time allowed.

But, unable to formulate the real exchange-value of wealth in terms of life, they adopted the legal definition in terms of money. Karl Marx, contrary to common belief, did not attempt to show that the origin of wealth was human labour, but rather that the exchange-value or money-price of wealth was.

Of wealth he was perfectly correct, so far as it goes, in his statement, "We see, then, that labour is not the only source of material wealth, of use-values produced by labour. As William Petty puts it, 'Labour is its father and the earth its mother.'"[14] It was rather the disciples of the prophet who forgot all about mother, until their memories were jogged by the recalcitrance of the Russian peasantry.

But the more orthodox of the followers of the Physiocrats, though at first they had some veneer of the natural knowledge of the latter, soon lost all scientific interest in wealth altogether. Like Adam Smith, they have been the tutors and mentors of property owners rather than scientific men. Their attention was diverted by the legal conventions under which the titles to the ownership of wealth are acquired, which they had the hardihood to describe as inexorable economic laws. After inglorious efforts to find a definition for the supposed subject-matter of their studies, they seem now to have given up the attempt. It is, of course, logically impossible to define the hotch-potch of wealth and debt, their various partial factors, ingredients, and even legal titles to ownership, comprised under everything which can be bought and sold, from land, labour, live-stock, fuel and other perishable commodities, houses and permanent possessions, factories, tools and agents of production, light, heat and power, to discoveries, inventions, goodwill of businesses, personal skill and aptitudes, rents, Stock Exchange securities, national debts, banknotes, mortgages and credit. Wealth as a real quantity – and, as such, subject to the laws of conservation – they failed to disentangle.

Out of the Frying-Pan into the Fire

Up to this point economics was a relatively simple subject compared with what it has since become with the development of

[14] *Capital*, Book I, cap. I, p. 10.

finance. J. S. Mill, following Adam Smith, could pour scorn upon the vulgar errors of the old Mercantile System, which regarded national wealth as synonymous with money and the coinage metals, thus:

> "The universal belief of one age of mankind ... becomes to a subsequent age ... too preposterous to be thought of as a serious opinion... It looks like one of the crude fancies of childhood, instantly corrected by a word from a grown person."

But, heedless of the fact that, even in his day, money was no longer necessarily specie or made of any precious metal, but might be, as now it mainly is, a mere paper acknowledgment of the community's indebtedness to the owner of the token, he fell into an error greater than that he ascribed to the Mercantile System in his own definition of wealth.[15]

> "Money, being the instrument of an important public purpose, is rightly regarded as wealth, but everything else which serves any human purpose and which Nature does not afford gratuitously is wealth also... Everything therefore forms a part of wealth which has a power of purchasing, for which anything useful or agreeable would be given in exchange."

This is as complete a confusion between wealth and debt as was ever made by the ordinary untrained mind, and the error vitiates all economic reasoning to this day.

Exultingly H. D. MacLeod pounced upon it, and with the utmost hardihood pushed it to its logical conclusion.[16] He twits the earlier economists for hesitating to include a merchant's Credit (or ability to run into debt) as wealth merely for fear of being forced to admit that wealth can be created out of nothing. This did not worry him. He defines pure economics as the science which treats of exchanges and nothing but exchanges. "A merchant's Credit is purchasing power exactly as money." Therefore, according to Aristotle and Mill, Credit is Wealth. In the grip of this syllogism MacLeod warms to his subject, and proceeds to demonstrate that wealth *can* be created out of nothing. But

---

[15] J. S. Mill, *Principles of Political Economy*, 1909 edition, p. 6.

[16] H. D. MacLeod, *The Theory of Credit*, Longmans, Green & Co., 1893.

before quoting from him a few words of introduction and explanation may be helpful.

In the first place MacLeod, as a barrister-at-law and legal expert on the subject of credit, uses the term *Debt* in its legal significance, as an amount owed by, say, A to B, *and* owing to B from A. In ordinary usage it is the debtor's rather than the creditor's position that the term suggests. To own a debt is to be owed it, so that people buy debts as they buy wealth if they can make a profit out of the business. To exercise or use one's credit is to run into debt. To grant or extend credit is to own a debt.

In the second place, the confusion being examined arises, so far as the wealth of individuals is in question, from the fact that an individual, independently of whether he has property and even if he has none whatever, may possess credit. If his penurious condition is unknown, or if people trust his business ability, he may be able to run into debt. By using or spending his credit he may obtain wealth, contracting at the same time an equivalent debt. So that the zero of no-wealth is, in his case, not the point from which the personal wealth of such a person must be reckoned in contrasting him with a person of no wealth and of no credit. We may count his credit, or unexercised power of running into debt, as part of his personal wealth, but to do so we must start to reckon his wealth from below zero – from a negative quantity, namely the amount he would owe if he had exercised all his credit and spent all he owns and all he owes. In a similar way the height of the ground, which is usually reckoned from sea-level, might, for some special purpose or survey, be reckoned from the floor of the ocean. But that would make it no easier to reclaim a Zuyder Zee or to drain and people an uninhabitable swamp. Let us now quote a few extracts from MacLeod's *Theory of Credit*:

> "How is a Debt created? By the mere consent of two minds. By the mere *fiat* of the Human Will. When two persons have agreed to create a debt, whence does it come? Is it extracted from the materials of the globe? No. It is a valuable product created out of Absolute Nothing, and when it is extinguished it is a valuable product decreated into Nothing by the mere *fiat* of the Human Will. Hence we now see that there is a third source of Wealth besides the Earth and the Human Mind, namely the Human Will."
>
> "Goods, Chattels, Commodities, WEALTH can be created out of Absolute Nothing and DECREATED again into the Absolute

> Nothing from whence they came, to the utter confusion of all the materialistic philosophers from Kapila to the present day and to the first school of Economists. The superlative importance of these considerations will appear when we come to exhibit the mechanism and practical effects of the great system of Banking."

And of this system over THIRTY YEARS AGO he was already able to say:

> "At the present time Credit is the most gigantic species of Property in this country, and the trade in Debts is beyond all comparison the most colossal branch of commerce. The subject of Credit is one of the most extensive and intricate branches of Mercantile Law. The merchants who trade in Debts – namely BANKERS – are now the Rulers and Regulators of Commerce; they almost control the fortunes of States.

As there are shops for dealing in bread, in furniture, in clothes and every other species of property, so there are shops – some of the most palatial structures of modern times – for the express purpose of dealing in Debts; and those shops are called BANKS.

> "And as there are corn markets and fish markets, and many other sorts of markets, so there is a market for buying and selling Foreign Debts, which is called the Royal Exchange. Thus Banks are nothing but Debt shops, and the Royal Exchange is the great Debt Market of Europe."

He adds triumphantly that "there is not one who ever had any more conception of the principles and mechanism of the great system of Credit than a mole has of the constitution of Sirius."

The interest about all this is that MacLeod – an acknowledged authority on the theory of Banking and Credit – is merely more candid than the economists in his treatment of this question. He is quite correct in pushing the definition of wealth as adopted by Mill and other economists to its logical conclusion, and in proving that if wealth is what can be bought and sold it can be created out of nothing in defiance of the laws of physics. It is the economist's definition of wealth that is at fault and which vitiates the conclusion. If we reasoned similarly in physics, we should probably discover that weights possessed the property of levitation.

Credit

It is thus of great importance to get as early as possible some real conception of credit, which always, in times of difficulty as at present, appears to the imagination of the sanguine to be vested with almost magical powers. There is this much to be said for these beliefs, that they have some foundation in National Economics as distinct from Individual Economics, in that – as we shall see when what is termed the principle of Virtual Wealth is discussed – a community can, and indeed must, act as if it possessed more wealth than it does possess, by an amount equal to the total purchasing power of its money, and need pay no interest whatever on the debt! But our present purpose is rather to avoid the national aspect of money, in so far as is practicable.

Ownership of wealth is transferable with or without the exchange of an immediate *quid pro quo* in wealth. The possession of goods brings with it the power of lending them to others, as well as of selling them or of consuming them. Thus a merchant with a reputation for business acumen can obtain wealth from the owners on account, and this power of contracting a debt is purchasing power as assuredly as money or wealth.

But it is not wealth in the sense of a part of the nation's wealth. The exercise of his power of running into debt temporarily changes the ownership of wealth and does not affect its totality. Even if a merchant's credit is, whilst still unexercised, regarded as a part of the merchant's individual wealth, it is clear that we must start to reckon his wealth not from the zero of no-wealth, but from a minus quantity.

The creditor, or lender of the wealth, again may transfer his right to repayment from the debtor to a third party in exchange for wealth, in which case the transaction is in no wise different from what it would be if the debtor had obtained wealth on credit from the third party in the first instance. But it enables the original creditor to act as though, having given up ownership of his wealth, he still had it, so long as he can find another willing to give up temporarily his ownership of wealth on similar terms. Money does no more and no less as a means of effecting the transference of ownership of wealth without a *quid pro quo* in wealth.

The distinction between money and credit, as purchasing power, is that the use of the former does not leave the user in debt, whilst the use of the latter does. In the case of money the buyer does not have to pay again for the wealth purchased, but the seller who receives the money passes on the token, as a legal claim to wealth on demand, indefinitely – that is, the claim circulates and is not cancelled.

In the first case, a merchant using his personal credit contracts a debt to an individual and gives him an I O U or promise to repay, which is returned to him and destroyed by him when the debt is repaid. In the second case, a buyer, using money as purchasing power, is not a borrower contracting a debt, but a creditor being repaid in wealth a debt due to him from the general community, in which the money circulates as legal tender. The money, or national I O U, passes to the possession of another member of the community and confers on him a similar right of repayment, and so on, indefinitely. Unless it is convertible into gold coin and is converted into gold coin and is melted into bullion, and in this form of wealth repays the debt to the owner of the money, the national I O U is not cancelled.

All of this has nothing to do with the totally different question whether a borrower uses the wealth more or less advantageously than the original owner would have done. The point – and it would be impossible to exaggerate its importance – is that, if the process is followed through, it will be found that all forms of purchasing power – other than wealth given in exchange for wealth by barter, but *including* money except when, as explained, it is actually destroyed and converted into bullion – are not a part of wealth, but merely devices for transferring ownership of it, without an immediate *quid pro quo* in wealth, for the right to a future repayment in wealth.

Usually the attempt is made to argue that there is "behind" the debt some equivalent of wealth in the possession of the debtor, just as there is in the case of gold money that can be melted and demonetised.[17] Thus Irving Fisher,[18] speaking of bank credit, remarks: "When the uninitiated first learn that the number of dollars which note-holders and depositors have the right to draw out of a bank exceeds the number of dollars in the bank, they are apt to jump to the conclusion that there is nothing behind the notes or deposit liabilities. Yet behind all these

---

[17] In this illustration the gold of a coin is regarded as the property of the King or nation issuing it until it is defaced and converted into bullion.

[18] *Purchasing Power of Money*, 1922, p. 40.

obligations there is always, in the case of a solvent bank, full value; if not actual dollars, at any rate *dollars' worth of property*."

But this is merely to confer upon one piece of property two owners at one and the same time. Clearly, if one piece of property with two owners can be counted as two pieces of property, then there is nothing at all remarkable in MacLeod's discovery that wealth can be created out of nothing and decreated into nothing by the mere *fiat* of the human will.[19] But, as Ruskin has sagely remarked, "It is the root and rule of all economy that what one person has another cannot have."

Credit *means* surely that the creditor *gives up* to the borrower the use of the property lent. It is true that in granting bank credit the bank gives up nothing whatever, but the community does, and the borrower receives it.

Mill, illogical and inconsistent as he was in his ill-fated attempt to define wealth, was under no illusion as regards the nature of credit. To him "the smallest consideration" was sufficient to dispose of the view that the lender and borrower could both have the use of the same property at the same time. Writing in 1848, he could hardly be cited as an authority on modern credit systems, but at least he was quite modern in stating that, as purchasing power, in their effects on prices, "Money and Credit are exactly on a par." In his definition of wealth the context leaves no doubt that he was defining national wealth in contradistinction to forms of individual wealth, neutralised by the coexistence of an equal debt, as, for example, a mortgage, which is not national wealth at all. Having defined wealth as the power of purchasing, and having stated that money and credit are on a par in this respect, clearly he was inconsistent in regarding credit as, like a mortgage, merely an addition to the possessions of one individual at the expense of another.

But we need not accept MacLeod's credit absurdities. It suffices to recast the argument in an unexceptionable form. *Everything is*

---

[19] MacLeod quotes the economist Say: "Those who consider Credit to be Capital maintain that the same thing can be in two places at once," but dismisses him contemptuously with the remark, "Say never thought out the fundamental principles of economics." This sort of thing seems to pass for argument in economics – a proof of how far it deserves the title of a science.

purchasing power which can be exchanged for wealth. Labour, money, credit, wealth can all be exchanged for wealth. Therefore these things are all purchasing power. Much as the syllogism may illuminate the nature of purchasing power, it leaves that of wealth still to be defined, with the chance that, after all, the laws of conservation of matter and energy may be true. It is curious that it should be left to a chemist to correct a logician's logic.

Since money and credit are on a par as purchasing power, how can money be rightly regarded as a part of wealth if credit is not? The essence of money, as of credit, is that the owner temporarily gives up possession of the wealth to which he is entitled for money – a token, like a merchant's I O U, but issued by the nation to signify that the owner has given up the ownership of the wealth and is entitled to repayment of it on demand. Thus money, so far from being rightly regarded as a part of national wealth, is rightly regarded as a part of the national debt, the claims of individuals on the national wealth, exactly like Consols or War Loan except that, being repayable in wealth on demand in every market, it does not and need not bear interest like a debt repayable, if at all, in the future.

This is no new view, but has been expressed by people as different as Ruskin and MacLeod. The former said: "All money, properly so called, is an acknowledgement of debt … a documentary promise ratified and guaranteed by the nation to find a certain quantity of labour on demand."[20] The latter said:[21] "The quantity of money in a country is the quantity of Debt which there would be if there were no money." "When there is no Debt there can be no currency." Again he speaks of money as a transferable debt against the general community.

But common sense surely is sufficient to convince the matter-of-fact moderner that a certificate declaiming various half-truths about George V being King of all Great Britain, Defender of the Faith and Emperor of India, is not of value to him on this account, but as evidence that he is entitled to wealth in exchange for it, just as a railway ticket,

---

[20] Unto this Last, *1862.*

[21] Loc. cit.

of even less artistic and informative worth in itself, is evidence that the holder is entitled to take a railway journey.

Thus in counting money as national wealth rather than national debt, economists have merely carried over to modern times a habit of thought which arose through the now almost entirely discarded practice of making the certificates of indebtedness out of intrinsically valuable metals. Paper and credit forms of money are absolutely necessary and beneficial debt, on which no interest can be demanded, but they are not wealth.

The experts in this question have confused the public rather than enlightened them, and fallen into the very errors it was their special province to avoid. The view that modern money is a part of the national wealth is as crude to-day as the view that money and the precious metals were the only real national wealth. The whirligig of time has brought its revenges, and the universal belief of one age is becoming to a subsequent age too preposterous to be thought of as a serious opinion.

Professor Cannan's APERÇU of the Science of Wealth

For a broad modern view of the position which orthodox economics has reached we cannot do better than to turn to one of the foremost teachers of the subject of the present day. At least they have learned to walk delicately and fight shy of definitions. It may be instructive to attempt to give a condensation of the first chapter of Professor E. Cannan's *Wealth*, "The Subject-Matter of Economics."[22]

We learn that that is to be regarded as wealth which it is usual and convenient to the science of wealth to regard as wealth. At first economists entered into controversies about national wealth, but the use of the term "political" is not intended to confine the science to the wealth of nations. Originally wealth meant weal *th* – the state of being well, just as heal *th* means the state of being hale. The controversies of the eighteenth century, and the realisation that wealth consisted of other concrete things than gold and silver, led to this meaning of wealth being

[22] E. Cannan, *Wealth*, 1924.

lost sight of in favour of that of material possessions. But the economist deals with the increases and decreases of quantities which involves the element of time, and searchers for formal definitions overlooked this. The question, "How much a year have you?" does not occur to a man of the lowest class or to a child of any class but rather, "How much have you got?" In cultivated society, however, the conception of a periodical receipt has forced its way in and overpowered the conception of a realised amount.

Economists without noticing the change came to use "wealth" to mean a nation's annual produce. At first the physiocrats did so with the eyes of the farmer, and denied productivity to all labour not immediately employed on the land. Adam Smith extended "productive labour" to include permanent improvements, and Say to "non-material products," so that, in spite of J. S. Mill, who in this as in other matters tried to furbish up the obsolete, the annual produce was regarded as including services as well as commodities.

But to avoid the duplication in reckoning annual produce, it was necessary to distinguish between the gross produce and the net produce, the latter signifying those commodities and services which actually reach the consumer, *plus* those added to existing stocks *minus* those deducted from stocks. But there is no way really of actually distinguishing between net produce and gross produce, and the practice arose of substituting "income" for "net produce." Marshall, in his great work, defined economics "as how man gets his income and how he uses it." Instead of starting from land and labour and tracing the product, excluding double reckonings, we look at the net results as shown by individuals' money incomes. But money incomes do not include a farmer's consumption of his own product or a wife's domestic duties, and even if we can estimate the money value of these, the question remains whether services of a mother to her child are economic and are to be appraised at the same money value as those of a wet-nurse. Then it is necessary to "go behind" the money valuation and consider "real" income as distinct from money income, owing to the complications introduced by the variations of the purchasing power of money. We find ourselves groping after a measure of the good effects of commodities and services upon those who get them. Hence the practice of economic teachers is more and more directed from outward objects and particular actions to considering utility and satisfaction. Democratic institutions now make it necessary to take into account the pain and irksome toil involved in the creation of utility and to consider also the interests of the working classes upon whom most of this falls.

The older economists hardly thought of this, and the idea of deliberately sacrificing positive utility to leisure scarcely occurred to them. But most recent economists would regard the economic condition of a people working ten hours a day as superior to that of a people with the same positive satisfactions working sixteen hours a day. So that our subject-matter becomes utility minus disutility, and wealth has reverted to its old meaning, weal *th*. But this raises questions usually considered to be outside economics. Though no satisfactory definition is possible, yet, in practice, no great differences of opinion or usage exist as to what is and what is not the subject-matter of economics. Economic things can best be defined as economic just as blue things can be best described as blue. But, as a second-best description, we must fall back on "having to do with the more material side of human happiness."

The Interest-bearing Theory of Wealth

Now all this as a review of the progress of the currents and eddies of economic thought is extraordinarily able, and, of course, to be properly appreciated the original must be read. But it is also exceedingly clever and politic in the modern sense of that much-abused term. We get to perfection the quiet shelving of the really awkward questions of the unsophisticated who have to work to produce wealth and who not only ask, "How much have you got?" but somewhat more critically and pointedly than Marshall, "How did you manage to get it?" We have at least a graceful, if unacknowledged and uncertain, echo of the ideas of Ruskin, who expressed himself profoundly uninterested in the conclusions of economic science and more concerned with the ultimate exchanges denoted by production and consumption, i.e. life for wealth and wealth for life. The change in the views of an individual growing from childhood to riper years, and from poverty to affluence, is shown to mirror perfectly the history of economics so far. But the question arises, Is this really political, i.e. national, economics at all. Individuals grow from youth to age and die, but nations must have an economy that enables them to grow and live.

The better educated and leisured classes, indeed, now usually regard the physical conception of wealth – i.e. actual goods, food, fuel and the like – as a crude and rude idea that civilisation has grown out of. To them civilisation means a much more advanced stage of society, and of "progress" in which wealthy people derive leisure without any effort in perpetuity as an interest payment on some form of communal debt.

The debt may be a simple debt like Consols, War Loan, etc., in which case they derive their livelihood without assisting in production of wealth from the communal revenue of wealth, as a payment of an annual sum in return for not being repaid their principal.

Or it may be derived as a hire-payment for the use of some agent or accessory essential to the production of wealth which they lend to the community. So used are they to living on the interest of debt that they do not realise sufficiently the absurdity of everyone trying to do so.

Whereas when we deal with the Wealth of Nations rather than of Individuals – that is, with Political Economy in any real sense – there is no question that whether the views of the manual worker, i.e. of "Labour," are crude and unsophisticated or not, they are in strict accord with the facts of life and the physical laws which regulate the production of wealth, as that which is necessary to maintain the life of the nation. In proof of this it is only necessary to point out that a perpetual motion machine is an impossibility. A man with, say, £20,000 invested at 5 per cent is in perpetual enjoyment without work of an income of £1,000 a year, and his heirs and successors after him. Consuming wealth every day of their lives, they always have the same amount as at first. This is not physics and it is not economics. Like all alleged examples of perpetual motion, it is a trick. It is, of course, perfectly possible for the individual or a class of leisured individuals to live after this fashion, and a very bitter commentary upon the age it is that the triumphs of physical and mechanical science are so largely stultified because of it.

The comfortable "income" and interest-bearing view of wealth may provide individuals with a source of livelihood. The development of it may be called Individual Economics, or the Economics of a Class, "the Art of acquiring a Livelihood as professed by Tutors and Mentors of Property Owners." But it should not be called Political Economy, for a system of Political Economy that cannot under any conceivable circumstances be applied to a nation is a contradiction in terms.

Neither is it a science, for one of the main principles of the sciences which have enriched – rather than impoverished – the world, and made it possible for this country to support some five times as many people as ever before in the history of man, is the denial of the possibility of perpetual motion schemes of all kinds as a vulgar delusion.

The Conflict between Wealth and Leisure

It, therefore, is of importance to commence studies such as these with an examination into the physical criteria of wealth. For wealth, unlike debt, rots if it is accumulated. Increment is not a property of wealth but of the use of it in production.

The accumulation of wealth as agents of production produces work, not leisure, for the more that has been accumulated of factories, cultivated land, and the like, the larger the number of man-hours required to use them and to produce wealth by their use. Suppose, at a certain stage of science and invention, that a nation's accumulated productive capital required an average of eight hours a day work-time on the part of the workers, and it be doubled. If the land is not to go out of cultivation and the factories and plant to depreciate by disuse and neglect, it must be worked. So that all must now work sixteen hours in the day instead of eight, and, if it be trebled, twenty-four hours. Beyond this it is physically impossible to go. Any increased accumulation of the agents of production beyond a definite limit is at the expense of leisure, not an addition to it. The *average* gentility of the community is *decreased* thereby, and if one class succeed in becoming perfectly genteel – under no necessity for the rest of their lives to produce anything at all of what they consume – it is perfectly clear that the gentility of the rest must be reduced to a degree greater than that of the increase of accumulated capital. So much, then, for the "income" view of wealth as the interest on communal debt, and its fundamental conflict with the weal *th* view.

Some Other Views

It would be idle to deny that this confusion between wealth and debt is to be found everywhere in economic writing at the present time, and no better example could be cited than the works of Mr. J. M. Keynes. As one of the most original and brilliant of contemporary writers he is, on that account, the more easy to convict.

The majority are of a more nebulous school, pushing caution to the point of fatuity.

Mr. Keynes, however, is giving signs of a rapid awakening. Thus, in his celebrated *Economic Consequences of the Peace*, he seriously seemed to think that the law of compound interest is the law of increment of wealth rather than of debt, and in pronouncing judgment upon the past century's passion for accumulating wealth, which he likened to a cake, he said:

> "In writing thus, I do not necessarily disparage the practices of that generation. In the unconscious recesses of its being Society knew what it was about. The cake was really very small in proportion to the appetites of consumption, and no one, if it were shared all round, would be much the better off by the cutting of it. Society was working not for the small pleasures of to-day, but for the future security and improvement of the race – in fact, for 'progress.' If only the cake were not cut, but was allowed to grow in the geometrical proportion predicted by Malthus of population, but not less true of compound interest, perhaps a day might come when there would at last be enough to go round, and when posterity could enter into the enjoyment of *our* labours. In that day over-work, over-crowding and under-feeding would come to an end, and men, secure of the comforts and necessities of the body, could proceed to the nobler exercise of their faculties. One geometrical ratio might cancel another, and the nineteenth century was able to forget the fertility of the species in a contemplation of the dizzy virtues of compound interest."

In the first paragraph Mr. Keynes is doubtless speaking of an accumulation, in a geometrical progression with the time, of real agents of production, which, even if Society had the appetite of an ostrich, it could not consume. The accumulation is supposed to continue until there is enough to go round. But then – hey presto! – we switch over to debt and the interest accruing to those who own this wealth by loaning it to those who do not. The security and leisure is not a consequence of the accumulation, but of the distribution, whereby those who work the accumulation productively pay a share of the produce to those who do not. So that as a result of this confusion between wealth and debt we are invited to contemplate a millennium where people live on the interest of their mutual indebtedness.

The passage is also remarkable in revealing the role in which the philosophical economist apparently regards himself in relation to the world, not as a scientific man examining cause and effect and obtaining by correct knowledge and theoretical reasoning a grip of the way the economic system works, but as the patient historical and statistical student and recorder of its mysteries, gravely attributing the key to the overriding omniscience of the human herd instinct. Possibly also the herd of Gadarene swine, in the unconscious recesses of its being, knew what it was about.

Or is it as Mr. W. Trotter has said in his *Herd Instincts in Peace and War* : "The survival of the wagoner on the foot-plate of an express engine has made the modern history of nations a series of breathless adventures and hair-breadth escapes"? So that at the end of the second decade of the twentieth century the chariot of the nation, which by the understanding of the laws of thermodynamics and the inventions of science has been harnessed to the sun, is, in the mind of the wagoners, responding to the whip and spur of usury and the magnificent conjuring tricks of the human will.

However, in the case of Mr. Keynes, there are signs of rapid advance, for in his latest work, *Tract on Monetary Reform*, he is becoming strangely inconsistent.

Thus on one page he speaks of the savings of the nineteenth century, accumulating at compound interest, having made possible the material triumphs we now all take (so very much) for granted, and three pages farther on he is expounding the necessity of debasing the currency to assist the new men and emancipate them from the dead hand and to arm enterprise *against* accumulation. On one page he is demonstrating the necessity for the nation to save £M250[23] per annum to keep up our standards of living from depreciation, and on the other he is arguing for a Capital Levy as the rational and deliberate method of adjustment in an individualistic society which depends for its existence upon moderation because the powers of uninterrupted usury are too great.

Mr. Stephen Leacock is a professional humorist as well as a professional economist, and the reader must judge in which capacity he wrote these words:

> "Our studies consist only in the long-drawn proof of the futility of the search after knowledge effected by exposing the

[23] £M signifies throughout £1,000,000.

errors of the past. Philosophy is the science which proves that we can know nothing of the soul; Medicine is the science which tells us that we know nothing of the body; Political Economy is that which teaches us that we know nothing of the laws of wealth; and Theology is the critical history of those errors from which we deduce our ignorance of God.

"When I sit and warm my hands, as best I may, at the little heap of embers that is now Political Economy, I cannot but contrast its dying glow with the vainglorious and triumphant science that once it was."

The natural philosopher is tempted to reply with the paradox of Poincaré:

"You wish me to tell you all about these complex phenomena. If by ill-luck I happened to know the laws which govern them I should be helpless. I should be lost in endless calculations and could never supply you with an answer to your questions. Fortunately for both of us, I am completely ignorant about the matter. I can therefore supply you with an answer at once. This may seem odd; but there is something odder still, namely that my answer will be right."

Poincaré was speaking about the directions of the velocities and magnitudes of the energy possessed by the individual molecules making up the community of a gas – each individual in ceaseless collision with others millions of times a second, at each of which the distribution of velocities and energies changes – in contrast with the simplicity of the problem as affecting the energy of the gas as a whole and the laws it obeys under every possible change of the conditions. So, in economics, if we first try to follow the changes in distribution of wealth produced by circulating bits of paper or gold about or depositing them in banks we shall be helpless, lost in endless calculations, and never able to supply an answer to the simplest questions affecting the welfare of the community as a whole. But when we consider the latter question first, and study the physical laws regulating the production of wealth rather than its acquisition and distribution, though we may not immediately be able to supply the answer to all the unsolved problems of national economics, some we can answer almost at once. It is odd, but in so far as the problems involve questions of physical reality we may rest assured that the answer will be right.

So in perfectly general and uncompromising form we get the answer to the question whether it is possible to consume wealth and still have it, and put by some to "accumulate" at compound interest, and whether nineteenth-century Society, in the unconscious recesses of its being, really did know what it was about. It is rather our business to put the finger of science upon the precise mistakes of the past.

CHAPTER V

UNORTHODOX AND POPULAR VIEWS

The Denial of the Existence of Absolute Wealth

Economists usually deny the existence of absolute wealth. MacLeod, merely more outspoken than the rest, says: "There is no such thing as Absolute Wealth, nothing which in its own nature and in all circumstances and in all places and in all times is Wealth. It is necessary that someone *not its owner* should desire and demand it and be willing to give something for it." He thus entirely ignores the primary object of owning and acquiring wealth, namely consumption or use.

He cites ancient authority for the view, and quotes the unknown Greek writer of Eryxias, who put into the mouth of Socrates this imitation gem of ancient wisdom: "If anyone could live without meat and drink they would not be wealth to him because he did not want them." If matter did not fall it would not have weight.

But all economists stipulate want or demand as essential to wealth in their sense of valuable or desirable things, though Sidgwick[24] has pointed out that if wealth is defined as possessing value, it would be more logical first to define value. Bluntly, the position they take up is that there can be no food without hunger, no drink without thirst. Such

---

[24] Principles of Political Economy, *1883.*

purely subjective considerations are, of course, at the root of commerce, whether between individuals or nations, but they are utterly at variance with national economics as concerned with the more material side of human happiness. They are merely a vicious survival of pre-scientific philosophy, which denied the existence, apart from perception, even of the physical world -- views peculiarly out of place in economic matters, unless they be regarded as the subject of religious faith rather than of common sense.

In effect, human wants and desires, changing from instant to instant with every change of appetite, taste, fashion and circumstance, are constituted the measure of wealth, so that a greater and more urgent want *increases* it, whilst abundance and satiety *diminish* it. We are, in fact, using a variable standard of measure and imposing upon the quantity measured the variations of the standard. It is a relief to turn to another type of economist.

Ruskin

Ruskin, in solitary and picturesque protest against the hallucinations of his age, pleaded in vain for an economics founded upon life. Hostile in spirit to science, or rather to the chrematistic pursuit of science which desecrated the countryside and doomed the workers to bestial conditions of existence, and a great champion of the cause of the higher spiritual and æsthetic values against the onrush of a sordid materialism, yet it is to materialistic science we must turn if we require the theory and justification of his philosophy.

But even Ruskin laboured heavily under the error he was trying to extirpate.

Wealth to him still was inseparably connected with the lower passions and avarices of the struggle for existence, and he did not realise that the materialistic sciences had already severed the bond. He railed at beneficent and humane applications of science no less than at the unbridled pursuit of it for money – at railways and the harnessing of water-power as at the reckless belching out of deleterious smoke and fumes which produce a Glasgow fog or the desolation of a Black Country.

Perhaps, even yet, science cannot wholly prevent some sacrifice of natural beauties and even of civic amenities. But the grosser forms of its abuse which characterised the industrial revolution were due not to science, but to the historical students of the world's systems of commerce scientifically pronouncing that the lures of private interest and unlicensed gain were safe and satisfactory substitutes for the more traditional forms and principles of government.

It was typical of the nineteenth century that the grosser forms of atmospheric pollution were soon abolished by the alkali and factory inspectors educating the manufacturers into uses of their deleterious waste-products more profitable than the devastation of the countryside. Thus the old Le Blanc alkali process at first belched out into the air with absolute recklessness hydrochloric acid gas. Prevented, the manufacturers found in it a most valuable by-product, but for which they could not have survived so long the competition of the newer and more elegant ammonia-soda process. The smoke problem, industrially, is in much the same category, and few are the industries where it would not be more profitable to consume smoke than to send it out to pollute the air. But in cities as important a source of this crying evil is the open domestic hearth, and, as yet, no satisfactory complete solution of the technical problem has been found. Still, there is no valid reason why scientific industries should not be carried on with full regard to the amenities of life. The small minority of offensive industries could, at the worst, be confined to definite localities where the nuisance is the minimum.

A much more real opposition between the claims of science and natural beauty and national amenities arises in the use of water-power. Waterfalls and foaming cataracts rank among the finest of Nature's works, but it must be confessed, from the scientific standpoint, that they represent a prodigal waste of live energy which humanity at present can ill afford. Ruskin was especially hostile to the harnessing of water-power. Yet had he realised the essential identity of the vitalising stream with that which courses through what he termed the purple veins of wealth – the full-breathed, bright eyed and happy human creatures he esteemed above gold – possibly (who knows?) he himself might have been the first to open wider the sluices and to drain even a Niagara if thereby he could enrich human life.

The peculiar world-position of this country in the nineteenth century as the first to develop the use of power and its temporary circumstances, in that it found it cheaper to export its products in exchange, in some small part, for the bulk of its food – though probably far more went in exchange for paper claims to future wealth – no doubt were the cause of the eclipse of political economy and the rise of what

Ruskin termed mercantile economy, or chrematistics. He alone in the nineteenth century seems to have had any appreciation of the distinction. His patriarchal attitude towards his less fortunate fellows and his oracular religiosity are nauseating to many in these days, sick to death alike of the charity of the Christian and the benevolence of the Jew, and needing only permission to get on with the nation's household management without their interference; but in seeing the reality beneath the appearance Ruskin was a true scientist no less than the true artist.

The Economics of Life as the Product of the Consumption of Wealth

In his *Unto this Last,* published first in 1862, Ruskin showed a profound insight into the nature of what passes for wealth, if not for that of wealth itself. His theory of the relativity of individual riches–"The art of making yourself rich, in the ordinary mercantile economist's sense, is therefore equally and necessarily the art of keeping your neighbour poor" – is of fundamental importance to the consideration of the obstacles which prevent reform. His dicta that there is no wealth but life, and that the wealth of a nation is to be estimated by what it *consumes,* are less unorthodox than of yore, if only because of the sheer impossibility of finding any conceivable use for the wealth science provides so prodigally, except by consuming it, if not for the enrichment, then for the destruction of life. Consumption absolute – i.e. not for future production – is, as he put it, the end, crown and perfection of production, not something to be reduced to the minimum as an unavoidable waste, as it appears in chrematistics. Even the very word "economy" properly should mean the efficient and abundant provision of the necessaries of life, not the parsimonious consumption of them. It is significant that only with the almost unbounded enrichment of the material life by scientific discovery the word should have gained this sinister meaning.

Ruskin's description of the chrematist's paradise–"capital producing nothing but capital, bulb issuing in bulb, never in tulip, seed issuing in seed, never in bread" – is scarcely any longer ahead of the times. His picture of the political economy of Europe, devoted wholly to the multiplication of bulbs, and unable to conceive such a thing as a tulip–"Nay, boiled bulbs they might have been – glass bulbs – Prince Rupert's drops, consummated in powder (well if it were glass-powder and not gunpowder)" – for any end or meaning in the accumulation, received its vindication on the stricken fields of Flanders. The next age may even erect a memorial to Ruskin there, bearing his words. But there are no stricken fields in America, as yet, to mark the end and meaning of capital accumulation, and it remains to be seen whether America is going to keep alive in the future the discredited political economy of Europe, so that once again it may work itself out to its inevitable end in the New World.

The century that has come and gone has seen a steady alteration in the significance of the word "wealth" from its original meaning, weal *th,* as the requisites that enable and empower life, to debt, the right of the creditor to demand wealth and the duty of the debtor to supply it. Adam Smith some hundred and fifty years ago pictured a rude state of society prior to the extension of commerce and the improvement of manufactures, where the only use of a large revenue was in maintaining as many people as it can maintain. "A hospitality in which there is no luxury, and a liberality in which there is no ostentation, occasion, in this situation of things, the principal expenses of the rich and great." The times to-day partake of the same character with regard to the end of the eighteenth century to which his system of economics referred, as they in turn did to the earlier condition he depicted. He bewailed "the progress of the enormous debts which at present oppress, and will in the long run probably ruin, all the great nations of Europe," when in this country the National Debt amounted to £M130 (1775), at the commencement of a new war which involved an additional debt of more than £M100. He noted that "when national debts have been accumulated to a certain degree there is scarce a single instance of their having been fairly and completely paid." At that time the whole debt was less than half the annual interest upon it to-day. The world has experienced different ways of distributing its revenue, but, in the ultimate analysis, the principle that the only use for a large or a small revenue is the maintenance of as many people as it will maintain is, and always has been, as true, in terms of *wealth,* as it was in the most primitive society.

The opening words of Marx's *Capital,* quoted from an earlier work published in 1859, gives his idea of wealth: "The wealth of those societies in which the capitalistic mode of production prevails presents itself as an immense accumulation of commodities, its unit being the single commodity." But Ruskin in the work quoted (1862) was conscious of the totally different meaning which the word "wealth" implied in the mind of the owner of property: "Mercantile economy signifies the accumulation, in the hands of individuals, of legal or moral claim upon, or power over, the labour of others; every such claim implying precisely as much poverty or debt on one side as it implies riches or right on the other."

In the early stages of the War the then Chancellor of the Exchequer deprecated a certain financial policy on the ground that thereby one-half of the capital wealth of the country would be destroyed. Even in war you could not so easily destroy an immense accumulation of commodities! Since then we have learned to regard even our real individual wealth as our annual revenue, and, if it is unearned, to divide it by the current rate of interest, whatever that may be, to arrive at its capital value.[25] We have yet to see a Chancellor of the Exchequer doubling the capital wealth of the country by resuming the pre-war rate of interest on Government securities.

But the idea of wealth, apart from a revenue, has almost lapsed even in individual economics. The immense accumulations of commodities implied by the existence of £M7,000 of legal claims to wealth as War Loan we saw destroyed as fast as they were produced. But, by the inexorable laws of thermodynamics, if not of economics, the immense accumulations of the nineteenth century in railways, canals, factories and slum cities, even if they did not get out of date, are all on the same broad highway to destruction. But debts neither get out of date nor wear out; they grow.

Ruskin's Failure to Grasp the Nature of Absolute Wealth

In *Unto this Last* the Preface states: "The real gist of these papers, their central meaning and aim, is to give, as I believe for the first time in plain English – it has often been incidentally given in good Greek by Plato and Xenophon, and good Latin by Cicero and Horace – a logical definition of WEALTH: such definition being absolutely needed for the basis of economical science…" It may be questioned

---

[25] Thus, when the rate of interest on Government securities was 3 per cent [0.03], an income of £100 a year was derived from Consols worth £100 ÷ 0.03=£3,333⅓. When it rose to 5 per cent, the same Consols would only fetch £100 ÷ 0.05=£2,000 in the market.

whether either he or the ancients succeeded. It is not unfair to conclude that Ruskin never got beyond seeing that what passes for wealth in mercantile economy, or jurisprudence, is *also* debt. On his own analogy, the two were commingled like the north and south poles of a magnet. He never seems quite to have divorced himself from a patriarchal attitude of mind, still prevalent but weakening to-day, where the use of a revenue is to maintain a retinue of happy and thankful dependents rather than a free people.

The physical reality of wealth, apart altogether from legal claims, escaped his analysis. He copies Bishop Berkeley in the aphorism, "The essence of wealth consists of power over the lives and labours of others"—a definition of debt, but not of wealth. Whereas the essence of wealth is not power over men, but power over Nature. Even the essence of ownership of wealth is not power over men, but rather over the fruits of their *past* diligence in embodying the energy of Nature or replacing it usefully by things into the making of which work has gone. Power over men is the essence of debt, not of wealth. The *not* owning and *not* possessing wealth owed to one individual by another or by the community gives that individual power over the other or the community *until the debt is paid*. When paid, the not-owner becomes the owner. The wealth he now possesses, but the power over men he loses. We had kings of nations and captains of industry. The captains and the kings depart, and leave us emperors of debt, rulers and regulators of commerce, controllers of the fortunes of States, for whom the one world is too small, and the whole universe capable of assuaging only for a moment an infinite thirst.

Before leaving Ruskin, it is interesting to recall an incidental remark in a footnote of the book cited, part of which has already been quoted, which shows how far ahead and yet how far behind he was of his own times: "All money, properly so called, is an acknowledgment of debt... The final and best definition of money is that it is a documentary promise ratified and guaranteed by the nation to find a certain quantity of labour on demand. A man's labour for a day is a better standard of value than a measure of any produce, because no produce ever maintains a consistent rate of productibility." That all money, properly so called – all genuine money – is an acknowledgment of debt, a documentary promise of the nation to provide a certain quantity on demand, is no longer the view of a few students, but since the war – which saw money multiplied without gold-mines, as science multiplies productibility – has become evident to all.

But what is the quantity promised? Is "a man's labour for a day" a consistent measure of productibility – in one age tilling the ground from whence he came, in another diligently watching a harnessed Niagara or steam turbine energise a community? Do not such views, like those of the Marxist, that the origin of wealth is human labour, sign, seal and deliver Labour over to bondage, whereby the machine competes with him and multiplies the debts of the community rather than its wealth or health? This seems to be the pivot upon which the whole future course of history will turn, and decide whether science is yet to prove itself a blessing or a curse. In brief, is the increment in productivity due to science to be available for the redemption or merely for the multiplication of debt? We shall have to revert again to this question.

Both Ruskin, who regarded human labour as a consistent measure of productibility, and Marx, who held that the value of commodities, produced for exchange, is determined by the labour-time socially necessary for their production, did not take into account sufficiently the effects of science in replacing animate by inanimate power. Both seem to have had a suspicion that science was dealing with things that would prove upsetting to their philosophy. Indeed, nowhere in *Capital* probably does Marx so excel himself in vituperation as in his description of the founder of thermodynamics as "an American humbug, the baronised Yankee, Benjamin Thompson (*alias* Count Rumford)..." Curiously enough, this is only for his daring to recommend, in his *Essays, Political, Economical and Philosophical*, "receipts of all kinds for replacing by some succedaneum the ordinary dear food of the labourer," and not his more famous recipe for replacing the labourer himself. For out of the work of this "American humbug" truly arose the modern 10,000 horse-power machine, each horse-power equal to that of 10 men, working not 8 or 10, but 24 hours in the day, and each machine tirelessly replacing the physical labour of a community of 30,000 labourers. How cheap things would have become if Marx had been right! Nor is it of much avail for his present-day followers to retort that the machine is the product of human labour as well as the coal that energises it. We may grant the machine, if they will grant the science and the invention, and, on the same terms, we may grant the coal in so far as the mining of it is concerned. But the power is neither in the machine nor in the mining; its origin is more ancient. The hated capitalist was in this case the tree patiently storing up the energy of the sunshine in the carboniferous era, millions of years before there was such a thing as a man.

The Physical Laws of Conservation can be applied to the Conception of Wealth

As Ruskin said, a logical definition of wealth is absolutely needed for the basis of economics if it is to be a science. The doctrine of energy, and the laws of thermodynamics do allow of this. In particular the eminently practical common sense underlying the second law is perfectly applicable. No exact science can progress until it has established within its province laws of conservation, and decided what are the real quantities which do not change with progress of time and circumstance. The law of conservation applies to the conception of energy itself, but the second law introduces what is, in practice, far more important, a sense of direction, by distinguishing between useful or available and useless or unavailable categories of energy. Wealth, as we shall more nearly examine in the next chapter, is essentially the product of useful or available energy. For every plus there is a minus, but for every minus there is not a plus. For every appearance or production of wealth there is a disappearance of available energy, but for every disappearance of available energy there is by no means a production of wealth; rather, the opportunity to so utilise it passes the same, whether utilised or not. It might be thought that the idea of conservation, whilst useful and necessary to the original formulation of the laws of energy, was, nevertheless, of the nature of a scaffolding that might be abandoned when the building was complete. This point of view is often urged with regard to potential energy. In every beat of a pendulum there is a conversion from kinetic into potential energy, and it is sometimes said that the conception of potential energy is a mere means of saving the face of the law of conservation. However, there is something physical and real to show for the disappearance of the kinetic energy of the full swing in the height the bob is raised against gravity, and the more correct view is that the term potential energy cloaks an ignorance as to the nature of the action at work – in this case gravitation – rather than the creation of an imaginary existence.

This is, as it happens, peculiarly demonstrable with regard to the continued existence of energy after it has passed into the useless form, as heat of temperature uniform with the surroundings. To the naked eye, we have reached a limit to the progress of change, and all appears at rest. But under the microscope there is no such thing as rest. Every particle suspended in a fluid, if small enough, is found to be animated with the lively Brownian movement, and the more minute it is the more intense its perennial agitation. The energy which before moved masses is there in undiminished amount, but it is agitating the individual molecules of matter, and the microscopic particles floating in a fluid serve as indicators of the perennial bombardment to which they are subjected. For larger particles these sufficiently nearly cancel out, and such remain at apparent rest, but below a certain size inequalities of the bombardment in different directions make themselves immediately felt, the light and responsive particles being driven first this way and then that, and never for an instant remaining at rest. Energy is eternal, but useful energy as we know it so far is an eternal flow in one direction.

It may seem a far cry from such topics to economics, but until the latter can be based upon the principles of conservation of the materialistic sciences, and every conjuring trick exposed, it cannot be said to have any proper base at all. Economics deals not with energy, but entirely with the flow of useful and available energy and its transformations into useless forms, and physical wealth as a product of the control and direction of this flow. Physical science joins here with the common sense of humanity that wealth can never be made with a wave of the wand.

The Confused Aspiration of Modern Communities

Before trying to solve the problem of the nature of wealth, let us consider a few of the more startling consequences of mistaking wealth and debt, which have become apparent in the present century. Doubtless so fundamental a change in the manner of living of the greater part of the habitable globe could not come about without grave dislocation, but the naïve and superficial arguments by which a whole world has been madly set chasing its own shadow are difficult seriously to examine.

First and foremost we have the deep intuitive instincts of humanity. If we refer to the chart at the end of the second chapter we shall see that it attempts to contrast the manner in which men derive energy, intuitively and by the use of the reason. The main course of natural intuitive evolution up to man, through the animal and vegetable kingdom, has been parasitic as regards the wherewithal of life. Men initially rose out of animal-like conditions of existence only by preying upon one another, as we still prey upon the animal and vegetable kingdom for our internal energy. But originally this dependence concerned the energy required for all external labour as well as that required for metabolism. With growing intellectual achievement, emancipation from this dependence, so far as external labour is concerned, has increasingly come about, and in course of time may not inconceivably be extended even to metabolism.

Possibly even vegetarianism may one day become a relic of barbarism.

Prior to the scientific era, all forms of government naturally reflected this physical dependence, and there always has been a relatively small and luxurious class living upon the fruits of the labours of the many, though the services, real or nominal, by which they justified their dominance have changed with every change of conditions.

The Grecian and Roman civilisations were based upon human slavery as an indispensable condition. The Jews were busy resisting it from without, but this did not prevent them from developing it within, whilst among the Mohammedans it still survives. Under Christianity, except for a brief term in America, slavery disappeared, but its place was taken in various ages by some form of economic or feudal servitude, which has always been sedulously inculcated, and virtually, if not openly, defended as necessary for the preservation of culture and leisure to pursue the higher values. Under science, with so much of the heavy burden of life removed from the backs of men and draught-cattle and placed on broader shoulders, dependence upon the animal and vegetable kingdom for internal supplies of energy persists, but dependence upon life for external labour increasingly disappears. Perhaps, so far, only a single step has been taken on the road to economic freedom, but the tragedy is that even this step humanity frustrates.

We have seen how aloof the educated classes have been, in this country especially, to the great revolutionary march of science. A democracy, on the other hand, is too prone to "put its wish-bone where its backbone ought to be." The result has been an interpretation of the social conditions of the time in terms of an inherited philosophy of class servitude and a mad democratic uprush into the possessing classes without changing by one iota its essentially parasitic character.

Because formerly ownership of land – which, with the sunshine that falls on it, provides a revenue of wealth – secured, in the form of rent, a share in the annual harvest without labour or service, upon which a cultured and leisured class could permanently establish itself, the age seems to have conceived the preposterous notion that money, which can buy land, must therefore itself have the same revenue-producing power. It is easy to understand the physics of seed-time and harvest, and, in general, the origin of the increment whether of a corn-field, chicken-run or a piggery. Plants or animals are sedulously collecting solar energy, and, wonderful as the process is biologically, there is no physical mystery about the appearance of ham and eggs and toast on the breakfast-table. Granted, first, land and sunshine in the ownership or possession of one set of people, and, secondly, human industry furnished by another set of people, the means of support of the gentleman, if not visible, are not very well concealed. From the contemplation of this mode of gentle livelihood, honoured by tradition and history, let us turn somewhat abruptly to the modern passport to gentility, the ownership of, say, £20,000, a ball of gold some 9 inches in diameter. As a possession it obeys the laws of conservation of matter and energy. As money in its original sense, something to be exchanged for wealth, it possesses no powers of self-reproduction. As a hoard or store used to buy goods it would diminish in quantity, like soap when you wash with it. But *lent* to someone else, and buried out of sight in the vaults of some bank, like a seed in the earth or a fowl laying eggs, it reproduces its kind. If the rate is 5 per cent per annum, it becomes capable of supporting in gentility and perpetual motion a whole family and their heirs and successors after them on £1,000 a year. It *may* buy a farm or some other source of revenue, and the labour of the farmer and his labourers, out of the increment of which they and our family together may be supported for ever after. It rises superior to the laws of physics and now energises even an entirely idle owner.

If its owner has sufficient independent income to do without it, he may lend the interest, so that the rate of increment changes from simple to compound. The revenue of the hypothetical farm is now hypothetically sold for more gold and more farms. In 1070[26] years out of our 9-inch ball of gold, disposed of in this way, there would arise legal claims to a golden ball equal in size to the earth, and weighing four times as much.

Or, if we are to get the best out of both possible worlds, let us maintain our chosen family in the state of the somewhat shabby

[26] In the original edition this was erroneously stated to be six hundred years. For this to be true the rate of interest would have to be about 9% instead of 5%.

gentility and diminished perpetual motion possible on £500 a year, "putting by" half the income to "accumulate." After enduring this for four centuries, our family would be in a position to supply a world population of 2,000,000,000 souls each with the same principal as itself it started with.

This is the celebrated fallacy of compound interest, and we have already indicated briefly its origin, and have still further to elaborate its nature, so far as orthodox technical economics is concerned. But its origin is more general. Society, "in the unconscious recesses of its being," remembers the day when there was neither economics nor science, nor even religions of the modern Sabbath and Sunday type. Older than these, and infinitely more powerful in its sway over the mind of man, there still persists, as a full-blooded weekday religion, the worship of the golden calf. That, at least, has survived, though lovelier religions have come and gone, and time has witnessed the passage "of all Olympus' faded hierarchy."

CHAPTER VI

THE TWO CATEGORIES OF WEALTH

The Nature and Definition of Absolute Wealth

Let us see from the standpoint of modern knowledge, whether light can be thrown on the difficult and vexed question of the real nature of wealth rather than on the particular modes by which its quantity or value may be measured. The physical or material necessities of the body must be satisfied before any of the further necessities of life – whether sexual, intellectual, æsthetic or spiritual – are even called for. A definition of wealth must be based upon the nature of physical or material wealth, in the sense of the physical requisites which empower and enable human life – that is, which supply human beings with the means to live, and, as an *after* consequence of living, to love, think and pursue goodness, beauty and truth. The enabling requisites of life, in this sense, constitute a short definition of wealth. The purely physical criteria of wealth demand consideration before the more special economic criteria.

These enabling requisites are derived from and produced by the flow of available energy in Nature, and represent drafts upon or deductions from this flow, in that for the production of all forms of wealth available energy is required from the natural flow, and either enters into the wealth produced or is used up in producing it – that is, is converted into waste heat.

The term *available* in this definition has the same meaning as in the second law of thermodynamics, which divides energy into two categories, useful, available or "free" energy, and useless, unavailable or "bound" energy, the latter also being designated *entropy*. But the meaning is not essentially different from, only rather more precise than, its ordinary significance. Only that kind of energy is available which has the tendency to transform itself into other forms. With unavailable energy the last form of natural transformation has been reached and the tendency to suffer transformation disappears. It must not be supposed, of course, that the reverse transformation is impossible, but it is practically impossible, because it requires the expenditure or degradation of a greater amount of available energy into unavailable than is gained in the reverse process. The thermodynamic conception of availability has, of course, nothing in it limiting it specially to life or to human life. Wealth as a form, product or result of a draft upon the flow of available energy consists of the special forms, products, or results which empower and enable human life.

A Debt of Life repaid in Life

In the continuous flow of available energy we find the primary absolute want of human life, without which it dies, and it is this want which wealth satisfies. The preposterous idea that there is no such thing as Absolute Wealth, but that there must be someone, not the owner, who desires and demands it and is prepared to give up something for its possession, is a mercantile view convenient in cities which live upon the produce of the surrounding country, but cannot be applied to nations.

Chrematistics, the science of wants and how they exchange is a very useful science for individuals to understand, but it is at best only one part of economics.

Thus the air is a most obvious want of life, and it is argued that because it is impossible to own it, it is therefore not wealth. But if you liquefy it and put it in a bottle, it can be owned, is wanted and demanded – very much so in a modern university, at least – and then it becomes wealth and a regular article of commerce.

A truer view is that the gaseous nature of air and the universality of the supply allow people normally to obtain their supplies without the expenditure of effort in the getting, whereas to obtain it liquid much work in the physical sense as well as diligence in the human sense are required.

So with food and fuel – which, no more and no less than air, and for an identical reason, are needed to supply the want of the energy without which life dies – it is true people want and demand them and are willing to give up something in exchange for them. But it is even more true that people have to give up some of their lifetime in order to produce them. Physical science, as distinct from physical, holds out no hope whatever that wealth will ever be produced without the expenditure of human-being-hours as well as of available energy. If new discoveries provided such food that corn was fit only to feed to cattle, and such energy that coal and oil were useful only to make soot, these would decline in value, and possibly even be entirely displaced, but only because the needs of life could be better subserved by other forms of wealth, themselves the products of available energy and human time. Science may multiply the efficiency of human time, but it does not abolish the necessity of expending it in production.

It has been argued that wealth must not only be useful, but usefully used. This is a metaphysical rather than a scientific standpoint. Rightly or wrongly, the scientific mind has decided to accept the theory of the conservation of physical realities, apart altogether from the faculty of apprehension. It points to the geological record of the rocks as proving that the rocks were there before – applying the Johnsonian test of reality – there were feet to kick them. The energy stored in corn and its power to nourish life are physical realities apart altogether from the consideration whether it is to be the future fate of the corn to rot or be eaten. Corn which rots and is not eaten is assuredly not wealth, but then neither is it when it is eaten and does not rot.

Admittedly, these conceptions of the nature of Absolute Wealth as a definite physical reality do not take us very far in economics because they do not lead to a precise method of relative measurement, whereas the exchange-value or money-price does. But at least they enable us to offer a blunt denial to the physical origin of wealth as something capable of being created out of nothing by the human will.

When we try to measure the relative value of different kinds of wealth, or of the different partial factors or ingredients that enter into its constitution, clearly the most important and least arbitrary consideration is what the wealth has cost of past human life to produce. But in this the value of one man's time differs greatly from that of another. Just as substances are esteemed in proportion to their rarity, if required for living, and are valued on the average in proportion to the time that must be spent in finding or winning them, so rare and exceptional skill or ability is esteemed above the average, but only if it conduces (in the present tense) to the business of living. But it has already been remarked that, as knowledge advances and the processes of industry become less empirical and more scientific, less and less exceptional ability is required to operate them. The optical pyrometer replaces the man who can judge furnace temperatures accurately with the eye, and rule-of-thumb metallurgical processes, that can only be operated by work-people born and brought up to the industry, tend to be replaced by more scientific and less uncertain methods requiring no exceptional skill. So, in business and banking, if the national requirements were foreseen in advance and a monetary system devised which worked automatically, as it was intended it should, special qualifications, certain of commanding a high reward when everything is uncertain, speculative and empirical, would no longer do so. The chief factors that oppose reform and progress and strive to keep things as they are by no means inertia and ignorance, but thoroughly well-informed individual self-interest.

Much has been said of the importance of genius and the essentially creative type of mind, and it might be thought that there would always be in industry and business glittering prizes for the brains that devise new methods. But in this we have the old heresy that wealth can be created out of nothing by the human mind or will. The man who composes a musical work is rarer than those who can sing or play it brilliantly.

Such qualifications, compared with origination, are mechanical, but they are the more highly esteemed and rewarded, because it is the performance and not the composition which subserves the needs of life. So it is with the exploitation of inventions as distinct from the inventive genius.

Value or Price

The money-price or exchange-value of wealth brings in a host of arbitrary considerations, such as the state of the laws regarding the land and property, the incidence of taxation, protection from competition, trusts, combinations and monopolies, the rate of increase or decrease of a community, of a locality, and so on, almost *ad infinitum*. The money-price integrates the whole of a host of complex factors, many of them in themselves too elusive to be traced. Yet it is the one quantitative fact about wealth that can be confidently asserted, and which is usually capable of being ascertained. In this work no attempt will be made to analyse it.

"We should be lost in endless calculations." From the point of view of national economics, in dealing with the relations between money and wealth, the average money-price of wealth, or price-level, is a fact of the utmost importance, absolutely irrespective of how it is made up and whether it is just or unjust.

But first it may be well to go a little deeper into the question of the real nature of wealth from the physical standpoint.

Labour and Wealth

Life itself, in metabolism, consumes continuously a flow of available energy – that is, converts it into useless energy – and one form or category of wealth of necessity consists of the food-stuffs which provide this flow. Life also requires means to conserve its vital energy and protect it from the rigour of the climate – clothes, houses and fuel, means for locomotion, transport and external forms of labour, and means to produce the tools, plant, equipment and other accessory requisites incidental to the purpose of producing the primary supplies. The only criterion which distinguishes this varied collection of requisites is that they all require and result from drafts upon the flow of natural available energy.

Usually, but not invariably or inevitably, the production of any form or category of wealth demands also the expenditure of human time and effort. In a state of nature, however, especially in the tropics, where human needs are few and sunshine abundant, there is a sufficiency of the available energy of nature already available for the purposes of human life, for a very limited population, without the contribution of any human factor to its production. Fuel and clothes are hardly needed, and food in the form of tropical fruits exist ready to hand, so that a very sparse and unambitious population can maintain itself permanently in a condition of almost complete *dolce far niente*. This fact alone controverts the Marxian doctrine – which, as already stated, is not that of Marx – that all wealth originates in human labour. Similarly, an occasional quantity of precious metals may be found native without human effort, though on the average a very large expenditure of effort is needed in the winning of them.

But in civilised forms of communities intensive forms of production are necessary to support, in general, larger numbers of people on a higher scale of living and plane of civilisation than would be possible in a state of nature. In those circumstances a human factor becomes essential to the production of wealth, and it takes the form of initial inventions and discoveries, hereafter applied continuously with human effort. At first the effort largely consists of actual physical labour supplied from the body of the labourer in supplement of the natural flow of energy; but, as civilisation advances, it consists more and more of diligence, pure and simple, in guiding non-human forms of energy to human ends. From the energetic standpoint the human contribution is always of the nature of a transformation of rather than a creation of energy, becoming, as civilisation advances, more and more direct, with the replacement of the intuitive metabolic process by others arrived at by reason.

An Electrical Model of the Productive System

An analogy which may prove of use is in the dynamo, or dynamo-electric machine, considered as a transformer of mechanical energy into electrical energy.

This is accomplished by driving electric conductors across the lines of a magnetic field – or a magnetic flux – a movement they actively resist. The energy so used reappears in the form of a flow of electric energy along the conductors, at right angles to the magnetic lines and to the direction of motion. Natural magnets exist as the lodestone, and from these permanent steel magnets can be produced in indefinite quantities. In the first forms of magneto-electric machines natural magnets or permanent steel magnets were used to produce the magnetic flux, and the transformation of the mechanical into electric energy did not involve any expenditure of power whatever in producing or maintaining the magnetic flux; but in the modern intensive form of dynamo-electric machine a part of the electric energy *produced* is expended in magnetising a soft-iron electromagnet, whereby, from a machine of given dimensions, a very greatly increased output becomes possible. It is significant that the mechanical energy produces not only the useful part of the electric energy generated, but also the part of the product which has to be expended in magnetising the iron, and that this latter part does not appear in the final product, but is degraded at once into useless heat by overcoming the dead resistance to the flow of the current through the copper conductors wound round the magnets. Moreover, theoretically, this loss is not essential. If a better conductor than copper were available, less of the product would have so to be turned into useless heat, and, if an infinitely good conductor existed, none would so be lost. Some conductors in the neighbourhood of the absolute zero of temperature are practically perfect. A current once started in a copper ring at very low temperature will go on circulating for hours before its original energy is wholly converted into heat.

So we may envisage the production of wealth as a transformation of the available energy of Nature into a flow available for the purpose of human life – a part of it actually into the energy of human life. In the natural state no expenditure of human energy is necessary. In intensive production it is, but the energy so used is deducted from not added to the product. It produces its useful results indirectly, and runs to waste without appearing in or being incorporated with the final product. Its function is to change the quality of the natural available energy into the form available for the needs of life, and the gain in quality is a consequence of a reduction in quantity. It is, of course, very useful in attempting to understand any process to have a concrete physical model, however crude, in the mind, and the analogy suggested seems to cover correctly the essential features alike of primitive, modern, and possible eventual processes of wealth production. Even the steady displacement of human labour in mass production, as the process becomes more and more automatic and self-regulating, finds its analogy in the reduction of the magnetic reluctance of the circuit by employing better iron and the electrical resistance of the field-magnet circuit by employing better conductors or conductors at lower temperature.

The Two Thermodynamic Categories of Wealth

We have found it useful in our consideration of the laws of energy to distinguish between the expenditure of energy in overcoming an active opposition, in which there is something useful, in energy, to show for the expenditure at the end of the process, and the expenditure of energy in overcoming dead resistance, in which the energy expended suffers immediate conversion into heat and there is nothing useful, in energy, to show for the expenditure at the end of the process. The idea extended to wealth enables us to distinguish at once the two main categories of wealth according to the manner in which the energy has been expended. In the first category are commodities which retain part of the energy expended in their production, as an internal store, which, in the consumption of these commodities, is released to serve the purposes of life. In the second category the energy is expended in overcoming dead resistance, in changing the form or nature of the materials worked upon, and does not remain in the materials as an essential to their use.

Perishable and Permanent Wealth

Commodities, in general, belong to both categories, and these categories are distinguished by the *opposite* qualities of relative perishability and permanence.

Commodities of the first category are valuable as stores of energy. In them the materials of which they are made serve as the container for a store of available energy. In functioning as wealth they are totally consumed or destroyed as wealth, and this perishability is essential to their function. Energy is of no value in itself, and the flow of energy from one thing to another and from one place to another alone is valuable. The material counterpart of the tendency of energy to flow is the tendency of materials to change. Liability to rot, decay, catch fire, suffer slow deterioration is thus an *essential* quality of this category of wealth. It comprises food, fuel, explosives, some forms of fertilisers, and similar materials, which actually fulfil the purpose which gives them the title of wealth only by suffering total conversion into waste matter and energy. Whereas in the second category permanence rather than perishability is the essential quality. It comprises clothes, houses, and their equipment and furniture, in general "possessions," as well as tools, plant, roads, vehicles, ships and other accessory requisites necessary for the production and supply of wealth.

Capital Agents of Production

In contradistinction to the first category, though destruction in use cannot be altogether avoided, it is not essential to their function, but a disadvantage. Rather they are required to resist wear and tear and to last *as long as possible*, and for this reason are often made of very refractory and resistant substances, which necessitate the expenditure of much energy in their conversion into wealth. In so far as the energy used upon them remains in the materials in a potential form, their durability and value as wealth are *adversely* affected. Thus distinctly opposite characters distinguish between the two thermodynamic categories of wealth.

The building of a house cannot be effected without storing up some of the energy expended in erecting it, and the presence of this store of potential energy causes the house in time to fall down again. Whereas the house is wealth only for so long as it stands. So it is with iron. Iron embodies in itself a large part of the energy liberated in the combustion of the fuel used to smelt it from its ores, the possession of which causes it to rust, i.e. to revert to its initial exidised state. But whereas the store of energy is *essential* to coal as wealth, it is an *unavoidable defect* in the case of iron.

To run a locomotive the coal must be consumed, but the combustion of the iron, though it cannot be altogether prevented, is no advantage, but a dead loss. If, with the same desirable engineering qualities, iron had the durability of gold or platinum, it would be even more valuable as wealth. But corn or beef with the durability of the noble metals or precious stones would not be wealth at all.

In engineering, the term *power* signifies, in contradistinction to *energy* or *work*, the rate at which the energy is spent or the work is done, and a power quantity is converted into an energy quantity by multiplying it by a duration of time. Life similarly, from the physical standpoint, has the dimensions of power, and is expressed in energy terms by multiplying it by the duration of time to which it refers.

Thus we have already seen that a million Calories – quantity of energy – suffice to maintain the food requirements of an average man for the duration of one year.

Now although the doctrine that all wealth is the product of human labour is not true, that all wealth is the product of work, in the physical sense of the expenditure of available energy, is for practical purposes absolutely true, and almost the only general and satisfactory definition of wealth that can be framed. Money, credit, and other legal claims to wealth are debts, rather than wealth. Labour and inventions are not wealth, though essential factors in its production. The physical definition of wealth is a form or product of energy or work which enables or empowers life.

Exceptions might possibly be found as regards the second category of wealth, but they do not invalidate the rule that, on the average, a definite expenditure of work and time is required for the production of a given quantity of any kind of wealth. The occasional find of a nugget of gold by accident without any special search may be cited as an exception, as the occasional find of wild-fruit is an exception to the rule that human labour is necessary to the production of wealth. But in national economics, dealing primarily with averages rather than exceptional events, they may be completely ignored.

The expenditure of energy is necessary for the production of all wealth, but the regeneration of the energy expended in a form available for the needs of life takes place only in the case of the first category. For brevity the two categories may be distinguished as Wealth I and Wealth II. We may denote, after the manner of a chemical equation, the production and consumption of Wealth I as:

Raw Materials + Available Energy = Wealth I.

Wealth I = Life-Energy + Waste Energy and Materials.

For Wealth II the production is expressed by:

Raw Materials + Available Energy = Wealth II + Waste Energy.

but there is no corresponding equation for consumption. The degradation of the energy has already gone to its last stage, *and in this sense Wealth II is already* "consumed."

An Illustration from Chemistry

Even in pure science, the distinction between the two different reasons why the production of a substance requires the expenditure of energy is not always very precisely made. Sometimes one has to climb a mountain, as it were, in order subsequently to be able to run down by the aid of the energy stored up, as with Wealth I. But often the climb is necessary because there is no level way round, as with Wealth II. Thus in the process known as the fixation of atmospheric nitrogen, whereby the nitrogen and oxygen of the air are caused to combine to give oxides of nitrogen by exposing them to the very high temperature of the electric arc, a very large expenditure of energy is required. This, indeed, is the origin of the description of the Swiss valleys as glacier at one end and 98 per cent nitric acid at the other. Yet the energy expended is not embodied in the oxides of nitrogen, but goes to waste as heat, as in the production of Wealth II. The process is analogous to a journey from one place to another on much the same level over a very high mountain, necessitating a great expenditure of work with nothing in the end but waste heat to show for it, unless a way round can be found.

In this case a way round was found, and it fixed more than nitrogen: it fixed the date of the Great War. For Germany, without any great natural sources of power, and cut off by superior navies from the external sources of nitrates – which are shipped from the Peruvian seaboard and form the raw material for the manufacture of all explosives – could otherwise hardly have waged war for three months. The Haber process was the result, in which the nitrogen is combined first with hydrogen to form ammonia, under high pressure but at moderate temperature, by the aid of a catalyst, and then the ammonia is oxidised by the action of air and water to nitric acid by the aid of another catalyst. This process requires no excessive expenditure of power.

So, in general, for Wealth II (which includes not only all permanent possessions, but all agents of production) new processes are continually finding a more level road around the intervening mountains, whereas for Wealth I this possibility of improvement does not exist. These new processes depreciate the value of all capital expended upon the old, and tend to destroy it as wealth by rendering it obsolete.

Repayments Given by Wealth

Since both categories of wealth are alike in the manner of their production, but completely different in their physical character and in the manner in which they, respectively, empower and enable life, the definition of wealth necessarily is based upon what is consumed or used up in its production rather than upon what it actually is or what, in turn, it yields. From the physical standpoint so much live energy and so much human time have been expended in its production and represent a cost or debt-charge incurred to Nature and to men. As regards Nature, it is the sun which is debited and the earth credited, so that from the standpoint of humanity the energy is a gift. Under natural conditions the whole revenue of available energy runs to waste, whether used or not, and wealth is the part of it man has salved. The expenditure of human time in salving the energy is the only real debt-charge upon the products in the ultimate analysis, when we narrow the point of view from that of physics to that of economics. If the product is useful and is used, the debt in man-hours is repaid in man-hours, and the physical possibility of the maintenance and expansion of life depends upon the repayment, on the average, being vastly in excess of the expenditure.

Economically this is an increment, but physically it is not, as we have already seen from the analogy of a dynamo. In terms of the actual fount of vigour which energises life, the expenditure goes to waste in overcoming resistance, and the increment is derived from the live energy salved from the natural flow.

As regards the first category of wealth, for which use means total consumption, the repayment is definite in quantity, and is of the nature of a lump sum of energy and living-hours. But as regards the second category, in which destruction is not essential to use, payment is of the nature of a revenue, neither energy nor living hours, but of living hours saved which otherwise would require to be spent – over a period of time which is quite indefinite. It depends not only on the relative durability of the wealth considered, but on purely independent factors deciding whether the wealth is actually used or not, and this involves the future state of progress and invention and the state of common sense of the community.

The point of view brings out the necessity of first expending the time and energy, whatever happens to the product, and the fact that, in real quantities, the wealth is paid for at the time that it is produced. The ability to pour out for five years a mounting tide of munitions is evidence of a nation's wealth. Conceivably *during* their production the nation might have had to go short of other requisites; but there is no physical reason, *after* they have been produced, why it should do so, or for the conventional belief that because so much has been blown up and wasted everyone must tighten their belts and endure a period of poverty. If national debt was repaid, some would, in order that others might consume, whereas the national creditors prefer a small annual repayment for not being repaid. The popular notion that because a nation has in the past generation produced it is unable to do so in the next, that God and usury provide so much and no more, and if we consume much one year we must make up for it by consuming less in the future, is in the inversion of the truth. It contains just enough of the truth as it applies to individuals – that wealth is a real quantity, incapable of spontaneous generation and multiplication – to be plausible; but in national terms it is as fallacious as abstaining from drinking from a river because last year was hot and everyone drank so much, or shutting down a power station until an abnormally high past load had been recouped.

Capital as a Form of Permanent Wealth

This is especially applicable to the second category of wealth, which includes all the agents of production, usually termed capital. Thus with a vague idea that wealth is "consumed" in use, which we have seen is essential to the first category but only incidental and a defect in the case of the second, people envisage wealth production as entailing a steady consumption of machines as well as coal, oil and food; whereas, in point of fact, this consumption *by use* is often not very serious, and is always, as far as possible, provided for, or capable of being provided for. A vast machine for making motor engines probably has the actual wearing parts, the cutting edges of the tools, renewed many times in a day, if not in an hour. The journals and bearings, similarly, are made renewable. Of far more consequence to the deterioration of capital agents of production – such as factories and cultivated land – is neglect through *not* being used, and, in the case of the former, new inventions which displace them. The other losses are often of lesser importance. In their production the process, as regards the degradation of the live energy, has gone one stage farther than in the production of consumable wealth, and in this sense they are *already* fully consumed. They are only productive by use, and if unused become simple unrepaid debt.

Psychologically, the economic aim of the individual is, always has been, and probably always will be, to secure a permanent revenue independent of further effort, proof against the passage of time and the chance of circumstance, to support himself in old age and his family after him in perpetuity. He endeavours so to do by accumulating so much property in the heyday of his youth that he and his heirs may live on the interest on it in perpetuity afterwards. Economic and social history is the conflict of this human aspiration with the laws of physics, which make such a *perpetuum mobile* impossible, and reduces the problem merely to the method by which one individual may get another individual or the community into his debt and prevent repayment, so that the individual or community must share the produce of their efforts with their creditor. We have examined the process in the traditional method of living by ownership of land, and now we have to consider the modern method of living upon interest on capital.

The second category of wealth divides itself naturally into personal possessions, which are necessary to the enjoyment or consumption of wealth, and organs of production necessary to its creation. The latter, being essentially permanent and not consumed by use, but actually productive by use, seem at first sight to offer humanity a way of escape from the laws of physics and from economic dependence, because they appear to repay the debt of time incurred in their production by a perennial revenue of time saved by their use.

Capital multiplies Human Efficiency

The first category of wealth contains, to offset the debt of time incurred in its production, a definite positive quantity of energy available for life, yielded up as a lump sum when the wealth is consumed. The second category pays the debt of time incurred in its production by time saved by its use, and which, but for the existence of the wealth, would have to be spent. But for the organs of production the payment is of the nature of a revenue of time saved over an indefinite period, which continues as long as the wealth is used to facilitate production. So that, if the use is *continuous,* as in the production of perishable wealth, the hours spent in its winning are saved over and over again. This apparently endless payment for a definite expenditure of time is, of course, the physical basis for the origin of interest, defined as the hire-payment for the use of organs of production in production.

Actually no kind of wealth is absolutely permanent and proof against wear and tear, and the durability varies from that of such relatively short-lived possessions as clothes to that of the diamond. In practice, in addition to the provision of the first category of consumable wealth, a community must maintain in repair its possessions and organs of production. But this does not affect the nature of the problem, and in practice it is customary to suppose a part of the time saved by the use of capital expended as required in its perpetual maintenance, leaving still a permanent net interest.

It may be said at once that there is nothing to prevent a dominant class in possession of political power from so arranging things that a certain *limited* tribute may be exacted in perpetuity from the actual producers of wealth by the hire-payment for the use of capital, just as there is no physical impossibility in living by the ownership of land under similar political circumstances. It was impossible for the landowner to set himself flagrantly against the laws of Nature. The failure of the capitalistic era is due to the nature of interest and "capital" being misunderstood, and to the idea of perennial interest being extended from payment for the use of organs of production in the production of perishable wealth to payment for the non-repayment of any sort of debt. There are well-defined limits to the possible interest that can be exacted from a community which cannot be exceeded by increasing the capital.

Capital cannot multiply Human Time

For capital multiplies the efficiency of the expenditure of human time, but it does not multiply human time, though it attempts always to do so by lengthening the hours of employment up to and beyond the limit of human endurance. This statement is historically justified by a very slight acquaintance with the industrial history of this country prior to the Factory Acts. The process is taking place before our eyes to-day in the East, where the Hong-Kong legislature have recently passed legislation prohibiting the working of children more than nine hours a day out of the twenty-four and six days out of the seven. In China, which has as yet not reached the stage of legislation regulating industrial hours of work, the conditions are described as very similar and as horrible as those that occurred in this country prior to the passing of the Factory Acts.

Whatever may be thought of the economics of Marx, which to the author appears no less metaphysical than and as divorced from essential knowledge of the physics of the productive system as the systems of the more orthodox, no one who has read *Capital* can fail to have been impressed with the stores of sociological erudition in that volume, for the most part in voluminous footnotes. Written at the time when the *laissez-faire* policy of Governments left unchecked the evils of sweating and the exploitation of the workers by the industrial system, it forms for all time a record of some of the almost incredible abuses that attended the earlier history of the great accumulation of capital in this country. To-day, a revolted public opinion and the growing economic power of trade unions has to some extent redressed the balance, but in the East and in other countries where the capitalist systems are still uncontrolled the first effects in lengthening the hours of labour, and in using women and children as the cheapest sort of labour, are as much in evidence as they were in this country at the time when Marx wrote his “Bible of the working classes.”

Capital Increases EITHER Leisure OR Wealth

The use of capital saves time *or* increases the output of wealth, and in so far as its return is taken in the one form, so much the less is available of the other. But the limit of production of wealth is fixed by the state of scientific and technical knowledge and business organisation, and the number of possible working hours in the day. Once the capital necessary to enable the workers to employ the methods of production which are dictated by the state of technical development has been accumulated, further accumulation is sheer waste. It can only be used by lengthening the hours of work, and then only to the extent of human endurance. The apparent perpetual productivity of capital wealth and its superiority over consumable wealth in this respect leads always to the covetous exalting the production of capital as thrift and the production of consumable wealth as extravagance, whereas the physical basis of perpetual interest is not in the production of capital, but solely in its use in producing the first category of consumable wealth. Its use in producing perishable wealth is permanent, but in producing permanent wealth is ephemeral.

For possessions, like capital, accumulate. Once a community has accumulated possessions sufficient to enable it to consume its wealth in accordance with the scale of living fixed by its rate of consumption, more possessions, like more capital, become a useless charge and a burden upon the possessors. In brief, both forms of permanent wealth, for different reasons, only accumulate to the point at which they come into equilibrium with the rate of consumption of perishable wealth.

A physical analogy would be a reservoir in a water supply. At first when the reservoir is empty, the water flows in faster than it flows out, until a certain height or head of water in the reservoir accumulates, sufficient to drive the water out of the reservoir as fast as it flows in, after which the water in the reservoir remains constant.

So with each increase in the flow of wealth by scientific discovery, at first part of the wealth accumulates as new possessions and capital, but the only possible permanent condition is when the rate of inflow equals that of outflow, or the rate of consumption equals that of production.

In future, if any class in the community desires to live upon interest, it must encourage and not discourage the production of consumable wealth, and discourage the production of capital except as required to produce perishable wealth.

Abstinence in this respect might preserve the method of livelihood, like that of ownership of land, for an indefinite period without conflict with physical possibility.

In practice the foregoing simple considerations are invalidated to the extent to which it is possible to export permanent wealth to foreign countries in exchange for consumable wealth, but in the long run, over the whole world, they must be true.

This is an important consideration as regards this country which, traditionally as one of the leaders in the use of mechanical power, has in the past succeeded in exporting considerable quantities of permanent in exchange for perishable wealth. But this can only be a somewhat precarious situation, for as the world fills up, not only do the new countries make more and more of their own machinery, but they consume more and more of the food they produce. Unless we again contrive to get the lead in technical inventions in the use of power, it is clear that the ultimate future policy of this country will have to be directed towards the home production of consumable wealth, i.e. its neglected agriculture will have to be revived.

The Limit at which the Accumulation of Capital Defeats its Object

Some of the foregoing conclusions may be put beyond dispute if they are stated in general algebraic terms. Let us suppose that by the expenditure of some large initial amount of time – equivalent to, say, T working years of the whole community – in the accumulation of the necessary capital certain technical advances can be got into operation, which will permanently increase the efficiency of the working-hour by the factor X. If the community produces wealth thenceforth at the same rate as before it will do so in $1/X$ th of the time, and save $[1 - 1/X]$ of its former working-time, i.e. will gain this amount of leisure.

Whereas, if the community works the same time as before and produces X times as much wealth as it did, its gain is in wealth to the extent of $(X - 1)$ of its former wealth. If T working years have to be expended to provide the necessary capital in the first case to produce the same wealth as before, to produce X times the former wealth, as in the second case, will require X times greater abstinence from consumption, or XT years of working-time.

If the community adopts some intermediate course and decides to abstain to the extent of YT years, so as to be able to produce Y times its former wealth, where Y is any factor between unity and X, it now works Y/X of its former working-time, saves $[1 - Y/X]$ of it as leisure, and gains $(Y - 1)$ of its former wealth. It is clear that if Y is made equal to X, as in the second case considered, the community has X times as much wealth as it had but no additional leisure in which to enjoy it, so that its abstinence from consumption to the extent of XT years does not reduce its working hours or result in any increase in its average gentility. At this point a still further expenditure of working hours on capital production brings a further increase in the daily task also, and the community as a whole still further from its object in initially abstaining from leisure to accumulate capital.

The gain in leisure is $[1 - Y/X]$, and though it is easily made zero when $Y = X$, it can never be made unity, but reaches a maximum when Y is unity and the community are content with the same wealth as before. This is the algebraic way of saying what is – political polemics notwithstanding – the most obvious common sense. However much an individual may contrive by being in possession of agents of production – accumulated by the expenditure of past working-time, whether his own or that of others – to live without any further contribution of present working-time, the community of which he is a member cannot do so, but must supply the working hours to operate the capital he owns, even when he has provided it by his own abstinence.

Of the two factors necessary for the production of wealth he provides but one.

Thus the principle, so clear when we consider the case of the average state of the community as a whole, give rise to quite unsolved, if not insoluble, social problems when one set of people own the capital and another set operate it. There is no known theoretical method of equating the sum-total of hours of past labour expended on the provision of capital against the continuous expenditure of present working hours necessary to make it productive, or of determining what is, ethically, the just distribution of the increment.

CHAPTER VII

MONEY OLD AND MONEY NEW

The Mechanism for Distributing Wealth among Individuals for Consumption

A study of how wealth originates and of its different categories logically precedes the study of its consumption and use. Life is, in the physical sense of human-being-hours, the product of wealth as wealth is the product of energy and human time. Such considerations obviously lie at the root of any inquiry into political or national economy, and take precedence over questions of ownership, distribution and exchange, which are of first importance to individual economy. The production of wealth is, in civilised communities, communal rather than individual. The process is so differentiated that a reversion to primitive individualistic methods of production would mean death to the greater part of the community. Those that would survive are by no means those generally considered to be wealthy as individuals, but the farmers and peasants actually engaged in food production. If, through political chaos, individualistic methods in the production of wealth came into operation, they alone could maintain indefinitely a rude uncivilised type of existence.

But the use and consumption of wealth, in the enabling and empowering of life, is individual and not communal. A man's life is his own personal and individual affair in a state of political freedom, and claims prior consideration even to that of the community. The life of the community in its physical aspect is the aggregate merely of the lives of its individual members, whereas the wealth of a community has no necessary relation to the claims upon its present and future wealth which constitutes the wealth of its component individuals. It is, in

Ruskin's phrase, "the rule and root of all economy" that what one person has, or claims, many others than himself have had, or will have, to exert themselves to make.

Money is the device which, whether consciously or intuitively, gives effect to this relationship between wealth and life, for it enables the individuals in a community, personally and as individuals, to indent upon the fruits of the total activities of the commonwealth and to own, use and consume, whilst contributing, if at all, only a limited and specialised part in the production.

The Dangers of Money

Money, or some equivalent, is, in consequence, a necessity in any civilisation or community above the stage where everyone produces all that he or she consumes.

But it is a dangerous necessity, for all that, only too apt to engender in the body politic social diseases potent enough to bring the proudest nations to the dust. It substitutes for the natural inalienable right of the worker to the produce of his toil a vague generalised claim upon the totality of the fruits of the community's efforts – a highly indefinite quantity, which opens the door to every kind of abuse. On the moral side, it divorces the conception of wealth from the dignity of labour, a sanctifying connection driven home by the genius of Thomas Hood in the simple lines – It is not linen you are wearing out, But human creatures' lives! and by Ruskin's words: "Luxury at present can only be enjoyed by the ignorant; the cruellest man living could not sit at his feast unless he sat blindfold."

The variation of the purchasing power of money exposes the community to wholesale injustice on the one side and undeserved gain on the other, as assuredly as if the one set had been despoiled of their belongings by the other by robbery and violence. But worse than all, it paves the way to the economic subjugation of humanity to monetary power because of the confusion in the minds of people between money and wealth. By substituting for the "conception of a realised amount" "a periodical receipt" of an infinitude of future interest payments, it tries to condemn to eternal slavery generations not yet born. It is therefore of the utmost importance that all those who wish to understand social problems should understand and make themselves masters of the subject of money. That no one yet understands it is a truism. Least of all those who have made a special study of it – starting always from the initial inversion that money is national wealth rather than debt – seem able to answer intelligibly the simplest questions about it that it would occur to the veriest tyro to ask.

The Simplest Questions about Modern Money are unanswerable

How is money made, by the King and Royal Mint, or by the banks? How much money is there? Does money bear interest? What is precisely the distinction between bad money and good, between what is issued by the King and Royal Mint, by a counterfeiter, or by the banks? What is the correct quantity of money needed for the conduct of a nation's business, and why cannot it be printed as railway tickets are, or as food tickets were during the War without an elaborate mystical apotheosis of the golden calf and a bowing down to vulgar fallacies concerning the fecundity of debt?

Even a child can understand the reason why money was made of a valuable metal. A commercial transaction in which gold bullion exchanges for goods is simple barter. When we pass from bullion to gold and silver coins, which circulate practically for ever, from these to a national paper money, like the papier mâché of Kubla Khan or the American "greenbacks," then to the modern bank-note and cheque which have practically displaced national money, and then to the various forms of elusive bank credit, "created out of and decreated into Absolute Nothingness by the mere fiat of the Human Will," the simplest questions that would occur to the mind of a child seem incapable of a definite answer. If it was once considered an elementary principle of honesty, and self-evident that the nation's currency should be of just weight and fineness and issued only by a duly authorised Mint, how are the vital national interests in the creation of money properly safeguarded now that the big transactions of the world are carried on by cheques, bank-notes, and other forms of paper credit that never saw the inside of a Mint?

It is absolutely unavoidable, before proceeding further, for the reader to try to understand the existing monetary system. In all the ramifications of the evolution of the conception of money it is essential that one main thread running through them should never be for one moment lost sight of. It is the same thread one must pursue in passing from the common conception of money, as it is thoroughly well understood by every *individual*, to the conception of money as a *national* instrument to effect the distribution and allocation of the community's wealth, for the historical evolution of money in the community mirrors the evolution in the mind of a learner trying to master the subject.

The Evolution of Money

The first or individual conception of money is that of a gold or silver coin – of definite value and intrinsic worth if melted into bullion and so demonetised – being exchanged for goods in general of equal value, a simple barter. The second or national conception of money is different because the gold money is never demonetised by being melted when used as internal currency. It circulates indefinitely. A simple sale of goods for a given piece of money has to be considered with respect to the previous transaction in which the seller acquired the piece of money by giving something in exchange first and the subsequent transaction in which he passes it on, himself buying something with it. It then appears that what really gives the coin its value is not that it is made of gold or silver, so much as that it is legal payment for debt.

A seller hands over to the buyer the possession of certain wealth, and, to discharge the debt, the buyer hands over to the seller money as legal payment, and so transfers to him a legal claim to anything he can purchase of equal value to that which he has sold, whenever he cares to exercise it.

In the case of a genuine loan of money from lender to borrower, or creditor to debtor, the borrower who receives the money incurs an equal debt to the lender. In the case of a sale of goods for money the buyer who receives the goods pays the debt he incurs with money, and so confers upon the seller in exchange for what he has given up an equal credit or right to be repaid in wealth on demand. In the first case the borrower gives his personal promise to repay the creditor; in the second case the buyer gives money, which is the nation's generalised promise to repay the seller the wealth he has given to the buyer, whenever he pleases.

We thus come to look upon money – quite irrespective of whether it is specie or paper – as a token certifying that the owner of it is a creditor of the general community and entitled to be repaid in wealth on demand.

The only difference between specie and paper money is that in the first case the nation's creditor holds in his hand not only the nation's promise to repay on demand, but also the means of enforcing the demand, if the nation should default, [27] by melting the coin and destroying it as money, so gaining the gold out of which it is made in repayment of his debt. In the case of an inconvertible paper money he has not that power. In the case of a paper money convertible on demand into gold money he has the power, but only exceptionally, as an individual, provided too many other individuals do not at the same time try to exercise their power also. If they did, there would generally be only a small fraction of the necessary gold in existence to satisfy their claims to it.

Thus the next step to a complete divorce between the original notion of money as a form of wealth to barter for equivalent goods and the modern token as a credit instrument that confers upon the owner a right to a repayment of wealth, merely awaits the devising of a suitable guarantee to the owner of the money that the nation will not default, which shall be as acceptable as the rude method of incorporating with the token of indebtedness an equivalent of gold or silver.

Let us now contrast the state of a nation under a gold or silver currency of full value and a credit currency respectively. The first certainly presents no difficulties.

The specie is part of the national wealth. No one in the community has a monetary claim to wealth beyond the wealth in the possession of the community, and no one part of that wealth has, on account of the money system, more than one owner at the same time. True, individuals may owe and be owed amongst themselves, and those owed may sell the debt to others, transferring their claims much as credit money circulates. But no one here would be so bold as to claim that by multiplying ownership you multiply wealth. If B owes A £1,000, B may or may not have real property to the value of £1,000, which can be regarded as behind the debt and as security for its repayment. But even if he has, no one in his senses could argue that, because A and B are to this extent joint owners of the same property, its value in joint

[27] The common mode of default is when the currency is debased or depreciated in purchasing power.

ownership is double that in separate ownership. £1,000 is a £1,000, whether owned by A or B or both at the same time, and does not in the latter case become £2,000.[28] This would be transparently absurd.

Under a credit currency, paper money, cheques and banknotes replace specie without any important difference, save that no gold or other valuable material is incorporated in the token of national indebtedness. There is no wealth in the possession of the owners of the money, and there need be none in the possession of the nation behind these claims. Hence, if we regard the owners of paper money as national creditors, just as in the case of the individual creditors and debtors, there is a joint ownership of the property of the nation, as between its legal owners and those with money and, as a consequence of the money system, part of the wealth of the nation has more than one owner at the same time. The monetary claim is limited to wealth in the market for sale and the debt circulates indefinitely, being transferred from buyer to seller and not cancelled. Hence it comes about that though there is nothing behind these claims, there need not be, because the nation is a continuing organisation, and, to distribute its wealth, some people must always actually prefer a *claim* on goods in the market in general, exercisable at will, to *possession* of the equivalent of any one form of wealth. From this necessity arises the further deduction that, even in the case of gold money, it is not the gold that is the real inducement that tempts a seller of commodities to exchange them for money, but the power a national credit token confers on the holder to satisfy his needs in wealth on demand.

Even with a golden guinea it is the guinea stamp and not the gold that constitutes it money. If a man wants gold he buys it from a jeweller or bullion merchant. Hence all the human toil and effort expended in winning the precious metals for the purpose of currency is unnecessary, so long as the coins circulate and are not melted down and demonetised. They represent a waste of the community's labour, which it has to make good in real useful wealth to the owner of the coin on demand, no more and no less than a paper-money token represents, without any such

---

[28] Throughout, for brevity, the symbol £ is used to express a pound-sterling's worth of wealth or goods, and is always to be read in this full sense.

wasted effort at all, that the community must make good to the owner the amount of his claim to real useful wealth on demand.

Virtual Wealth

Hence we arrive at the conclusion that, in the one case as in the other, the monetary system of distributing wealth does so because of the power it confers upon individuals *not* to possess but to be *owed* wealth to which they are entitled, in order that any kind or quantity desired may be obtained as and when required without effort. Money is not wealth even to the individual, but the evidence that the owner of the money has *not* received the wealth to which he is entitled, and that he can demand it at his own convenence. So that in a community, of necessity, the aggregate money, irrespective of its amount, represents the aggregate value of the wealth which the community prefers to be owed on these terms rather than to own.

This negative quantity of wealth I termed the *Virtual Wealth* of the community because the community is obliged by its monetary system and the necessity of having one, to act as though it possessed this much more wealth than it actually does possess.

As a community grows in numbers and in revenue or income, so does its Virtual Wealth grow too, as indicated in the diagram (Fig. 1). Thus at a time *t* 1, if the real wealth of a community offered for sale is represented by *ab*, its virtual wealth may be *bc*, so that it can and must act as if it possessed wealth to the extent *ac*, of which *ab* is owned and *bc* is owed. At a later time *t* 2, if its real wealth on the market has grown to *de*, its virtual wealth will correspondingly have grown to *ef*, so that it can and must act as if it possessed *df*. There must be a rough, though not necessarily exact, proportionality between the positive and negative components, and both must start from zero, as the diagram indicates.

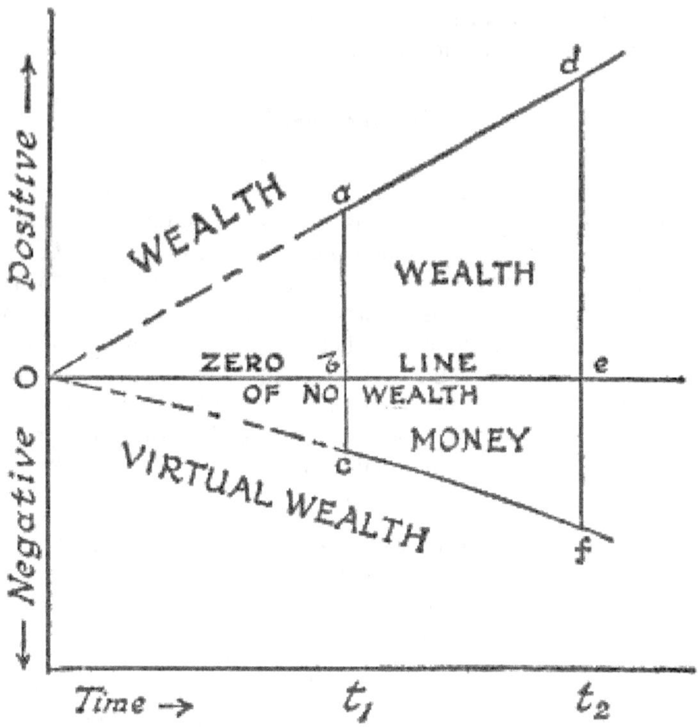

FIG. 1.– *The Principle of Virtual Wealth.*

The Two Kinds of National Credit

In this way we come to see that, just as in reckoning the wealth of an individual – if he possesses personal credit or power of running into debt – we must start, not from the zero of wealth, but from a negative quantity – what he would owe if he had spent all he owns and all he owes – something similar is necessarily true of a nation.

But the origin of this "credit" is entirely different in the two cases. In the case of an individual it is exercised at the expense of and with the consent of another individual, usually as a business accommodation or concession for which the debtor pays interest. In the other case, it is a necessity inherent to the communal nature of production and individual nature of consumption, and which arises out of the monetary system of distribution. It benefits all the members of the community, in proportion to their monetary holdings, to be owed rather to own a certain part of the wealth to which they are entitled. This Virtual Wealth is thus a peculiar part of national credit, and is sharply to be distinguished from the rest, which, indeed, is the only part of the national credit usually recognised, and which is in no way different from that of an individual. Thus, when MacLeod says, "So also the Credit of the State by which it can purchase Money and other things by giving persons the Right to Demand a series of future payments from it is National Wealth," he really means that the national credit enables the State to *acquire* wealth and claims to wealth owned by its individual citizens without immediate repayment, and this is no more national wealth than a merchant's credit is. Exercised, it creates interest-bearing National Debt, in which repayment is *not* indefinitely avoided, as it would be if the State printed money in the correct amount and exchanged it for goods. The National Debt must continue to be paid for until it is repaid. Whereas the Virtual Wealth of the community, although it is National Debt in one sense, is permanent, necessary, beneficial, normally non-repayable and non-interest-bearing debt. It is, of course, the confusion between these two kinds of national credit, and the carrying over of what is only true of a community to the individual, that is responsible for the almost mystical powers with which Credit is associated in many people's minds.

The expert, on the other hand, will say: "Have you not by a roundabout way arrived at what the economists have asserted, even though it involved them in logical blunders, namely that money is rightly to be regarded as part of the National Wealth?" The answer to this is clear. It is true that the nation must act, and continue indefinitely to act, as if it possessed more wealth than it does possess, by the aggregate purchasing power of its money, but the important thing is that this Virtual Wealth does *not* exist. It is an imaginary negative quantity – a deficit or debt of wealth, subject neither to the laws of conservation nor thermodynamics. But it *is* a quantity which has reference to *wealth* and not to *money*. It is not the amount of money people have that is of any real importance, but the amount of wealth they are in a position to obtain any time in the future on demand, and therefore go without in the present, that is of importance. It is the quantity of goods that the community abstains from possessing that is definite, and the number of units of money this definite quantity is worth is all the money, whatever that *all* may be.

It is the virtual wealth which measures the value or purchasing power of money, and not money which measures the value of wealth.

Although the money value of the aggregate virtual wealth is necessarily identical with the aggregate of the money possessed by the community, this identity merely obscures the real truth. The virtual wealth has, in fact, very little to do with the quantity of money. True, it may tend to change because people try to change their habits owing to an inflation or deflation of the currency, but the habits of a community are essentially conservative, so that it can only change within comparatively small limits. Whereas the quantity of money, on the other hand, is absolutely and entirely arbitrary, and can theoretically be made as small as or as great as the nation pleases without any limit whatsoever. However large or small, the total money is, of course, the money-worth of the virtual wealth, so that if the latter does not change, the level of average prices is proportional to the quantity of money and the purchasing power of money is inversely proportional to the quantity of money.

With this much preliminary description of the point of view about money stressed in this work, we may revert to what was termed the main thread the course of monetary evolution has followed. It has been the substitution for a money consisting of actual wealth possessed, a money denoting wealth owed to but not possessed. To the individual the latter means, or should mean, that that individual has done some service for the community not yet repaid in wealth. But to the community the significance of its money is totally different. It means, since the repayment of such services in wealth only transfers its debt from one individual to another, that such debts need not be repaid at all, and indeed can only be repaid by the community itself obtaining possession of the money and destroying it. These are the only kind of debts that are wholly beneficial to the community, and, being instantly honoured by transfer from one individual to another, so long as they are honoured at an unchanging price-level they need not bear any interest whatever, whether made of metal or paper. For money interest is essentially payment for the privilege of being allowed to defer the payment of a money debt. Let us now proceed to the consideration of actual monetary systems.

Sketch of the Origin of the Present System

Money, as an authorised token of the indebtedness of the whole community to the individual possessing the token, is, of course, a very ancient institution, and these tokens were even sometimes quite devoid of value in themselves, apart from the social convention of honouring them as legally enforceable claims to actual wealth. In the token monies of Athens and Sparta, between the tenth and fifth centuries B.C., in which metal discs of no value were employed as coins, the essential principle that the number of tokens issued should be limited and publicly known was perfectly appreciated. But no doubt the simplest communities found difficulty in checking the unauthorised and fraudulent imitation of the tokens. The connection with barter, where commodities of equal value change hands, was preserved in the precious metal money that still to some extent persists. The principle underlying it was perfectly correct to the principles of modern physical science. Since wealth cannot be created out of nothing, but is a product of human effort expended on the raw material and sources of energy of the globe, no individual should be able to manufacture a new money claim to wealth out of nothing, and the purchaser should give up something equal in value to (as difficult to come by as) that which he so acquires. It is in this vital point that the modern methods of multiplying claims to wealth fail.

But even more fatal to democracy has been its failure to provide any proper authority and mechanism for the making and issue of money, as and when it is required, to keep pace with the growth of its wealth. *National money* – whatever it is made of – does not bear, and never has borne, interest, which is the *raison d'être* for the issue of most modern money. Whatever ends it may be supposed to subserve, bank money is created primarily for that end, and, what is worse, then decreated again when that end is served. But a sovereign issued in the reign of George III is now worth no more than when it was issued, and obeys the ordinary law of the conservation of matter. It does not mysteriously appear and as mysteriously disappear like bank money. The whole expense of minting it, and of maintaining it against loss of weight due to abrasion in use, is borne by the State without charge to the user. In this country the loss was to some extent made up by the issue of silver coins worth, as bullion, only about half their face value and of copper coins of no definite metal value; but the currency was safeguarded from debasement thereby by limiting the validity of these silver tokens, as legal payment for debt, to sums up to £2 and the copper tokens only up to 1s.

Although, by making the main coinage of gold, the holder is given an equivalent in wealth for what the coin will purchase, actually stringent regulations prohibited the defacing of the coin and prevented its being used except as a token of the communal indebtedness. In a community in which mutual trust was not highly developed the precious metal in the coins ensured their ready circulation, but serves no other purpose so far as the internal currency is concerned. They are really one form of token money.

According to our definition of wealth, gold and silver bullion are clearly wealth – so long as they serve the needs of the community. Apart from their use in currency, they are, and will probably always be, wealth to the jeweller, who otherwise would have to search the earth, or pay others for searching, for the raw material of his trade. If so, they would still possess value as a store of wealth for hoarding purposes. So that even if demonetised, though their value would probably much decline, they would still be wealth, in the second category, along with permanent possessions and organs of production. Some of the complexities of the subject are due to this triple origin of the value of gold and silver.

With the growth of productive power due to the growth of science metal coinage ceased to be adequate, although, if it had been still retained, it is doubtful whether the consequent evils would have been greater than those which have come upon us as a consequence of paper money being substituted without the original principles of money being preserved.

Though scientific methods have, especially in comparatively recent times, very greatly cheapened the processes of winning gold and silver and have enabled very much poorer ores to be worked at a profit, these metals cannot as yet be made artificially at will. The supply of them has not kept pace with the supply of those forms of wealth that can be made by scientific methods, given the necessary workers, to any reasonable extent required. As the result of the Industrial Revolution and its secondary, but no less important, consequence in making the produce of practically the whole earth available everywhere by the use of mechanical transport, there should have occurred an immense fall in the money price of commodities if the currency had been restricted still to the precious metals, though possibly the demand created for them would have so stimulated the supply that the fall would have been only temporary. Because, price being under the system a weight of gold given for goods, if goods increase in abundance relatively to gold, less of the latter than before exchanges for the same goods. The price of the latter would therefore have fallen gradually, and the relatively increasing value of gold in goods would have stimulated the search for gold. But the actual course of events was the rediscovery of the use of credit or token money in the Western world.

Kubla Khan's Currency

Paper money is in itself a fascinating study, and it is perhaps worth while tracing its invention to at least one of its origins in the East. Kubla Khan, the great Mogul emperor, as Marco Polo records in his travels,[29] "had the secret of alchemy to perfection, for he makes his money of the bark of a mulberry-tree, and this they cut up into something resembling paper, but black… Everyone takes them readily, for wherever a person shall go he will find these pieces of paper current, and be able to transact all business just as if it were gold." The Great Khan must have arrived by intuition at many of the principles that we are so slow to accept. He realised that the bulk of his subjects had no need for gold for their internal currency, but required only a medium of exchange, of definite and constant purchasing power and safeguarded from counterfeiting, whereas for foreign trade the precious metals were essential.

Thus we read that all merchants from India bringing gold or silver, or gems or pearls, were prohibited from selling them except to the emperor, who paid a very liberal price for them in his own paper notes without any delay. The merchants found them vastly lighter to carry forth than gold, and bought with them whatever they liked anywhere within the empire. But the nobles, or indeed anyone else so ever, having need of precious metals or gems for girdles or the like, could always buy as much as they wished from the emperor with the paper money. The first issue was in 1260–1287, and some of this paper is still extant, and can be seen occasionally in museums.

The Origin of Modern Paper Money

Very different is the history of its rediscovery in the West. The kings, in need of gold and silver as much, no doubt, as the Great Khan, used in emergency to borrow it, sometimes without the formality of the owners' consent, so that it became extremely risky to deposit it in the Tower or other stronghold provided for the purpose. In these

[29] *Travels of Marco Polo*, edited by Cordier, translated by Yule. John Murray, 1903, vol. I, book II, p. 423.

circumstances the goldsmiths obligingly acted as caretakers for the spare cash of the merchants and others, and in course of time developed into bankers. Holding the stocks of money of their various customers, they were loth to allow such vast sums of "wealth" to remain "idle" and "barren," and they lent a safe proportion to reliable people at interest, knowing by experience that not all their depositors would want all their money back on the same day. But when merchants with mutual dealings happened to deposit with the same goldsmith, they found it convenient to issue a written order to the latter to pay one another out of and into their mutual accounts, rather than themselves to draw out the money for the purpose.

Thus the modern cheque originated, whereby, instead of remitting cash to pay an account, a cheque, or order to the banker to pay from the depositor's account, is sent.

Such an order, or cheque, as a substitute for money, has two sources of uncertainty. First, it may be worthless because of the insolvency of the signatory, and secondly, because of the insolvency of the bank. The first of these effectually prevents cheques from passing current as money, save, possibly, among a few to whom the signatory is personally known to be solvent. But the ability or otherwise of a bank to meet its liabilities is much more widely known, and is a matter of common repute among the business fraternity. Hence, among merchants personally unknown to one another, the practice arose of sending the goldsmith's receipt for the deposited gold. This eliminated the first uncertainty, and such receipts would circulate as money everywhere where the goldsmith was known to be reputable. In this way the bank-note originated. The depositor obtained receipts for definite sums of gold, with which in course of time the community got to be familiar. The receipts circulated as money as easily and more conveniently than the gold itself. At this stage there *was* the gold behind the note. It was a promise of the banker to pay the holder of the receipt or note the sum of gold specified on demand in exchange for the note.

The Displacement of National Money by Bank Money

The goldsmith, now turned banker, found by experience that he was in permanent continuous possession of a stock of gold far greater than he was ever called upon to pay out. So long as a bank-note circulated, the gold it was a receipt for remained unused in his safe. But there was a far more important effect produced by the rise in popularity of the cheque system. The banker's own clients, when they issued to one another orders to pay, or cheques, clearly *did not in the least affect the amount of gold he held*. Their cheques merely transferred *ownership* of money from one of the banker's clients to another. The settlement of mutual indebtedness between those banking with the same bank by the cheque system is merely an affair of bookkeeping, which goes farther than the bank-note and *dispenses altogether with money*. The money is thus freed for use over again by the banker, who can, and does, lend it to reputable producers for definite periods, to be repaid with interest out of the proceeds of wealth-producing enterprise. But, again, the money itself need not be used for this, as a cheque-book serves the same purpose everywhere[30] so long as the bank's reputation for solvency remains good. The original money is thus used over and over again, and out of an original quantity of wealth claims to many times this amount of wealth in the possession of other quite innocent and unsuspecting people are created literally by the stroke of a pen.

This is the *pons asinorum* of banking, and at this point its apologists always seem to be distracted from the principles that money is supposed to subserve in a community to an *ex parte* defence of the system. It certainly does seem odd to a tyro to discover that the law proceeds with the utmost severity against the fraudulent counterfeiter for uttering new money tokens, but allows the banks in effect to create it wholesale to lend at interest by these methods, which is a far more profitable business and infinitely more serious in its consequences to the general community than counterfeiting. To any other age it would have been the most obvious form of treason against the State.

The Private Issue of Money; A Chance Result of the Bank Cheque System

No doubt there are still many people, if not the majority, who will be frankly incredulous that money vastly exceeding in amount the total national money can be, and is created and destroyed by the moneylender with a stroke of the pen. How frequently does one still

[30] The borrower simply "overdraws his account," but the banker posts to the borrower's credit the sum in question, and on the other side of his ledger he posts it to his own credit as owing to him from the borrower.

read in the Press that the banks can only loan their customers spare money! Most people still think of what money once was, "a public instrument owned and controlled by the State." They naturally conclude that those who essay the thankless task of looking at the question from the national standpoint cannot understand it themselves. For this incredulity there is, however, no justification.

The main facts are in no dispute. They are set forth clearly in all works on money. If the uninstructed reader wishes to read the best attempted apology for the system he is recommended to the works on the subject by Mr. Hartley Withers. The point of view is that of the enthusiastic financial publicist, who sees the great rise of prosperity not in terms of invention, diligence and energy, but in terms of money, and to whom the marvellous growth of recent times is the effect rather than the cause of the wonderful banking system, particularly the British banking system, not to say the London banking system.

A few paragraphs may be cited:[31]

> "The broad conclusion arrived at is that banking deposits come into being to a small extent by cash paid into banks across the counter, to a larger but still comparatively small extent by purchases of securities by the banks which create book credits, and chiefly by loans from the banks which also create book credits.
>
> "There is nothing alarming in the conclusion, though people who have been accustomed to regard bank deposits as so much cash paid in are sometimes startled when the other side of the matter is put to them, and feel that banking credit is a kind of questionable conspiracy between banks and their customers. A little reflection shows that it is a beautiful piece of evenly working mechanism, by which coin is economised and a perfect currency is provided with extraordinary ease and cheapness. Nor need any sense of disillusionment be felt when it is realised that bank deposits, in so far as they are borrowed, are evidences of indebtedness quite as much as of wealth.

[31] *The Meaning of Money*, chap. V, "The Manufacture of Money."

> "Everybody knows that in all long-established, well-ordered and industrious communities vast stores of wealth are accumulated; and even if they could be heaped up in banks and expressed in figures nothing would be gained by the information. But the contemplation of this mass of indebtedness, and of the cheque currency with which it is passed from hand to hand, is novel, stimulating and unique.
>
> It is a wondrous example of human ingenuity applied to the cheapening and furtherance of trade, finance and speculation. There is nothing quite like it anywhere else, and its development has only been rendered possible by the confidence, based on solid experience, of the majority of Englishmen in one another's commercial probity, and readiness to carry out a contract at all costs.
>
> "The only defect in the system is its perfection."

He warns the uninitiated that bank deposits include deposits proper, in which the money is really deposited and cannot be taken out except after a stipulated time, and current accounts in which the money can be drawn at will by cheque. He then shows how the greater part are created by loans. He takes the latest (1909) available balance-sheets of half a dozen of the biggest joint stock bankers and puts their figures together, with the result that "the greater part of the banks' deposits is thus seen to consist, not of cash paid in, but of credits borrowed. For every loan makes a deposit, and since our balance-sheet shows 180½ millions of loans, 180½ out of the 249 millions of deposits have been created by loans."

So capable an authority at least must be respected even by those who still pretend to believe that the banks only lend their customers' unused money. Indeed, to some people it seems sufficient to prove this that a bank's balance-sheet balances. Whereas, of course, when a bank credit is created, both sides of the balance-sheet are written up to the same extent. It is not merely the old lady of fable who overdrew her account and sent her banker a cheque for the amount. Her misfortune was merely that she was not her own banker.

The following quotation from *The Times*, December 9, 1925, p. 21, City Notes column, should convince the most skeptical: "… Issuing houses and underwriters must remember that capital available for investment is not, like bank credit, a thing that can be manufactured by a bookkeeping entry; it can only be provided by genuine savings."

The Moratorium and After

At the commencement of the War the ugly fact of the Moratorium needed some public *apologia*, and we read in a work by Mr. Withers published in 1914: "It came upon us like a thunderbolt from a clear sky. At the end of July 1914 any citizen of London who was asked what a moratorium meant would probably have answered that there was not such a word. Possibly he might have said that it was a large extinct woolly beast with big tusks. If he was exceptionally well informed in matters of finance he would have replied that it was some sort of device used in economically backward countries for blurring the distinction between *meum* and *teum*. On the 2nd of August we had a moratorium on bills of exchange. On the 6th of August we had a general moratorium… It was an unpleasant string of surprises, but it was not brought about by any internal weakness in the English banking system.

The fury of the tempest was such that no credit system could possibly have stood up against it. In fact, as will be shown, the chief reason for the suddenness and fullness of the blow that fell on London was nothing else but her own overwhelming strength.

She was so strong and so lonely in her strength that her strength overcame her."[32]

And at the close of the same work:

> "Summing up the effects of the War as far as it has gone, on Lombard Street, we may confidently claim that they have given a striking proof of the resourcefulness and adaptability of the Bank of England, the prudent and successful courage of the Government in pledging the national credit in order to maintain our trade, and the masterful power of England's wealth."[33]

In *Bankers and Credit*, published after the War, when the country is experiencing some of the consequences of its improvised efforts to take some small part in its own finances, it is the politicians, never the banks, that are to blame:

---

[32] *War and Lombard Street*, Hartley Withers, 1914, chap. I, "The Moratorium."

[33] Ibid., p. 131.

> "Political rulers have lately shown amazing capacity for creating chaos in the world of banking. Under the stress of war they seized and warped for their own purposes the banking and currency system of this country and of all other countries engaged in it, and of many of those that were only affected indirectly, with the result that the system which had been brought to something very near to perfection is now "Like sweet bells jangled out of tune and harsh," a melancholy mockery of its former beauty and efficiency."

The book ends on the proper functions of the politician:

> "The gold standard frees us from muddling with our money by politicians, has worked right well in the past and may do so again, whenever the politicians succeed in doing their proper job, of giving us peace and security and confidence and goodwill."[34]

Whereas most people who have any experience of responsible administration would probably agree that an administrative Government without any real power over finance, and with that power located elsewhere, can be little more than a figure-head. "The king is dead. Long live the king!"

The Change from the Old to the New "Money"

At this stage it may be helpful to revert once again to the critical point that the banking system, without uttering a single false coin, can and does multiply the money of the country for usury many times.

At first the legislature were strongly opposed to the banks issuing bank-notes.

The general feeling of the public was intuitively against any form of credit money, unbacked by the equivalent of gold. The early State interference with banking seems to have been directed rather towards the object of weakening the banks and making the business precarious both to the banker and the depositors than with any

---

[34] Bankers and Credit, *1924*.

intelligible object. It has been urged very ably[35] that the whole evils of the Industrial Revolution arose from State interference with banking, and that it is as essential for banking to be as free from restriction and as open to competition as any other form of commerce. Historically, it is claimed, the instincts of the banker has been uniformly social, and that banking has become what it has through these instincts being thwarted.

The criticisms of the system in this work must not be taken to reflect upon the bankers as practical business men, but are directly to the theory of credit upon which the system has been based. Nor is it suggested that there is the slightest taint of illegality in *their* actions, whatever may be thought of the way our ostensible rulers have abdicated their functions and left the country in the lurch. The forces at work in the Industrial Revolution were gigantic, and none, probably, understood them. The power of increasing production conferred by the harnessing of mechanical power called for a means of increasing the currency and economising in the use of gold. But the Governments of those days would neither allow the banks to do it in their own way, nor openly and frankly do it themselves by the issue of a national paper money.

In this situation the invention of the cheque system practically solved the problem. It has virtually displaced the bank-note and relegated to quite a minor role the money authorised and issued by the State. It has altered the very nature of money itself without the public and the legislature as yet realising what has occurred.

It is characteristic of the dizzy virtues of compound interest that they are not at all dizzy at the start. It is only after they have been in operation a certain time that they show any disposition to become marvellous and to transcend the bounds of the physically possible. But now that the increments of indebtedness are mounting up, it is hardly a sufficient defence of the system to say that it served the country well in the past, and only needs to be left alone to work further miracles in the future. A single grain of corn doubled as many times as there are squares on a chessboard represents more corn that the present population of the world could consume in a period longer than that covered by the records

---

[35] *Industrial Justice through Banking Reform,* Henry Meulen, 1917.

of history, whereas doubled only half that number of times it would scarcely suffice to give London a square meal. This means that a system might show no signs of breakdown for a century and yet become absolutely impossible during the course of the next.

Reverting to the transition from the old to the new system, before banking started there was a definite amount of gold and silver coinage only. The first step on the downward path, from money for use to money for usury, was the power conferred upon the Bank of England to issue bank-notes to a limited extent in return for the loan of money to the Government – a power they still possess under the Bank Charter Act of 1844. Their uncovered note issue was then limited to £M14, beyond which they were required to keep gold in reserve. The whole intentions of the latter Act, which is still the law – namely, to prevent the issue of paper money uncovered by gold – were frustrated by the development of the cheque system. The latter effectively killed the bank-note as a form of currency by establishing a much more insidious and uncontrollable form. It is only the latter that needs any further elucidation.

The Pyramiding of Credit

As the banking and cheque system developed and people got into the habit of depositing their money more and more in banks and using cheques, in lieu of cash, to settle their accounts, the banker at first would, as we have seen, always possess a much larger stock of gold and silver than he required to meet such demands for cash as the public still made. It is therefore clear that the banker can safely lend part of his depositors' money; but what is not so clear is that he can lend many times as much as the whole nation possesses – in fact, create it to lend at will.

Before the War it was considered "safe" for the banker to keep some £15 per £100 of cash against deposits. That is, for every £100 deposited £15 of cash sufficed for the small cash demands, most of the depositors' purchasing power being exercised by cheque. We may take this 15 per cent for purpose of illustration only.

It is doubtful if as much has been necessary for a very long time.

Now the whole secret of the system is contained in the fact that when a bank creates a loan and lends £100 to a borrower, to do so it need only have £15 of its depositors' money, or whatever the "safe" ratio may be.

Thus, dealing throughout with averages, against the original depositor of £100, £15 of legal tender must be kept in the till, leaving £85 available to be lent to a borrower. It is true this borrower might demand it in cash, but, on the average for him no less than for the original depositor, only 15 per cent of cash, or £12 15s. is necessary, leaving £72 5s. free to be lent to a second borrower. Of this 15 per cent, or £10 17s., again suffices to be retained, leaving £61 8s. available to be lent to a third borrower. So it goes on until each £100 of original cash becomes a total of £666 13s. 4d. Of this £100 are due to the depositor and £566 13s. 4d. is owing to the bank from the borrowers.

The borrowers have to deposit with the bank acceptable collateral securities, which, if they default, the bank can sell, or try to sell, to recoup itself. But such securities are usually not sold. The bank charges interest upon the fictitious loan. At the modest 5 per cent bank rate the interest on £566 13s. 4d. is £28 6s. 8d. per year, which is, it must be admitted, not a bad return on £100 which the original "depositor" *has not lent.*

If the truth were known it would probably be found that this estimate is altogether too modest.[36] At least since, if not before, the War the figures suggest rather a 7 per cent "safe" limit than 15 per cent. On this basis a client depositing £100 of cash in current account enables the bank to loan £1,330, which at 5 per cent brings in £66 10s. 9d. per annum.

It is therefore not surprising that banks are usually so ready to keep their depositors' accounts for nothing. Economists, in their analysis of how a man gets his income and how he spends it, regard this interest apparently as payment for services in banking, and have never to the author's knowledge tried to assess its cost to the community. Clearly if they were deprived of these powers, the banks would have to charge their customers for the trouble of keeping their accounts like

[36] Hugo Bilgram (*Journal of Political Economy*, XXIX, November, 1921) takes the total of cash reserves held by deposit and reserve banks in the United States as not less than 8 per cent of the total deposit currency, and of this 40 percent must be gold.

other businesses. But whether such a system of economics that overlooks the virtual wealth of the community and treats it as the property of the bankers rather than of the nation – a mere perquisite for the performance of certain clerical duties – is of much help to the nation's government is another question.

Puzzle – Find the Money

Still, many features in connection with the process of "pyramiding" credit are likely not to be wholly clear and will repay careful examination. So let us trace so far as possible the change from the old system, when all money was legal tender – gold and silver money – to the modern system, when only a small proportion is. It is necessary to remember that those who are accommodated with loans from the bank really need goods of one form or another. They do not pay interest charges on borrowed money to hoard it. They very quickly exchange the money with others for goods. Once this has happened all distinction between the two kinds of money – genuine money owned by owners and bank money created to lend – disappears. All is then genuine money lawfully owned by its owners. A man who has sold goods to another for money created by a bank has as valid a right in law to the ownership of that money as though it were genuine, whereas a man who is so unfortunate as to become the possessor of a counterfeit coin has his claim to wealth decreated into the Absolute Nothing so soon as the coin is detected and nailed to the counter. Property in wealth does not pass on delivery, but property in money does. The owner of stolen goods may recover them even from an innocent receiver of them, but the innocent receiver of money is confirmed by the law in his ownership, even though the money can be proved to have been originally stolen from someone else. Even if it could be shown that the banks have broken the letter of the law in creating money, as they have certainly driven a coach-and-four through its spirit and intention, it does not in the least affect the conclusion that, for all practical purposes, there is no difference between genuine money deposits and those created by loan. Each is a valid claim to the wealth of the community.

This was certainly a definite stage in the author's own efforts to understand the problem. Thus one may be tempted to think, when one reads that, of the total amount of bank deposits, three-fourths or four-fifths have been created by loans, that only one-fourth or one-fifth is really money genuinely belonging to the depositors, and that the rest is borrowed from the bank and owed to the bank at the same time and by the same people. This is not so. The people who owe the money no longer have it; they have for the most part exchanged it for goods. True they are continuously repaying it, but, as continuously, the bank is granting new loans to take the place of those so repaid. Practically the whole of the deposits are genuine claims to money lawfully owned by the individual depositors, but the money they claim has no existence.

Money imagined to Exist for the Purpose of bearing Interest

We have thus reached a very interesting conclusion: that whereas the old form of metal money could not and did not bear interest to the owner, and could only bear interest when he parted with the ownership of it and lent it to another, the new form of credit money – at least prior to the War, which saw the birth of the Treasury note – has no existence, but imagined to exist and lent to borrowers as though it existed for the purpose of bearing interest. This non-existent money passes by sale into the hands of those who give up something in exchange for it, and who now therefore own what is not in existence. Absurd as this description may appear, it is none the less undeniable. Let everyone with money that is his very own – borrowed from or lent by nobody – present himself at the bank at the same time and ask for it. The proof of the statement whether this money does or does not exist will then be apparent. As everyone knows, they would be lucky if they got 2s. in the £. Even if the banks do keep 15 per cent of their liabilities in cash, they would only get 3s. in the £. As the owners of it have not got the money they own, and as the banks have not got it, and as the people who borrowed it have not got it, where is it? Obviously nowhere. It is imagined to exist for the purpose of charging interest upon it.

Those who have followed the earlier exposition of the Principle of Virtual Wealth; will have no difficulty in recognising money as wealth imagined to exist for the purpose of lawfully obtaining it on demand as and when required. But that is old-fashioned money. The modern bank money carries the process of imagination one stage farther in imagining money itself to exist for the purpose of lending it and charging interest upon it. Purely fictitious money, which the nation has not authorised the issue of, is fictitiously lent without anyone giving it up, and then creates perfectly genuine deposits and legal claim upon the community's market for the supply of wealth, indistinguishable in every respect from those the nation has authorised.

How the Community is robbed

It is easy in criticising the monetary system to give a false impression of what it really was. Though by the creation of money and the inflation of the currency by bank credit the community as a whole are robbed of the wealth equivalent to the new creation, it must not be supposed that the banks ever had or claimed any legal title to the ownership of the money so created. They got the permanent use of it and the ownership of the interest it was issued for. The industries to which the money was lent got from the community for nothing – at the expense of the general purchasing power of money – the wealth they purchased with the new money, but had to restore it when the loan was repaid and the credit cancelled. In practice it was never more than temporarily cancelled; it was renewed to other borrowers on the first opportunity. So that a continuous succession of different people without money were empowered by the banks to acquire wealth temporarily from the community to which they were not entitled and for which the whole community paid.

The banks traded on a monetary capital they created themselves, but made no pretensions to possessing. If they were wound up and their businesses discontinued all of the excess of their liabilities over their assets would have to be made good by those to whom they have lent money. The quantity of money would be reduced then to, say, one-sixth of the present amount or less. Prices, "in the end," would be reduced to one-sixth unless a corresponding quantity of genuine national money were issued to take the place of the fictitious money destroyed, though, as Mr. Keynes has sagely observed in a similar connection, "in the end we are all dead." If this were not done, the last loan to be recalled would have to be paid in money worth six times that at which it was issued, and the average for the whole amount of the loans would be over twice their initial purchasing power. This is a somewhat vital distinction between real money and the phantom money being described. With the repayment of a genuine loan the quantity of money is not affected. With the repayment of fictitious loans there is so much less money in existence, so that repayment becomes increasingly difficult as it is enforced. If issued in boom and cancelled in slump they are repaid in units of money worth more than when borrowed.

Some Monetary Data

Very few people outside the banks know much about the amount of money in the country and how it is accounted for. Even Mr. Hartley Withers says:

> "Banking statements and balance-sheets were always designed rather to veil discreetly the modesty of our monetary institutions than to let the full light of day fall upon the beauties of their figures and proportions. Since the War this has been more than ever so. Much of the information that used to be made public has been withheld."[37]

H. W. Macrosty[38] complains that:

> "The published figures regarding our banking transactions, which are certainly abundant and are commonly considered to be sufficient, are neither clear nor sufficient…"

On the important ratio between real deposits, not capable of being drawn upon except after due notice – or "time deposits" – and money in current account he says:

> "It is not improbable that the proportion of time deposits in British banks is one-fifth of the whole amount of deposits, as is the case with the 800 chief banks of the Federal Bank system of the United States."

The Rt. Hon. Reginald McKenna, ex-Chancellor of the Exchequer and Chairman of the London Joint City and Midland Bank, has given the public a good deal of information. Speaking on January 29, 1920, he estimated the spending power of the public as gauged by the total amount of bank deposits, added to the total amount of currency in circulation, as £M1,198 in 1914 and £M2,693 in 1920.

The currency held by the banks in June 1914 was £M75 and in December 1919 £M191. He estimated *the increase* in bank deposits over the period as £M1,230, of which *increase* he attributed £M1,114

---

[37] Bankers and Credit, *p. 4.*

[38] H. W. Macrosty, *Journal Statistical Society*, March 1922, vol. LXV, p. 177.

to bank loans. Macrosty estimated that the currency in the hands of the public amounted to £M128, and in the hands of the banks £M75 in June 1914, whilst at the end of 1919 that in the hands of the public was £M393 and in the hands of the banks £M116. The two estimates are considerably at variance as regards the 1920 figures.

But it would seem perfectly safe to conclude that some two thousand million pounds sterling, ranking in all respects equal to real money, is created by the banks and bears interest at the bank rate, and that an annual toll of the order of one hundred million pounds a year is extracted from the national revenue by this means.

Nor is there any risk worthy the name, for the loans are all no doubt well covered by collateral securities which would be sold up if the debtor defaulted; or, if that were not possible, a moratorium would be declared, as in August 1914.

These data are of the utmost importance to the subject, and it is a great pity that they are not authoritatively and less ambiguously available to the public. It is interesting to know that the monetary value of the virtual wealth of the community was about £M1,200 before the War and about £M2,700 in 1920. One of the few data that is accurately known is the amount of the cheques, bills, etc., annually cleared through the Bankers' Clearing House, London. In 1924 it came to the stupendous total of nearly £M40,000, which is three times the total of 1913 and four times that of 1900.

It will be observed that the annual sums expended by cheques, etc., amount to some fifteen times the total amount of Bank Deposits, and no less than one hundred times the currency in the hands of the public. The amount of the latter is astonishingly small, in comparison with the population, amounting to only some £6 or £7 per head, and even the inflated totality of Bank Deposits is only about £40 per head.

Considerations of this character cause the economists to dismiss contemptuously as an illusion any scheme of social reform by "tinkering with the currency." If we mean by that printing continuously ever more and more money, against expenditure, the reason is obvious. Wealth is consumed, but money goes on for ever. Apart from a very small loss, possibly, due to fire or similar accidents, a coin or note once put into circulation goes on circulating until it is withdrawn from circulation. £1 purchases not £1, but £1, *every month* or so, for ever after, on the average. Here, again, the average "time of circulation" is very imperfectly known and has been variously estimated at different periods of history, but one month seems a sort of probable guess. One might as well try to estimate the velocity of a stream which flows in some parts through broad lakes and at others over foaming cataracts, most of which has no physical existence, but disappears mysteriously underground in one place and, at a different time, reappears in another.

Modern Money a New Institution

These considerations may serve to show how little is known as to the facts of the existing monetary system, but they are probably sufficient to give a general idea of the order of quantity involved, and, in so far as the evils afflicting society are monetary in origin, to suggest reform. The foregoing brief analysis of the origin of modern money reveals that a complete and unsuspected alteration has come over the very nature of it with the discovery of financial devices for economising the use of currency. It is necessary therefore to regard it as an entirely new phenomenon and to go back to first principles in examining it. Almost by accident, certainly as a by-product unforeseen when the cheque system originated, the power of issuing and withdrawing currency has passed entirely beyond the control of the nation into the hands of the banker. If anyone claims that this power is exercised, according to a properly thought-out and intelligible system, to distribute the abundant wealth a modern community is empowered by scientific methods to produce in order that the members may obtain wealth for consumption, let him look around. The money is now issued primarily for usury. Even to the most convinced individualist this must seem to be pushing the principle of liberty rather far. If some people are to have the right of issuing new money, why not the nation as a whole, as and when required?

The financier points to the achievements of science in the past century as a tribute to the soundness and adaptability of the British monetary and banking systems. At the best they must be regarded as a temporary makeshift, extemporised to meet a particular phase of the rapid progress in the materialistic sciences, and, now that that phase is past, obviously unsuitable for the one that has succeeded it.

The continued coexistence of unemployment and poverty in a scientific era is its sufficient condemnation.

The system allows a nation with only at most some £M500 of money in existence to lend to the extent of some £M2,000, and to spend to the extent of some £M40,000 a year by cheque alone. Especially since the great banks have combined – over 90 per cent of the business is in the hands of one group known as *The Big Five* – the purchasing power exercised by cheque exerts no very great influence upon the magnitude of the "deposits," for the cheque merely debits one account and credits another at the same time, save for the small part actually cashed, without affecting the aggregate. Yet most people still believe that the banks only lend the monies their clients are *not* using.

To any business man a knowledge of the truth ought to be sufficient to condemn the system according to the canons of ordinary competitive business. Where else in the whole realm of human activity is it possible to create capital by an act of imagination and to derive from its supposed existence a perennial revenue, just as though it were real wealth put to productive use?

We have seen how in cultivated society the conception of a periodical receipt has forced its way in and overpowered the conception of a realized amount and how we regard our annual income as the really important consideration, dividing it by the rate of interest for the time being to arrive at its aggregate value.

What, then, in "cultivated society" is the difference between the utterer of false coin and the banks? The one pretends to the ownership of a fraudulent realised amount, while the other does not, but will assuredly fight for, as their own property when challenged, the periodical receipt derived from an imaginary realised amount.

Bankers as Rulers

But this is only a minor question in comparison with the effect it has in making the banker the real ruler of the nation. Bankers certainly may be trusted to know their own business, but it is not the business of government. The prerogative of issuing money has down the ages been regarded as the essential prerogative of government.

Possibly it is the only prerogative that is essential. Whereas a banker is not responsible for the government of the community, but for the interests of his own clients. Government by banker is essentially, and in its purest form, government in the interests of the propertied at the expense of the property-less. Better, indeed, that the knowledge of science had been buried, like that of finance, under a mystic jargon in the keeping of a secret hierarchy than that it should exploit and enslave rather than liberate the poor.

> "Whose image and superscription is this?" The coins and Treasury notes still bear the imprint *Georgius V. D.G. Britt. Omn. Rex*, but the vast bulk of the currency omits the first word preceding the big five. So that one is reminded of the schoolboy's version of the scriptural quotation: "He said, 'Bring me a penny.' And they brought him a penny. And he looked at the penny and said, 'Whose miserable subscription is this?'"

CHAPTER VIII

THE PURCHASING POWER OF MONEY

Gold-Value and Goods-Value.

The task of trying to understand how money is multiplied by means of bank credit – apart altogether from the ethics of the transaction – is, however, simple in comparison with the task of trying to determine exactly what, under the system, fixed the total quantity of money in a country, and to this extent its value or purchasing power. We have seen that this quantity, whatever it may be, expresses the *monetary* value of the virtual wealth of the community. It is simple to visualise the latter as the aggregate of wealth of all the kinds required in living, which the aggregate individuals of the community abstain from buying, though able to do so.

Or, as the individuals themselves would look at it, that part of their total possession they have to retain in the form of money to carry on their business and domestic affairs. Regarded as what the money would be used to purchase, it is probably a very definite and conservative amount, growing with the number of people in the community and their material prosperity or income, affected, but only very gradually, by changes in financial and banking methods and habits, altered, but reluctantly and only temporarily, by changes in the price-level or purchasing power of money, but a fairly definite quantity and a very good gauge or index of national well-being and prosperity.

If, as in this country before the War, the money is kept on a gold basis by being exchangeable on demand for gold coinage, and if gold can be freely imported and exported at a price fixed by law, minted into sovereigns or melted back into bullion as required, the purchasing power of the money is kept constant in terms of gold, though not in terms of goods in general, which is the true measure of the virtual wealth. If we suppose the latter does not change, and the value of gold relative to goods in general falls, we shall have a rise of the general level of prices, and, conversely, a fall, if the value of gold appreciates with reference to goods in general.

So on a gold basis we express virtual wealth which is a fairly intelligible and constant quantity in terms of daily life and its necessities, as a variable quantity of gold, the exchange value of which in terms of goods is one of the most elusive and little understood factors in human experience. We may think we can analyse it and understand it as it operates and has operated in any one country – as, for example, in this country – only to find that, just as a change comes over the nature of money when we consider nations rather than individuals, so a change comes over gold as international money when we consider not one country, but the whole world.

Concerned with its outgoings and incomings between one country and the rest of the world, we overlook that, though the general level of prices is equalised as among countries on a gold basis, we are still as far off as ever from determining what that price level may be and what, in fact, determines it. But, the reader may inquire, does it greatly matter? Certainly if there were no debts, or none of more than a few weeks' or months' duration, and no traditional ideas as to the magnitude of salaries, wages, etc., it would not matter so much; but in a world which is one inextricable tangle of more or less permanent mutual individual, national and international indebtednesses and contracts nothing can possibly matter much more. In the following quotation we have the economist at his best, with cold scientific precision and crystal clearness setting forth principles it would scarcely be politic economy to apply to problems nearer home, as they are operating in a foreign country:

> "If we look ahead, averting our eyes from the ups and downs which can make and unmake fortunes in the meantime, the level of the franc is going to be settled in the long run not by speculation or the balance of trade, or even the outcome of the Ruhr adventure, but by the proportion of his earned income which the French taxpayer will permit to be taken from him to pay the claims of the French *rentier*. The level of the franc exchange will continue to fall until the commodity-value of the

francs due to the *rentier* has fallen to a proportion of the national income, which accords with the habits and mentality of the country."[39]

It would perhaps not be untrue to generalise this to explain the world-wide phenomenon of currency depreciation through the ages. If we look ahead, averting our eyes from the haphazard discoveries of gold that can make and unmake fortunes, and the irregular growth of knowledge and invention, the purchasing power of money is settled in the long run neither by science, finance nor trade, but by the proportion of his earned income the worker permits to be taken from him by the *rentier*. It will continue to fall until the commodity value of money due to the *rentier* falls to that proportion of the national income which accords with the habits and mentality of the growing world.

How the Gold-Value of Money was maintained

Quite briefly we must notice the ordinary explanation of the method by which in this country before the War the value of money was kept constant with reference to gold.

The monetary system before the War was based on gold, in the sense that the money could always be exchanged for gold coins on demand, and these, at a definite invariable rate fixed by the Bank Charter Act, for gold bullion for export, to pay for any balance of goods imported from foreign countries over those exported to them.

For foreign trade is at bottom necessarily, in the first instance, barter still. With more settled political conditions and the growth of mutual confidence it became unnecessary, in order to secure the circulation of money, that it should be made of gold, and the mere power of being able to demand gold in exchange sufficed. So that, although still largely used in minor transactions, metal money or *cash* became relegated to a small proportion of all that now functions as money in the community.

In a report to the House of Commons on this crisis in 1857 one of the leading bankers stated that, in his house, specie entered into

[39] J. M. Keynes, *Monetary Reform*, 1923, p. 73.

transactions little more than 2 per cent, and in the case of other banks to only 0.25 per cent. Naturally in retail trades cash is used to a much greater extent than in wholesale trades.[40]

But the power of the public to demand gold – then the only legal tender for large amounts – and the legal necessity for the banker to supply it or go out of business, put the onus of seeing that there was a sufficiency of gold in the country upon the banker rather than on the Government.

The vast superstructure of bank credit was prevented from depreciating the currency in terms of gold, and could only be expanded as fast as the community increased its virtual wealth (reckoned in terms of gold) by the following automatically acting mechanism: If too much money were created so that prices rose, the power of demanding gold in exchange for money, though normally useless to the ordinary citizen, was of great importance to those engaged in foreign trade. Though the price of every other commodity had risen, that of gold could not, being kept constant by law. So that the cheapest way of settling foreign debts was to export the equivalent of gold rather than of any other goods. This reduced the amount of gold legal tender in the country, so that the banker, to maintain solvency, had to cancel credits to many times the amount of gold coin melted and exported, and by thus reducing prices in the home market stop the drain of gold. Hence it became necessary for him to contract credit. He attempted to get his clients to do so themselves voluntarily by raising the bank-rate of interest, *but*, if this did not suffice,[41] he arbitrarily called in loans already granted. This destroyed money in circulation as literally as the granting of credit in the first instance created it, and by lowering the quantity of money "in the end" lowered prices in proportion. We need not at this stage do more

[40] For the United States the figures given by Professor Fisher are, for 1896, 14 per cent money and 91 per cent cheque; for 1909, 9 per cent money and 91 per cent cheque. Credit money is growing rapidly in the States, but has not attained yet to the same dominating position as here. (*Purchasing Power of Money*, 1922, p. 318.)

[41] E. Dick, in a recent work, *The Interest Standard of Currency*, 1925, argues that raising the bank-rate of interest increases rather than decreases the demand for credit, and that the correct course is to lower the rate in order to contract the currency.

than touch on the mechanism of the process. To go into the ethics of the question and trace out the arbitrary losses and risks it imposes upon perfectly innocent and defenceless people, doing their best according to their lights to serve the needs of the community, would take us too far afield.

But it must not be too hastily concluded, as has often been done, that the free market in gold at a fixed price, which this country offered to the world, was a mistaken policy, or that foreign traders were acting unpatriotically in draining the country of its gold in time of need, forcing up the rate of interest and condemning those who whose loans were called in often to bankruptcy and ruin. The foreign trader is merely the unwitting instrument for enforcing an unpleasant necessity.[42]

Foreign trade is at basis barter, and is paid for in goods, sometimes in securities or claims to wealth in the future, never by money, which is a claim to wealth on demand valid only in the country of issue. To enable a merchant in this country to buy abroad, the merchants abroad must buy the equivalent here. In the long run, if the transactions do not balance, gold must be sent to redress the difference. In this restriction foreign trade differs from the simplicity and freedom of domestic housekeeping.

Thus, at the stage we have reached, the bankers of any one nation appropriated as their own property some four-fifths of the virtual wealth, or money of the country under the system, as interest-bearing debt, but were unable to affect or depreciate the *gold* value of the money in a permanent fashion. Whether banking, as an international organisation, has the power to depreciate the *real* value of the currency is a much more difficult question, and demands more attention than it has yet received. For the mechanism only keeps the level of prices in different countries on a gold basis roughly alike. It does not pretend to keep the prices of goods in terms of gold constant with the progress of time, and, as a matter of fact, has allowed them to vary enormously.

---

[42] The rise of prices and outflow of gold is shown later to be the physically necessary consequence of the issue of the fictitious loans in the first instance.

The Present Position

The moratorium declared in this country in 1914, actually before a shot had been fired in the Great War, showed that banking has become so vital to the interests of the nation that the banks can call upon the national credit to save them and their depositors from ruin in the face of any great emergency. The public at that time not only shouldered the burden, but lost their right to demand gold in exchange for their money, and suffered the debasement of the currency. So both restrictions to the expansion of credit have now been removed. The banks need not fear a run on their cash reserves, nor is there any automatic regulation of the gold-value of money. That their policy at the moment is to deflate rather than inflate the currency is beside the question. It is they and not the political Government which really regulate the economic affairs of the country. They make the profits and the taxpayers and citizens shoulder the losses under the system.

At the moment of writing (1925) the gold basis has been partly restored, as regards foreign transactions, though whether it can be maintained without repudiation of liability for much of the thereby grossly magnified National Debt still remains to be seen. But it is now open to a merchant to pay for goods bought abroad in gold if he elects to do so. The system which regulated in this country the quantity of money in existence ceased in 1914, and, whatever happens, is certain not to be fully restored.

The subject, so to speak, is suspended in the air at the moment, and all the monetary text-books have become out of date and misleading.

In this field it is as though men had just admitted the possibility that day and night are due to the earth rotating on its own axis, and not to the sun revolving round the earth and that, in spite of its manifest impiety, there may, after all, be something in the new helio-centric view. In absence of any real analysis of the physical nature of wealth, and owing to the universal confusion in both popular and technical economics between wealth and debt, monetary theory has hitherto been as impressionistic as the Ptolemaic theory of the universe now appears.

The Variability of Gold

Professor Irving Fisher, among orthodox economists, has been foremost in calling attention to the evils of a variable monetary standard, and has done much to get the importance of the question more generally recognised. But among the unorthodox, Silvio Gesell on the Continent, and Mr. Arthur Kitson[43] in this country, have been like voices, crying in the wilderness, years before any others realised its vital interest. The following are excerpts from a lecture given by Professor Fisher in 1924 before the Boston Ethical Society.[44] Discussing the United States, he says:

> "Let us look at figures in this country back in 1860. If we take 1860, before the Civil War, we find the purchasing power about the same as in 1913, before the Great War. We may call the level of 1860 or 1913 'the pre-War level,' and think of it for convenience as normal. The dollar then was, so to speak, a dollar. In terms of this pre-War dollar we can measure the dollar at any other time.
>
> "We find as we pass into the Civil War, from 1860 to 1865, that it was worth only 40 pre-War cents. From that time on it began to appreciate, first very rapidly and then more slowly, until it reached its maximum in 1896, when it was worth 152 pre-War cents. From 1896 to 1913 the dollar fell from 152 pre-War cents to 100, or 'normal.' From 1913 it continued to fall, from 100 pre-War cents until it got down to 40 again in May 1920. Then there was deflation, and rise in the value of the dollar. So the dollar changed again from 40 until it reached 72 pre-War cents in January 1922. Since that time it has been more stable than we have had it for many years, and yet it has danced about week by week a little... Our unstable dollar has picked the

---

[43] Compare *A Scientific Solution of the Money Question*, 1894, Arena Co., Boston, U.S.A.; *A Fraudulent Standard*, 1917; *Trade Fallacies; Unemployment*, 1921, and other works by Arthur Kitson; and by Silvio Gesell, *Aktire Währungspolitsk*, 1908, and *Die Natürliche Wirtschaftsordnung durch Freiland Freigeld*.

44 *Ethics in the Monetary System*, "The Standard", published by the American Ethical Union, January 1925, p. 145.

> pockets of the bondholder… The extent of this subtle robbing is prodigious.
>
> "Professor W. I. King, one of the best statisticians I know, when appearing in favour of a Bill on this subject in Congress a year or so ago, said that as nearly as he could reckon it out there had been a sort of pocket-picking of forty billions of dollars in the United States during the last half-dozen years…
>
> "When, at last, we really stabilise the dollar, as we now stabilise every other measure, to help make business honest, we shall have taken a great step forward in safeguarding and improving commercial ethics."

In his book, *The Purchasing Power of Money* (1911), he states that the purchasing power of money a thousand years ago was five times, and from 1200 to 1500 A.D. two to three times, what it was in 1911. During the last century before the War there have been five well-marked periods in all countries, as regards the change in the purchasing power of gold. In the forty years between 1809 and 1849 prices fell in the ratio of 5 to 2.

The Evils of a Variable Standard

After the bitter experiences of the last few years few people can remain unaware of the crying injustice of a variable monetary standard. The ethical principles underlying the institution of money appeal intuitively to the common sense of humanity. Just as we concede, without arguing the point, that the use of false weights and measures is indefensible in any circumstances, and that our standards ought to be invariable and placed beyond the possibility of being tampered with, so the same principle ought to be unquestionably conceded with regard to the value of money. A variation in the value of money, in terms of wealth, arbitrarily robs one class in the community for the benefit of others. In such matters people are apt "to compound the sins they are inclined to by damning those they have no mind to." A fall in the value of money, or rise of the general level of prices, defrauds those in receipt of wages, salaries and incomes of fixed monetary amount and advantages those who live by buying and selling. It lightens the past indebtedness of the community, and if the old currency becomes worthless, as it has done in Russia, Austria and Germany, wipes it out. So that a man may awake to the fact that his life-savings are not worth a farthing, and that an empty bottle is now worth more than the money before received from the sale of the vineyard. Nor is a fall in prices and rise in the value of money in relation to wealth less disastrous. It falls upon another set of people, and puts out of action the merchant, the industrialist and their wage-earners. We cannot progress a step in this subject unless we can devise a monetary system in which the money is issued neither for usury nor in response to political pressure from this or that particular interest, but by the nation solely and freely as it is required to keep its value in relation to wealth as constant as is possible from century to century. Any ideal short of this is simply to accept Stephen Leacock's definition of political economy as that which teaches we know nothing of the laws of wealth.

The Evils of a Shortage of Currency

It is extraordinarily difficult, but at the same time essential, to understand the real ultimate factors that, during the period from the Bank Charter Act of 1844 to the issue of national Treasury notes in 1914, really did limit the expansion of the currency and with it the prosperity of the country and its rate of producing consumable wealth. That the forces in operation were not even remotely understood is shown by the alternating periodic sequence of trade booms and slumps, called the trade cycle, which was, like the weather, regarded as completely beyond the wit of man to understand.

It may be of assistance to try to understand what would have been the result if credit money had not so largely replaced the precious metals as currency, and the latter had remained the sole medium of exchange. According to the current view, prices would have tended to fall greatly as the new powers of production outstripped – not, as usually stated, the rate at which gold was won, but the aggregate of it in existence. Economists have made many such errors through failing to distinguish clearly between the two categories of wealth – permanent and perishable – already insisted upon, but this point will be taken up later.

Gold and silver mining, being essentially very speculative and dependent upon chance discoveries, a long time necessarily elapses before a demand for precious metals can much increase the aggregate quantity available for currency. But their use as commodities, for jewelry and as hoards, enables the currency to be increased from these sources if their value or purchasing power increases to such an extent as to induce people to give up their ornaments and spend their accumulations. The triple function of the precious metals as coinage, jewelry and hoards is responsible for much of the complication of the subject.

If prices of goods rise in terms of gold, a given quantity of gold, though its winning consumes the same wealth, as food, etc., buys less and less wealth until gold-mining becomes unprofitable. *Per contra* a fall of prices stimulates gold-mining.

A practical example of the effect, though not the cause, was seen during the War, which, though it produced an enormously stimulated demand for gold for the expansion of the currency, made gold-mining relatively unprofitable! For the demand was met by the partial demonetisation of gold and the creation of an inconvertible paper money. This raised prices and made gold-mining unprofitable, exactly as if the gold had really been won.

Reverting to the probable course of events, if credit money had not been invented, in the end no doubt the fall of prices would have been checked. A larger and larger proportion of the world's energies would have been diverted to the financially profitable, but socially barren, task of accumulating gold and silver for currency, until sufficient had been accumulated to distribute the increasing revenue of wealth without a further fall of price-level. The effect of the great improvements in the knowledge of gold-mining due to scientific discovery, later to be alluded to, would have told in the same direction.

Admittedly there would have been very great and distressing evils and dislocation. The actual course of historical events, when successive waves of commercial prosperity resulted from each of the major gold discoveries of last century, shows that, even with the increasing use of credit currency, these evils were not wholly escaped. Usury would have risen to altogether extortionate rates, though probably the toll taken would have been insignificant in comparison with that extorted to-day under a monetary system perverted to that end. In general all debts would have appreciated in real amount, as money prices fell. The dead hand of the past would have been heavy on the land.

Production reduced rather than Prices

But the really vital evils of a currency scarcity are due to its reducing production rather than prices. The quantity theory of money[45] works beautifully *one way.*

Increasing the quantity of money temporarily increases, but makes no very lasting difference to, the aggregate virtual wealth, and prices very quickly rise in proportion to the increase. What some gain others lose. But decreasing the quantity of money is apt to decrease virtual wealth in proportion much more permanently, leaving prices unchanged and production reduced through the ruin of those engaged in enterprise.

This is dead loss, not as in the former case merely a redistribution of wealth, and it is reflected in a very much more permanent reduction of virtual wealth.

Whereas an excess of money is an inducement to a sale, a deficit is a fatal barrier. To the vendors, whose business it is to sell wealth for money, money is the primary consideration. To the buyer and consumer wealth is. The consumer is exposed to increased competition with others, due to an increase of the quantity of money, and is powerless to resist a rise in price. But no one in his senses, who has produced wealth for sale or caused it to be produced, and has, over a period of past time, incurred the charges involved in production, is going willingly to sell it at a loss to suit the quantity theory of money. If his competitors essayed to do so, they could hardly compete long. The result is that less goods are bought with the less money at the same price, not that the same goods are bought at a reduced price. Or, in the case under consideration, that the opportunity to increase production by new inventions remains for long unexploited, and, with increasing powers of production, the production of wealth, as in this country now, stagnates.[46]

---

[45] For an exposition of the quantity theory of money see Irving Fisher *The Purchasing Power of Money.*

[46] For a very clear exposition of this question, see John Strachey, *Revolution by Reason, 1925.*

For a period of inflation (money increasing relatively to the revenue of wealth) the quantitative theory is a rough guide to the facts. Whereas for a period of deflation (money decreasing relatively to the revenue of wealth) the older mercantile, or commodity, theory, which regards money as itself a commodity or valuable article, this being the vendor's conception of money, is a better guide. If it is any comfort to the advocates of the former theory, it may readily be admitted that, no doubt, it would work if it did not have the unfortunate consequence of ruining those committed to enterprise – labour and capital alike – and, in the end, in Mr. Keynes' sense of the word, "after we are all dead," no doubt must work.

What is left of the Value of the Standard of Value?

From these considerations we may begin to understand not only the extraordinary fascination which gold has exercised from the earliest times upon the human mind and the persistence of the worship of the golden calf implicit, if unacknowledged, in contemporaneous thought, but also the extraordinary influence which some of the most profound students of history have not hesitated to ascribe to the abundance and scarcity of the precious metals. Equally we may regard it as not at all a small permanent gain to humanity if the experience of the Great War has thrown fresh light upon and, at least in part, explained some of these profound influences.

Let us revert to a very curious fact, that the War produced at one and the same time a great demand for currency *and* made gold-mining temporarily unprofitable, because the paper substitutes raised prices just as if the same quantity of gold had really been won. If the price of gold had not been fixed arbitrarily higher than that stipulated by the Bank Charter Act, although still much lower than proportionally to that of goods in general, probably few mines would have been able to continue work. Now the same factor must have been operating, in gradual but continuous fashion, ever since the currency began to be expanded by credit money, thus artificially cheapening the relative value of the standard which we are accustomed to regard as invariable. Not only have we to consider the great technical achievements in gold-mining – cyaniding, dredging, and the general rise in power and efficiency of mining plant-operating upon the standard of value exactly in the same direction, though not necessarily at the same rate, as upon every other kind of physical wealth, increasing the quantity produced by a given expenditure of human effort, but, in addition to this, we are supplying for one of the major uses of the precious metals a costless substitute, and removing from the standard of value one of the main reasons for its value. The growth of banking is removing another – the practice of hoarding.

As for the remainder, gold teeth and even gold stoppings have long gone out of fashion. The general rise of education has made, and is making, personal adornment by massive golden chains and rings too obvious a relic of barbarism. The modern desire to avoid all ostentation, and at the same time to indulge in the maximum possible expense, is leading to the substitution in jewelry, even for wedding-rings, of gold by platinum, a metal which looks like silver and costs five times as much as gold – greatly to the disgust of chemists who, whatever it costs, must have platinum, and look back regretfully to the day when it was much less valuable than gold. So what is left of the value of the standard of value?

Clearly a gold basis of currency nowadays must be a rapidly depreciating currency. In the race between science, on the one hand, and finance, education and fashion on the other – the one cheapening the cost of producing all wealth in general and the other the standard of monetary value in particular – the see-saw of price-level which marked the past century is likely to be succeeded in the future by a rapid continuous rise of gold prices. Indeed, even to-day, if the gold that flowed to America during the War were let loose instead of being kept chained up, the results in this direction would probably be devastating. This is a temporary situation, with the outlook on the future.

Gold as the Spur of Civilisation

Let us, from a more general point of view, examine the effect of gold in past history. If we do not find in it exactly the cause of human progress, we shall have to admit that it must have been a powerful spur. Civilisation has never asked itself what exactly it has set itself to in adopting as the standard of value, the store of value and the medium of exchange, the metal gold. All the conventional qualities which are supposed to make the metal ideal for money are, in fact, fatal to its use. Consider first its permanency and imperishability. Men may come and men may go, but gold goes on accumulating for ever. The quantity of gold in existence is the physical factor regulating the total quantity of money in existence, as much under a currency based on gold as in the past, and this quantity is the integral of all the increments of gold contributed during the history of mankind. In literal truth, gold is not imperishable, as it suffers abrasion in use, but is so nearly so that its period of average life is greater than that of almost any other permanent form of wealth.

The value of money is given by the virtual wealth divided by the total quantity of money, so that the seeds of continuous depreciation are innate in the choice of gold.

If we stereotyped the existing scale of virtual wealth and the material prosperity it connotes, the increment of the quantity of gold would still go on, and, even with a dwindling revenue of wealth, the quantity of gold in existence would continue to increase so long as it was money.

Society, in effect, says to its workers, whether we want more gold or less, nevertheless if you bring gold, even when what we really need is food, you may have the pick of the market for it. The loss falls not on you, but on the whole community, though if you contributed stage-coaches or wind-mills no one will take them off your hands. So that, even in a period of dwindling revenue, when, if the money is not to depreciate in purchasing power, some of the stock ought to be buried in the earth again or sunk in the sea, the accumulation of gold still goes on.

In mathematical terms, society, in adopting gold as its measure of value and its medium of exchange, is attempting to keep a differential coefficient proportional to its own integral, for it must make the proportionate increment of its revenue of wealth always as great as the proportionate increment of its aggregate quantity of gold.

There is one mathematical function for which this is true, and it is the exponential function.[47] This is the function which regulates the dizzy virtues of compound interest.

Living in an age of relatively sudden expansion of productive power, the task may at first be easy. But it is quite a different proposition over long periods. It is not a question of maintaining any given level of production, but of maintaining indefinitely the proportional rate of

[47] $\int {}^{ax} \partial x = (1/a)\, {}^{ax}$.

increase of production. So that in the end, when this becomes physically impossible, the currency must undergo depreciation.

In this we may possibly find a physical justification for the existence of interest upon a monetary debt, as distinct from the hire-payment for the use of organs of production in production. During the War, when currencies were being rapidly debased, the astute found that it paid to borrow and to borrow and to borrow, whatever the rate of interest. For by the time the loans had to be repaid, principal and interest were worth, in goods, less than the original principal was when it was borrowed. But we have seen that the continuous accumulation of the precious metals must be a depreciating factor on the value of the currency, absolutely independent of all other considerations whatever, so that on this account to repay a debt of £1 lent in the past more than £1 is required to-day, or regarding £1 as the wealth obtainable for £1 originally, to buy it to-day requires more than £1.

The other reasons why gold is unsuitable for currency trench upon a question the discussion of which, hitherto, we have avoided. But, we may take it, meantime, as a fact of experience without as yet attempting the explanation that an increase in the quantity of money is a great stimulus to productive enterprise.

Not only during the War, but also after the gold discoveries of last century, trade greatly flourished, and general prosperity resulted. Now this prosperity directly stimulates the luxury demand for gold for jewelry and ornament, and in countries – still the majority – without a highly developed banking system, for saving. Thus the money tends to disappear again, the stimulus due to abundance of money receives a check, and a period of depression ensues. Then these hoards and stores, before taken out of the circulation, tend to reappear and again help to inaugurate a boom.

The trade cycle, in some part at least, must be due to the use of a metal as the basis of currency, which is gradually withdrawn as industry expands and comes back as it contracts, exactly the opposite to what is required of a currency. Even the ease with which the precious metals can be melted up without loss, and converted from coin to merchandise and back again an innumerable number of times at trifling cost, which has been held to make them especially suitable for coinage, is a fatal defect. Just as the industrial system has been laboriously tuned up to a higher level of production, the medium of exchange turns into an article of luxury, and with it goes the wave of prosperity.

Gold now a Fraudulent Standard

Summing up, we may say that with a gold currency in an era of expansion there will be a long period of currency shortage, attended with dislocation of the economic machinery of society. But the causes which expand production act in the same direction, though not necessarily at the same rate and to the same extent, on gold. So that the standard of value tends to be affected in the same way as the goods it measures, and gold prices tend to revert in time to their former level.

With a currency based on gold, the currency will adapt itself to the expansion very much more quickly. The human effort formerly spent in accumulating gold for coinage is saved, but under existing systems, the saving benefits, not the community as a whole, but the banker. So long as convertibility with gold is maintained, even international banking can only debase the *gold* value of money to a definite extent.

For, consider the case of a uniform inflation in all countries to the same degree at the same time. There is then no tendency for gold to flow from one country to another, as in the case of an inflation in one country relatively to another. But gold would, as the demand for it as merchandise absorbed it, disappear entirely from the currency, because the money will buy of gold more than its value in terms of other goods and more gold than could be obtained by expending the same sum in gold-mining. The coinage is thus hoarded or melted down and used in the arts, and would disappear in time from circulation entirely with the debasement of the currency, though the effect at first would be to cheapen gold as a commodity and the standard of value.

But by the use of credit money, based upon a small proportion of gold, the quantity of money becomes subject to much greater and more violent variation than before, and the exchange value of gold in terms of goods oscillates. The causes which are inherent in the use of gold as a luxury article, as well as a medium of exchange, are greatly exaggerated, producing the trade cycle.

The increasing use of bank credit and paper robs gold of one of its main uses, and, after the oscillations of the past century, we may look forward to a continuously rising gold price-level. So that credit money, having largely rendered gold obsolete, the device of making it convertible into coin on demand has ceased to be effective against its continuous depreciation, and has already come to be deceitful.

Hence arises an increasing necessity for stabilising the currency entirely without reference to gold, and reducing the latter to the level of a commodity, possibly honouring it meantime as international money at its market value, in redressing international indebtedness, under some equitable convention agreed upon by the League of Nations.

Real Wages and Just Wages

Before embarking on this inquiry, it may be pointed out that we are as far as ever from any Absolute Standard or Measure of Value, and it may be instructive to restate in a new form some of the preceding points. Economists, when they have taken into account the variabilities of the exchange value of gold and corrected for it – by means of index numbers, which enable them to reduce money prices to some former price-level taken as a standard of reference – arrive at what they term the *real* value of incomes, wages and the like; that is, values entirely independent of the money totals in which they are expressed, but representing the *quantity* of goods in general these incomes, wages, etc., will buy. But the *real* values, though real enough in representing definite *quantities* of purchasable goods and sufficient for economics as a science of exchange or commerce, are not measures at all of the human-being-hours *expended* in their production. If the efficiency of the processes of production did not change, or if civilisation were stagnant, then they would be – in fact, their use tends to stabilise wages and incomes and the consumptions they represent, so that we have the interminable argument, already alluded to, as to whether the worker to-day is economically better off than, at least as well off as, or only slightly worse off than, his predecessor in prescientific ages!

Now, if we are considering debt and its repayment, a currency stabilised so as to maintain the price-level of goods in general constant solves the problem – that is, commerce would be freed from all the legally unrecognised forms of theft attendant upon a variation of the standard of monetary value, which are of much the same nature as would result from fraudulent weights and measures. Business men and others could make contracts ahead without fear of being caught in a trap by variations in the general price-level due to monetary manipulation. But if we are considering the reward of work and the right of a worker to the produce of his work, clearly we have to take into account not merely the quantities of goods by which he is remunerated, but also what he produces. His *real* wages, in the sense used in economics, has to be expressed *relatively* to what he produces to arrive at his *just* wages.

The fact that it may be difficult to assess this, or to solve the problem as between the reward of present and past labour, does not in the least affect the question of the right of the worker to a just wage or the certainty that with growing knowledge and power he will not rest until he has secured it. Economics is, or ought to be, a far wider and more important study than commerce. Those who deny that it ought to concern itself with anything else may save themselves the trouble of thought, but do not add to the dignity of the subject.

CHAPTER IX

A NATIONAL MONEY SYSTEM

The Social Importance of the Study of Money

From the standpoint of society, the study of money is, in its social significance and effect on human welfare, as uplifting and as ennobling as from the individual standpoint it is apt to be selfish and degrading. Its technical jargon of the market-place make it appear a repellent subject, and it is capable of being made drier and duller even than a mathematical treatise on thermodynamics. Indeed, its absolute novelty to most people, and their preconceptions, derived from undue absorption in its individual acquisition, make it a difficult subject, the more so as very powerful vested interests depend for their continued existence upon the public being kept in ignorance of its mysteries. Those essaying the study often at first over-estimate the direct importance of money in the social economy – its indirect importance could hardly be over-estimated – and the "unsound money-men" have always been a special *bête noire* to the orthodox economist, though it would hardly be possible to have anything more fundamentally unsound than modern monetary systems, the principles of which the economists have never seriously challenged. It is essential to have clear physical conceptions of money and finance, as such, to enable us to understand their more important indirect bearing upon the admittedly still to be solved problems of achieving industrial expansion without the unwelcome concomitants of unemployment and the trade cycle. Those who have penetrated most deeply into the study of human history find it impossible to exaggerate the importance of the institution of money. As Delmar[48] has said: "It is a study that none can afford to approach with rashness or leave with complacency."

Among the list of master-minds he cites as having essayed its study in the past it is encouraging to a scientific man to read the names of Newton, Copernicus and Tycho Brahe. This indicates that scientific men in the past have not always interpreted their function as narrowly as is the custom to-day, or been so ready to leave with complacency to others the application of their work to the daily life of the world.

> "Unheard, unseen, unfelt, it has the power so to distribute the burdens, gratifications and opportunities of life that each individual shall enjoy that share of them to which his merits or his good fortune may entitle him, or contrariwise, to dispense them with so partial a hand as to violate every principle of justice and perpetuate a succession of social slaveries to the end of time."[49]

Again, one could hardly better describe "Europe after twenty centuries of Christendom" than by this passage from Ferraro:

> "The Imperial Democracy that held a world beneath its sway, from the senators who bore historic names down to the humblest tiller of the soil, from Julius Cæsar down to the smallest shopkeeper in a back street of Rome, was at the mercy of a small group of usurers."[50]

Sir Archibald Allison traces the fall of the Roman Empire to the decline of the gold and silver mines of Spain and Greece, and the Renaissance to the discovery of the mines of Mexico and Peru. Whilst it is almost in the memory of living men how the successive discoveries of gold in California, Australia and South Africa ushered in wave after wave of economic prosperity. More recent and striking still, we have the fresh experience of the Great War, when, apart from the destruction of life and property and the effects of blockade on the Central Powers,

---

[48] *History of Monetary Systems.*

[49] Delmar, loc. cit.

[50] Ferraro, *Greatness and Decline of the Roman Empire*, VI, 223.

there was a degree of economic prosperity and abolition of crime and poverty in the belligerent countries unknown in the time of peace.

We have seen that in modern times a fundamental change has come over the nature of money. Not only is it now a simple token of the community's indebtedness to the individual owner of it, but it is created not by the national authority, but by private institutions for lending at interest. It is therefore essential to go back to first principles in considering it. We must be on our guard against carrying over unchallenged into the modern era the earlier views of the evil power of money and the stigma attaching to usury deriving from ancient and mediæval times when money was a totally different institution.

Analysis of Usury

In its original meaning usury simply meant the interest upon a loan of money, whereas to-day it has come to be a term of opprobrium, referring rather to excessive and extortionate interest, increasing in proportion to the debtor's inability to repay.

The mention of this form of petty usury, as it exists in the underworld of great cities and among the swarming populations of India, conjures up possibly in the mind a memory of evidences of human terror and anguish one had never expected to meet this side the abode of the damned, and gives rise to a feeling of physical loathing as of something at work, ghoulish and inhuman, battening upon, if not responsible for, the extremity of misery.

Whereas, at the other pole, interest upon a money loan to the strong and adventurous, to enable them to develop the resources of the earth and to climb to positions of influence and power within the State, has nowadays occasionally even replaced the ladder offered in earlier times by the Church to the gifted offspring of the poor, and has been endowed not only with respectability, but even with an odour of sanctity.

Both in the ancient and the mediæval world there is undeniable evidence of the evils of usury. We have quoted the striking passage of Ferraro on its power in ancient Rome. The Christian Church at first universally condemned it. Indeed, the bar on usury was not removed in the Roman Catholic Church till quite recent times.

But there is little doubt that these evils arose not so much out of the practice of lending money in itself as from the comparative ease with which the currency metals can be monopolised. A period of great Imperial expansion, such as those of Rome, Spain and the modern Western world, demands an increase of currency. But it never seems anyone's business to supply it. The world may be thirsting for gold, the finding of which is, at best, a long and hazardous business, and against the real interests of those with gold to spend in the search. For if there are many borrowers and few lenders, the rate of interest rises just as the price of a commodity rises if there are many buyers and few sellers. The evil of interest upon money is not difficult to understand with money made of naturally very scarce materials. "Get your man into your debt for what he has not got and cannot get, and you may take the skin off him," is a financial aphorism which sufficiently indicates not only the cause of the evils of usury, but of those of monetary power in general. Make debts repayable in wealth, which, if people have not got they can make, and you strike at the heart of both evils.

With paper money this question, like the question of "hoarding," is utterly different. A nation printing and issuing its own money as required for use would be absolutely free from the *auri sacra fames* due to the monopoly of the coinage metals, and from the cause of the main evils of money as they arose in the past. It could regulate usury, absolutely within its own judgment, as the national interests demanded, by its control over the issue of money. In a time of abounding productivity due to science, it could, if it wished, repay, or at least redeem, its debts, neither in gold nor "pounds of flesh," but *mirabile dictu* in wealth in general. If it thought in real terms of wealth, not in that of money, it would not, in a time of greater powers of producing than the world has ever enjoyed, with millions of unemployed, large-scale organs of production lying idle and cultivated land reverting to grass, see the exact point in paying its creditors perennial interest for not repaying them, though, as we shall come to see, an individualistic society[51] can only redeem debts by levying taxation on the general wealth of the community.

[51] An individualistic society owns no revenue-producing property, and derives its revenue solely from taxation.

Genuine and Fictitious Money Loans

It was necessary at the risk of wearying the reader in Chapter VII, to go with great minuteness into the transition from the old national metal money to the modern money created by loan. Because the real charge against the modern system is not so much that it has caused an enormous increase in the practice of carrying on industry upon borrowed money, as that the bank loans are not genuine money loans, but are entirely fictitious, in that no one gives up the money *lent*, which is new money created for that purpose.

The owner of money is absolutely within his moral as well as his legal rights to spend or lend or hoard, but if he spends or lends it is to be understood that he really does give up the money spent or lent. With *cash* the lender must do so. Even a bank deposit is technically distinguished as a current account or a deposit account. With the first, the owner has not given up his power to spend, and cannot, in this country at least, obtain interest on it, though in America interest is, or at least was, commonly given even on current accounts. In the case of a deposit proper, the owner of the money does give up and transfer temporarily to the bank his purchasing power, and in return for the loan he receives a payment of interest on the deposit. In this distinction we see the original restriction that applies to metal money still lingering with regard to bank money. But obviously the question of usury is totally different, whether we consider a genuine loan, as in the case of a loan of cash, or of a sum deposited and not recoverable without due notice, and interest upon money which the owner has never given up at all. It will certainly be argued that the depositor, although he does not give up the right to spend at will, in fact does not exercise it, as is shown by the existence of the deposit, so that between the two classes of account there is a distinction without a difference.

Lending Money in Current Account Indefensible

This position, though it is very far from justifying what actually does occur in banking where "every loan *creates* a deposit" (Withers and McKenna), appears plausible, but can easily be shown to be indefensible. For one has only to remember the undeniable fact that the total quantity of money in a country is not affected by its being *spent* or *not spent*, to see that the argument is not concerned with the lending of money at all, but with its existence.

Let us suppose that cheques entirely replace cash as purchasing power and that everyone has a bank deposit. This is now so near the actual state of affairs that for the purpose of this argument it may be taken as already to a very substantial extent true. Now if we concede to the banker the right to lend the deposits on the score that their existence shows the owners are not using them, we thereby double the money in the country, *and double the deposits*. The existence of the doubled deposits is as clear evidence as before that their owners are not using them so they may be lent again, and now the deposits are increased four times. So we may go on and create an infinite quantity of money.

It is interesting that J. S. Mill, nearly a century ago, contemplated precisely such a case, payments being universally by cheque and

> "no money anywhere except in the hand of the banker, who might then safely part with all of it by selling it as bullion or lending it, to be sent out of the country in exchange for goods or foreign securities."

He concluded:

> "There would be in all this nothing to complain of, so long as the money, in disappearing, left an equivalent of other things, applicable when required to the reimbursement of those to whom the money originally belonged."

Why he confined the consideration of the case to lending the money to be sent out of the country is one of those mysteries that may never be solved. If he had not done so he would have made the interesting discovery already deduced, and which even at that time must already have been made by the bankers themselves. Nor do later economists seem to have pointed this out, though the finicking distinction they seem always so careful to preserve between money and bank deposits, without being able to point to any practical difference whatever, suggests that they may have known. MacLeod, the barrister, lays great stress upon a bank deposit not being money, but a right of action against the banker. Irving Fisher, having arbitrarily defined circulating media or currency as anything, whether generally acceptable or not, which serves as a means of exchange, and money as "what is generally acceptable in exchange for goods," says: "But while a bank deposit transferable by check is included as circulating media, it is not money. A bank *note*, on the other hand, is both circulating medium and money. Between these two lies the final line of distinction between what is money and what is not. True, the line is delicately drawn…"

These distinctions may have had some significance a century ago, but their retention to-day seems the merest hair-splitting for the purpose of confusing the issues.

We thus come back to the point that, in the case of the old-fashioned usury, the moneylender did give up the money he lent and received interest upon a genuine loan. In the case of money lent by a bank, it is given up by no one and the loans are entirely fictitious except in the case of genuine "time deposits," which Macrosty estimates, both for this country and the United States, as one-fifth of the whole deposits. Even these, in so far as they exceed the cash held by the banks – the only money not of its own manufacture the bank has to lend – were created in the first instance by the banks themselves. It is true that, up to the time of the War – which then saw the money of the country multiplied almost suddenly two and a half times – the creation of this money was a gradual affair extending over a century. Custom has confirmed the banker in his enjoyment of it, and made it quite out of the question ever to decreate it. But it is not his, as he himself would probably be the first to admit, if it were a question of his spending instead of lending it. It is, as we have seen, the virtual wealth of the community as a whole.

The Breakdown of the Monetary System; The Moratorium

The outbreak of the Great War revealed the complete unsoundness of our currency system. On July 24, 1914, Austria sent its ultimatum to Serbia. The world's Stock Exchanges, of course, took fright and ceased to function. On the last day of that month the London and New York Exchanges followed the example of the Continental Bourses and closed their doors. Securities of all kinds became temporarily unsaleable. By August 6th a general moratorium was declared. The banks only possessing a small reserve of money against their money liabilities to the public were quite unable to call in their loans and to attempt to recover the money which the system had allowed them to loan without possessing. It could not adopt the usual plan of selling at any sacrifice the collateral securities deposited by, and the property of, the borrowers so long as the Stock Exchange remained closed. The country had so "economised" in the use of money that *there literally did not exist* in the country one-sixth of the amount that those owning money were legally entitled to, or one-fifth of the amount upon which industry was paying interest. If the Stock Exchanges had not shut and it had been attempted to sell the securities to repay the loans created, this fact would have become most painfully obvious. Those to whom the credits had been granted, of course did not own the money, but had exchanged it for wealth with the owners of wealth, whereby former owners of wealth and not the borrowers now legally owned the money that had no existence. The loans could only therefore be got back, if recalled, by a forced sale of the borrowers' collateral securities at any price they would fetch. "In the end" the currency would have been reduced to a mere fraction of its former amount, and prices also. Whereas we have seen that it is very difficult to reduce prices by constricting the currency, because the producers of wealth will not sell below cost price unless forced to do so. The fraction of the currency that the banks would have recovered by the forced sale of their debtors' collateral securities and of all that they themselves possessed in the way of wealth would have been insignificant. In other words, they would have been hopelessly ruined, and those who had deposited their money with them would have lost it but for the moratorium.

Naturally the Government had to resume the responsibility for the regulation of the currency which the nominal political rulers of the country in the nineteenth century had shirked and passed on to private firms. *It did what ought to have been done from the very commencement of the Industrial Revolution.* It printed real money – money, that is to say, which the owner owns, not money on an unseen string to be called back and put out of circulation at the first financial panic by a power behind the throne. But unfortunately every Treasury note so printed and exchanged for wealth to pay for the cost of the War was multiplied in the old ratio by the banking system, now restored to solvency, and quite relieved from any risk of failing under any circumstances. These credits being only lent passed, of course, into the circulation without paying for anything at all. The necessity for financing the War was unavoidable, but the question has been much discussed as to the methods adopted.

Let us examine them.

War Finance

Patriotic people in this country – and for that matter in Germany – were urged to invest money in War Loans to help win the War, and did so. Some of the very curious consequences that arise from the fact that the same money circulates in an endless round, though the production and consumption of wealth is continuous, were then seen in their proper light probably for the first time. The more the nations spent the more they found they could spend – the flow idea, as contrasted with the store idea, that the more you spend the less you have left to spend, and the more you have to abstain from spending in future to replenish the store. The more people lent to finance the War, the more they found they had to lend among those classes of the community engaged in production. But all classes were encouraged to lend, and if they had no money to lend the country to help it to win the War, they could run into debt to the banks, and pay out of what they expected to have in the future. For every Treasury note printed and deposited in the banks enabled them to lend six or more pounds as credit, and the new War Loan the borrower would receive was a sufficient collateral security for the loan. The Bank of England issued circulars offering to lend at 3 per cent the money necessary to secure War Loan upon which the taxpayer was to provide 4 per cent. So that for each pound the taxpayer contributed, the bank would receive 15s. and the bogus subscriber 5s. The bank took no risk, for it would hold the new script as collateral security for their loan until the debt was redeemed. This transaction is merely a rather clearer example than usual of the process of saddling upon the taxpayer the interest charges upon fictitious loans.

The amount of the War Loans so raised, apart from the American debt, was of the order of £M7,000, and the charges for interest amount roughly to a million pounds a day. The total amount of money in the possession of the public we have seen was about £M1,200 before the War and about £M2,700 in 1920. A small part only of the increase was due to the issue of Treasury notes, probably not more than one-fifth. It is a great pity that the exact amount issued does not seem to be publicly known.

The point has been argued whether a larger part, or even the whole of the War expenditure, could not have been levied by taxation, since if people have spare money to invest, in theory at least, the State ought to be able to get at it by taxation.

It will be generally admitted that taxation is too indiscriminate and impersonal to extract only money from the pockets of those with spare cash and to leave those who have none uninjured. In the stress of war more urgent matters call for consideration than the devising of new methods of taxation to strike at the affluent and miss the indigent. It would have made the War unpopular in the City, and that is the same as saying that, for good or evil, it could not have been "fought to a finish."

Apart from printing money, taxation and selling foreign securities to pay for goods received from foreign countries, all of which methods the State employed, it relied upon the patriotism of its citizens to subscribe liberally to War Loans, which they did to the extent of £M7,000, of greatly depreciated money. The *ostensible* object was to stop the people who subscribed from spending either what they had, or, in the case of those who borrowed from the banks, what they would receive in the future, so that they should not compete in the market for and inflate the prices of the goods the State needed, or would need, for the conduct of the War, or, now the War is over, for its normal life.

Observe the nature of the contract. We, the taxpayers, are pledged to pay you, an individual, £5 a year for ever after, till the loan is repaid, for every £100 of purchasing power you have agreed to forgo. If the State had not been afraid of individuals exercising their purchasing power, it could have printed and not borrowed the money.

The Reductio ad Absurdum of the Modern Monetary System

It is perfectly legitimate for an individual to recover his purchasing power by selling his script and *so reducing the purchasing power of somebody else*, thereby leaving the total unchanged. But as things are, he need not do so. He merely needs to deposit it at the bank, and, as a gilt-edged security, it would be acceptable immediately as collateral security, though really productive wealth, such as a factory as a going concern, might not be so acceptable. This is one of the by no means minor absurdities of private banking: dead debts are preferred to wealth as security simply because backed by the national powers of taxation.

When the bank accepts War Loan as a collateral security the borrower pays the bank the current bank-rate of interest to do precisely what the State pays him out of the pockets of the taxpayer 5 per cent per annum not to do. Actually the taxpayer pays the tax, not to but only *via* the bond-holder to the bank, for doing precisely what the tax was imposed to prevent being done. Thus easily in this simple case we arrive at the *reductio ad absurdum* of the modern money system.

How the Taxpayer pays £M100 a Year Interest on Non-existent Money

We have seen that something of the order of two thousand million pounds have been created by the banks. Lent at interest, it brings in a revenue of some £M100 a year at a bank-rate of 5 per cent. The effect of this creation on prices is completely and absolutely indistinguishable from that of national money. It is unnecessary to print £M2,000 worth of £1 Treasury notes, and put them into circulation. They would merely take up storage room in the vaults of the bank until the next war or financial panic, when they can be so much more easily printed if required. But there is no reason to continue to pay the £M100 per annum out of the taxes. Although the money has no physical existence, and, except in times of crisis, does not need to have, owing to the popularity of the cheque system, the legal titles to claim it exist and are owned by genuine depositors.

If anyone wants a loan of currency on the security of a holding of War Loan, and can get it in a roundabout way by an increase of the total currency, clearly it is an elementary principle of business that the State should cancel the debt and itself issue the money to pay for it. *The money is issued in either case* with effects indistinguishable whether it is bank credit or national money. But, if the State issued it in exchange for fresh currency, it would relieve the taxpayer from the necessity of paying interest, and the original contract would thus be terminated in a business-like manner fair to both parties.

The old extreme *laissez-faire* policy of individualistic economics jealously denied to the State the right of competing in any way with individuals in the ownership of productive enterprise, out of which monetary interest or profit can be made, and this was ignorantly extended even to the virtual wealth of the community.

Individualistic economics, regarding money as wealth instead of debt, hands over to individuals the power of issuing money, and leaves to the taxpayer the duty of paying interest for the issue. The State, at any time it wishes, can relieve the taxpayer of some £M100 a year, or 2s. 6d. in the £. It has merely to buy back in the open market £M2,000 of War Loan with genuine new money to replace that created by the banks, £ for £ of the bank credit they issue, so enabling them to meet their liabilities at all times. The State must recover its sole prerogative in the issue of money, and make it impossible for the banks to issue money which they do not possess or which has not been surrendered into their charge by the owner as a definite time-deposit as distinct from a deposit in current account. This would terminate the absurdity of taxing one set of people to prevent the currency being increased and handing over the taxes to another set who are increasing it. The situation is that £M2,000 is in circulation by cheque and forms part of the total currency which determines the level of prices, but the formal tokens acknowledging the indebtedness of the community to the holders have not yet been issued by the State, and no valuable consideration has been received for them by the State.

Therefore, let them be issued.

The Remedy

Let us consider the nature of this transaction a little more in detail. We have seen that the purchasing power of the nation, as gauged by the total amount of Bank Deposits added to the total amount of currency in circulation, was estimated by McKenna in 1920 to be £M2,693. For the purposes of illustration, we will assume that the total amount of national money (coins and Treasury notes) to-day is £M700, and of bank credit £M2,000. It is of about this order as a maximum, but does not seem to be exactly known to the public. It is simpler to have concrete round figures in mind, but, of course, the argument does not depend upon the figures assumed being correct. Whatever they may be, the appropriate adjustment can be made by the reader, as the principle only is under discussion.

The State having decided to recover its lost prerogative of issuing money legislates to that effect, and notifies the banks that henceforth, after a reasonable interval, they must not lend money in current account, but only money surrendered into their keeping for a definite period under a proper deed of transfer or other authorised legal form. A suitable scale of stamp duties on such deeds could be devised, so that it was not profitable for them to be taken out for finicking periods, in order to avoid the intentions of the Act being made a dead letter by some new development of the system of purely fictitious loans.

The situation then is:

(1) The banks now lose one of their sources of income and must be conducted on the same principles as other business services, charging their clients for keeping their accounts.

(2) The debtors – owing the banks £M2,000 in aggregate, and owning for the most part collateral securities or other property against which the loan has been issued – must either sell their securities or find someone who has the money – either individuals or the State – genuinely to lend it to them.

(3) The State has ultimately to issue £M2,000 of new national money, and with it buy back and cancel £M2,000 worth of National Debt.

(4) This new money has in future to be held by the banks, £ for £ of deposits in current account, so that instead of their keeping in a *safe* proportion of their depositors' money as at present, they must keep the whole. #/

There is no difficulty or danger to be feared in carrying out this operation, provided it were conducted with ordinary financial prudence and acumen. The banks themselves could, with the co-operation of their clients, no doubt easily provide the whole £M2,000 of national securities to be liquidated. It represents less than one-quarter of the amount in existence, and, if they had not so much in their possession already in the form of collateral securities, it would be a simple Stock Exchange matter to exchange other non-national collateral securities for them to the requisite amount. Mr. Withers'[52] office-boy in the City no doubt would be able to explain, if consulted.

The position, then, is that all purely fictitious loans have been terminated. The amount of money in the country has not been affected by the transaction, and, indeed, the general public would only know that it had been carried out by the consequent reduction of taxation.

---

[52] *Bankers and Credit*, p. 200.

The banks are now solvent in foul financial weather as well as fair. Not a single legitimate feature of their business as moneylenders has been touched. They can lend money at interest as before provided they, or the owners of the money lent, genuinely do transfer the ownership of it to the borrower and give up the use of it. In so far as the loans to industry were due to simple deficit of legal tender, they will have been repaid and industry freed from the incubus by the sale of collateral securities in the debtors' possession. In so far as they are not, they would be continued as genuine and legitimate transactions between the industries and the lending public.

The way is then cleared for the future task of keeping the index number of prices and the purchasing power of money constant by issuing or withdrawing it, as the virtual wealth of the community grows or diminishes. We have dealt with how the issue could be effected. Its withdrawal, if necessary, is the converse – the State issues a new loan to the public and destroys the money so issued. Or, alternatively, the State imposes *ad hoc* taxation destroying the currency so obtained.

The still unsolved Problem

But we have still much ground to cover if we are to understand the laws to be obeyed by a community before it can keep its money from depreciating *and* its production of wealth a maximum, so that neither capital nor labour is voluntarily unemployed. That is a task which has never yet been achieved, and a problem that has baffled the entire world. It is insoluble if we permit money to vary in purchasing power and do not distinguish between genuine and fictitious loans. But if we say our money shall be made of constant purchasing power and issued for that sole end, and ensure that all loans must be genuine, we can then easily find the general form of the law as regards the relation between that issue and the accompanying abstinence (*genuine* loans) required to tune up industry from one level of production to a higher level until all available capital and labour are absorbed.

CHAPTER X

THE PRINCIPLE OF VIRTUAL WEALTH

High Finance or High Treason?

Let us take a breathing space, to come out from the trees and look again at the wood. At the close of the War, which had shaken us all out of ourselves, it did seem that a favourable atmosphere had been created in which to mould our national life nearer to the heart's desire. New things were then not necessarily untrue. But now we seem back to a resigned and fatalistic habit of mind which regards our failures as inevitable and part of the natural order of the universe. The upshot of our incursions into the scientific aspect of the social question is that the monetary system of the world is false and absurd, and that without minute attention to this little understood mechanism for distributing the products of industry, it is not much use thinking about where we all want to go and the supreme importance of our getting there. Politicians of all parties never tire of this easy theme, but each and all seem anxious to discuss anything and everything rather than money, which has us all in its absolute uncontrolled grip. There is an almost complete boycott of the subject in the Press. It seems impossible to get any of the essential data plainly and unequivocally made public, and for definite statistics one usually has to go to the U.S.A. for illustration.

The British public surely has right to information about its own system and to public and impartial inquiry and discussion concerning this new power, into whose hands it has been delivered over without its knowledge or consent.

Science, as was plain enough to everyone during the War, is amply capable of providing more than can possibly be required to enable everyone, able and willing to earn their livelihood, with the opportunity to live a decent life in healthy and adequate dwellings. The reward it should offer for efficient work should not be ever more and more work in competition with machinery, but leisure, honest and well-earned, to cultivate higher faculties and live on a less animal-like plane. True, there are plenty of people of mediæval views, carefully fostered by lack of education in our schools and universities, still ignorant of this, but facts in the way of masses of unemployed, factories working part-time, and land being allowed to go back out of cultivation, tell their own story. The conflict plainly is between science and finance.

It is, at best, but the counterpart of the busman's holiday to attempt to get people to devote their leisure hours to the study of the mechanism that drives them about their daily routine. But for all that, it is fascinating to think of ourselves at the wheel instead of being driven. It is the first step towards understanding the difference between the money we all know and the high finance so few get the opportunity to learn about. Instead of spending our whole working energies in the endeavour to find some employment, however uncongenial, in which to exchange our undervalued services for crisp new Treasury notes – which in these days of mass-production cannot cost very much more than postage-stamps to print – would it not be a change if we woke up one morning to find somehow ourselves running the printing machine and everyone else offering us everything they have to give in the way of labour, services, commodities, and the produce of industry in exchange for our coveted pieces of paper? High Finance has obvious advantages considered as a vocation.

But this the unimaginative and stolid politician will tell us is not High Finance, but High Treason against the State. That is precisely what it has from the dawn of history been always considered, and, before it got Britain by the nose – if a bulldog can be said to have a nose – it would have been thought worthy of publicity rather than concealment.

The Principle of Virtual Wealth

Let us take a survey of ourselves as we are – many of us priding ourselves on our hard-headed business and commercial acumen, some on our intellectual curiosity, others on our common sense, and none of us obviously escaped lunatics.

We all of us have wants and desires of every description, which we should satisfy if only we could "afford" it, of every degree of urgency or expediency, from a lack of proper nourishment and raiment to a mild hankering after a better motor-car or the latest in fashionable Russian footwear. Yet we all carry on our persons legal claims in the way of money to these things, and we do *not* exercise our claims to these things.

Rather we *prefer* paper tokens setting forth various 10 or less per cent truths about George V being, by the grace of God, King of all Great Britain, Defender of the Faith, and Emperor of India. But these tangible and existing tokens, which the public prefer to the things they really need are, as it were, the small change of commerce, almost insignificant compared with vastly greater equally valid claims in bank accounts for which no tokens exist.

Every one of us, as individuals, regard these monetary holdings as at least as valuable as the actual wealth they would exchange for. There is no compulsion in the choice other than the individual's own preference. It is, moreover, the normal and permanent condition of society, for as each individual in turn exercises his purchasing power and obtains the reality in lieu of the token or credit, he merely exchanges it with another individual, who then in turn abstains from the wealth to which he is entitled. Though the vast majority have none too much money, yet the aggregate of all our individual possessions of this Virtual Wealth is colossal. In 1920 it amounted, according to McKenna, to two thousand seven hundred millions sterling. As the annual total production of wealth in this country is estimated as of the same order, about £M3,000, it thus appears that there is nearly a year's production of the wealth of this country literally going begging, "glittering prizes" waiting to be picked up by sharp brains without producing anything whatever, and once picked up, well able to hire the sharpest swords of law, and every other weapon that can be bought for money right up to the nation's privately owned Press, in its defence. If we calculate in hard cash how much it is worth to spend in the defence of an unearned income of some £M100 a year, we may be sure it will not be a case of sinking the ship for a ha'porth of tar. But this, again, is a mere nothing compared to the power which the granting, withholding, and arbitrary cancellation of credit money confers on those who exercise it. Only one industrialist in the whole world, so far, Henry Ford, of motor-car fame, has dared to brave it and has escaped bankruptcy.

It is as well to picture sometimes what crude realities our idealism comes up against, if we wish to understand the complete rout of the forces working for progress in the past century, and their inability to take a step forward without the ground beneath their feet seeming to slip back farther than they have advanced. The world is getting very tired of the idealist, and the contemplation of an ever more distant goal. Surely a knowledge of the muddled idiocies of public finance is worth many a headache to acquire, and is the first necessary step to restore to the nations their sovereignty and inheritance.

The Value of Money measured by the Virtual Wealth

As indicated at the end of the last chapter, our problem falls into two distinct parts, which must not be mixed up but must be considered in logical order. There is the quantity of money, which must be always proportional to the virtual wealth of the community if its purchasing power is to be constant, and there is a very much more complex question, the circulation of this money from hand to hand interlocked with the endless flow of wealth from production to consumption, much as in a mechanical movement known as the rack and pinion.

In a rack and pinion, each complete turn of the pinion moves the rack a definite distance in a uniform straight line. A stabilised currency corresponds with such a mechanism, each circulation of the money sends forward from production to consumption or use the same quantity of wealth. A currency of variable value corresponds with a rack and pinion, in which the number of teeth in the pinion, and, consequently, its diameter, are never the same, but are continuously varying as it turns. Such a mechanism it is mechanically impossible to make, whereas hitherto, for reasons that will later be apparent, it has been politically impossible to distribute wealth by means of a currency of constant purchasing power. Violent alternations over short periods, and an average decrease of purchasing power over long periods, have been inevitable.

We may briefly recapitulate the position with regard to the first part of the problem, and put some of the points in a slightly different manner. The quantity of money in a country is the quantity of a peculiar sort of debt that would exist in that country if there were no money. It is not the only sort of debt, but it is the only sort of debt repayable in any form of purchasable wealth upon demand at the option of the owner of the debt. There are, of course, plenty of other sorts of debts, but they are not repayable in wealth, but in money. So that all of them have first to be repaid in money and then becomes repayable in wealth in general.

Now this debt, though expressed numerically by the sum total of the country's money, represents a deficit of real wealth, composed of all the actual things which the owners of the money are entitled to possess but voluntarily go without, or abstain from possessing, to suit their business or private affairs.

If we think of our own circumstances and the reason why we need money and have to keep a stock of it, the same reasons apply to the community as a whole. It suits some of the people's convenience and affairs all of the time, and all of the people's some of the time, to be owed rather than to possess wealth, so that they may be at liberty to select at their own time the sort and quantity they need at that particular moment in the market and receive it upon demand in exchange for their money. The quantity of wealth which it so suits a community not to possess, though legally entitled to possession on demand, is worth all the money in the community.

This negative quantity or shortage of wealth is termed in this book the Virtual Wealth of the Community. We may suppose it to be G – where G means the aggregate of goods, or real things, the community are abstaining from possessing, and we will first assume that this does not change. If the quantity of money in the community is £X, each £1 is worth G/X. Now suppose – whether by the action of the State, the banks, or of counterfeiters, it matters not at all – the quantity of money £X is increased in a certain ratio r to £rX, where r may be 2, 1.5, 1.1, or any ratio whatever, greater than unity, G is now worth £rX, and each £1 is worth G/rX. The owners of the original £X now have claims to XG/rX or only G/r; i.e. to only the $1/r$th part of what they had before. The issuers of the new money, or those to whom they pass it off, hold claims to the rest $G(1 - 1/r)$. If the State issues the new money, it will be to pay for public expenditure which otherwise would have to be defrayed by taxation, and if they withdraw it again from circulation it must be by imposing taxation and destroying the money so raised. Similarly if a bank issues it as loan credit, and cancels that credit when the loan is repaid, instead of re-issuing it, the community as a whole then regains in additional purchasing power of its money what before it lost. If a counterfeiter passes it off, what he so gains the individual, in whose possession the bad money is ultimately found, loses. But until it is detected, everyone in the community suffers a permanent loss in the purchasing power of their money, and for this reason, no doubt, the law has always regarded the uttering of false money as a treasonable offence rather than theft, though the actual counterfeiter gains no more in the one case than in the other.

If, now, we regard *G* as growing gradually and the money permanently and gradually increased to follow suit, so as always to keep the purchasing power of the £1 the same – i.e. now rG/rX, which is the same as G/X – then no injustice is done to money owners, but the increase of virtual wealth of the community is appropriated in the first place by the taxpayer, in the second by the bank, who pass it on to those who borrow money from them, and in the third by the counterfeiter.

But how is *G* increased or diminished? Only by people *abstaining* from possessing what they are fully entitled to possess, without any payment of interest as reward of abstinence, to a greater or to a lesser degree than before. In this the desires and intentions of individuals are not at all the same as the aggregate effects of those desires. People may think there is too much money and that there is going to be less, so that the price-level will fall, or too little and that there will soon be more, so that the price-level will rise. They may in consequence try to reduce or increase their holdings of it, but this has clearly no effect on the total money in existence.

What they give up or acquire others acquire or give up, and it is therefore a very complicated inquiry to ascertain under what circumstances their desires and intentions have any effect at all on the aggregate virtual wealth of the community and the purchasing power of money. We may state without fear of contradiction that, since the owners of money do not know, in general, whether money is being increased or decreased until the subsequent *effects* on the price-level manifest themselves, the temporary effect of an increase of the quantity of money, by conferring new virtual wealth on those before without it, is to increase it, and conversely a decrease of money temporarily decreases by cancellation part of the virtual wealth. But these are only the initial effects, the increase in the first case soon being neutralised by rise of price-level, but the decrease, in the second case, since the price-level is reduced more slowly, is more permanent.

The Musical Chairs Analogy

One can best illustrate this vitally important feature of all monetary problems by a very homely analogy.

In the game of musical chairs, when the music stops the ring of players moving round the chairs all instantaneously try to sit, but there is always one chair less than the number of players. This gives us easily the fundamental idea in the institution of money. If the instantaneous state of the nation could be similarly immobilised, there would always exist, in addition to those in full possession and enjoyment of all the wealth in the country, others with legal titles to demand it for whom no wealth whatever either exists or need exist. If a nation's affairs were liable to be wound up and the liabilities and assets apportioned, like those of an individual, then it would be necessary for the nation to keep in store, or put into the token itself, a quantity of wealth equal to the quantity of money. But a nation is a perpetual going concern. In so far as it may through adversity have to withdraw and cancel part of its money, it possesses through the right of taxation all that is required for this purpose. Hence it is quite mistaken to insist that there must be the equivalent of wealth behind a token currency. The first essential is that the community should not be robbed by the issue of token money in the first instance, and that it should be put into circulation to pay for costs that would otherwise be defrayed out of taxation. There need not be any backing of real wealth. What is behind the token currency is the necessity for the members of a modern community to abstain from possessing all the wealth to which they are entitled, in order to be able to get what they want in the form and at the time they require it.

The second essential is that the new money must not be issued more rapidly than the virtual wealth of the community increases. If the issue is conducted solely according to the desires of the State to defray expenditure without imposing taxation, by the banks with sole regard to the issue that yields the maximum gross amount of interest, or by the counterfeiter to obtain the greatest quantity of wealth for nothing, the currency is depreciated and the creditor class is robbed. If there is no issue, or insufficient to keep pace with the growing prosperity of the community, the much larger debtor class is defrauded. The dead hand of the past becomes excessive, and the payments to the *rentier* an exorbitant fraction of the national income. Labour, being without agents of production and forced to borrow the use of them, is in the debtor class and is permanently depressed by a fall of prices. Being also remunerated by wages fixed largely by custom and long term agreements, it is temporarily injured by a rise in prices. Though, as we have seen, fixing the level of prices is not a means of ensuring a *just* wage, but tends, if the nature of the standard is misunderstood, to stabilise rates of remuneration, yet it is absolutely essential to have a definite standard of monetary value before any progress at all in these further economic problems is even possible.

Why a Standard is essential

If politicians decide that it is essential for easy government that people should be led or tricked along the way they should go for their own good, and that the object in view had best be secured by some such rapidly depreciating standard as the gold standard, to lighten the dead hand of the past without arousing too openly the furies of private interest, the nation may rest assured that at the game of deceit in money matters the politician will not prove a match to those who have made the study of these questions a means of personal livelihood. So for the rest of this book we shall accept the advisability of stabilising the purchasing power of money, with reference to the general price-level of commodities, as an essential preliminary to any attempt to secure justice between all classes of the community. If, then, further adjustments are required as time goes on, it is far better that they should be made in the open by the State's powers of suitably graduated taxation than deceitfully, and with much unnecessary transference from the pockets of one class to another, by tampering with the standard of value. It is understood that the standard is essentially a debtor-creditor standard, and does not attempt to settle the just wage. It merely clears the way for possible reform, so that, in future, each step towards progress will not be more than offset by the ground on which we are attempting to progress slipping backward beneath our feet.

Index Number

There is no space in this book for any sufficient explanation of the methods by which economists of recent years have been able to determine the real value of money, apart from the large continuous variations of the value of gold. Those who have developed the subject can best be consulted.[53] It is a technical study much as the absolute standardisation of weights and measures is a highly technical and specialised branch of science. But in the one case, as in the other, this

---

[53] Compare Irving Fisher, *Purchasing Power of Money.*

is not in the least a barrier to its usefulness. The fact that no ordinary person is competent to say whether a pound weight, a yard-stick, or a quart measure is just or unjust – and on a desert island without any such existing measures could not reproduce them unaided – does not prevent the use of just weights and measures in commerce. In the end,

> the question as to correctness is decided in this country by the National Physical Laboratory, who check the sub-standards issued to the inspectors. So one must suppose a body of statisticians, who have devoted their lives to the work, enrolled and charged with the duty of ascertaining the general trend of the price-level and periodically reporting their conclusions to the national authority issuing the currency.
>
> The general level of prices is a fact capable of being ascertained by independent people without important disagreement in their several conclusions, and it should nowadays be as impossible for Governments secretly to tamper with the purchasing power of money as with the standards of weights and measures.

The Hypocrisy of Standardising Weights and Measures and not Money

If the State is to keep faith with all parties the value of its money must remain constant. It is obviously a pretence to set up a bureau of national standards and to maintain an army of inspectors of weights and measures to ensure that those who buy coals by the ton, cloth by the yard, or beer by the gallon, shall receive the quantities which they pay for, when the money itself which is exchanged for these commodities buys of them more or less according to the quantity of it that is put into circulation by purely private lending concerns.

If the nation does not control the issue of its money, it should give up the pretence of controlling the standards of weights and measures. It is the very acme of hypocrisy to enact laws against the utterers of false coins for use, and against usurers who, however exorbitant their interest, do, presumably, give up the money they lend, whilst allowing a creation of the order of two thousand million pounds sterling of new money for usury by the banks.

The only satisfactory test of the honesty of the currency is the constancy of its average value in terms of the goods for which it exchanges. In other words, the Index Number, which measures the relative cost of living in terms of monetary units, should remain constant at a definite prearranged value from century to century.

With the expansion of wealth-producing-power due to science and invention, we have seen that if the quantity of money in circulation were not increased, the value of money would increase, but that owing to the ruination of industry if it is compelled to sell its goods below cost due to the rise in the value of money – what actually occurs is that the shortage of money tokens paralyses industry, and instead of *prices* being reduced, *production* is. So that the scientific advance remains utilised, and the nation preserves its former state as regards production with fewer employed in the work, whereby unemployment and idle land and factories are the result. In fact the existing inversion of science and its consequences, from internal destitution to external insecurity and the phenomenon of world war, are the consequences of the nations not deliberately increasing their currency FOR USE, *pari passu* with the growth of their prosperity and virtual wealth.

A Currency based on Index Number

We have seen that the purchasing power of the £1 sterling is the virtual wealth of the community divided by the total quantity of money. Or, Virtual Wealth=Quantity of Money × Purchasing Power of Money.

The virtual wealth of a community refers to all the kinds of wealth that are about to be purchased both in consumption and production, each kind in relative amounts the same as those actually being purchased. The Index Number is the modern way of representing the average price of goods in terms of the monetary unit, and the purchasing power of money is inversely proportional to the index number at the time.

Thus an index number of 230 means that prices on the average are 2.3 times what they were at some former time, taken as a standard and given the value 100. The purchasing power of money with an index number of 230 is only 100/230 of what it was at the standard purchasing power of 100. Many index numbers are used, some concerned with wholesale prices, some with retail prices, and some dealing not only with the cost of commodities but including other expenses of living, as rent, rates, and so on. What is wanted is an index that so expresses the average money cost of the quantities of the things required in due relative proportion to maintain an average family, and then to keep that index number constant by regulating the currency so that always the total cost of these definite quantities of things shall not vary, however much they vary in price among themselves. It does not matter greatly how the various expenses of living are averaged in computing the index number, so long as the index number adopted is always calculated on the same principle and not departed from. There might be small variations in index numbers differently computed at the same time, but they would be of quite secondary importance. It might favour one class slightly more than another to reckon a greater proportion of the total living expenses going to food, for example, but the differences would be small, sometimes one way and sometimes another. Fixing the index number, and altering arbitrarily the total money so as to keep the index number always the same, would suffice for all practical purposes. Exactly how the index number was made up, if the averaging of the living expenses was at all reasonably done, would be of minor importance, and is a matter for expert discussion.

At what Value should Money be Fixed?

At what value to fix the index number, or rather, at what purchasing power of the £1 sterling to call the standard index number of 100, is, of course, of very great importance, for thereby the community fixes the ratio in which its income is to be in future divided as between the present and the past. If it makes the standard correspond to a low purchasing power of the £, it lightens the burden of its past debts – the National Debt and similar securities or debentures which yield a fixed monetary rate of interest, and in general all claims which do not depend upon present earnings. It will temporarily depress the real wage of labour, and all professional incomes and salaries in which the remuneration is fixed by custom and tradition, also such services as those of transport, where the charges are fixed by statute, and will temporarily increase the profits of those who live by buying and selling, and who receive as profits the balance left over after working expenses are paid. But "in the end" these will find a new level. Society has unfortunately become recently accustomed to large variations in the value of its money, so that the new level would to-day be more quickly attained, whereas before the War it would have been a long-drawn-out fight and the cause of much injustice and hardship on those adversely affected. But all those calls on the communal income which derive from fixed monetary payments will not alter in absolute amount, once the index number is fixed. As Mr. Keynes has put it in the paragraph already quoted, in discussing the internal affairs of France, and the future value of the franc, but altering the words italicised to apply to the question of the index number and to this country.

> "If we look ahead, averting our eyes from the ups and downs which can make and unmake fortunes in the meantime, the level of the £ sterling is going to be fixed not by speculation or the balance of trade, nor even by the outcome of the *return to the gold-standard*, but by the proportion of his earned income which the *British* taxpayer will permit to be taken from him to pay the claims of the *British rentier.*
> The level of the £ *sterling* will continue to fall until the commodity value of the pounds due to the *rentier* has fallen to a proportion of the national income, which accords with the habits and mentality of the country."

The times are highly abnormal, and it may not be yet possible to do more than provisionally to fix the price-level. But, even so, it would be a great political advantage if this vital question could be decided openly and above board, and due and sufficient notice given of the nature of any future change of price-level if that should prove necessary. This and the issue of the money are the nation's affair, not the bank's. It is their function to keep accounts and *lend* money, not to *create* it, and so determine price-level. In practice their interests are purely those of the creditor class, and although under the system they cannot help raising the price-level by their fictitious loans, they are always striving to force it back, though their decisions invariably condemn those, who have staked their fortunes upon producing the things which the community needs, to loss if not ruin; and the community to an artificially increased burden of indebtedness.

If the price-level is held constant, money values express real values, and the total quantity of money accurately expresses the virtual wealth of the community.

Relation between Price and Goods

Thus although at first sight a highly curious and uncertain quantity, virtual wealth is a very definite one, and its measurement presents no real difficulty. With constant quantity of money, it is proportional to the purchasing power of the money or inversely proportional to the index number of price-level. With constant index number of price-level it is measured by the quantity of money. Its use avoids certain difficulties which beset the quantity theory of money, which we have seen only works in practice one way. The latter pretends to correlate price not only with the quantity of money, but also with the positive quantity of existing goods, rather than with the negative quantity of goods abstained from, though whether the quantity which affects the price is the total quantity, the quantity of stocks in course of production as well as already produced, or the quantity actually in the market awaiting sale at the moment, is not made clear.

In reality it correlates price with the amount of money expended on the goods *bought and sold* in a year, which is a definition rather than an explanation of price, and the amount of money expended on goods in a year with the quantity of money and the number of times it is expended, which again is repetitional. It establishes no other relation whatever between price and goods, beyond that in the equation Price = Money expended · Goods sold and purchased.

Whereas the virtual wealth is quite independent of this complication, as itself, like the quantity of money which it measures the value of, it is a quantity and not a rate.

The causes that produce a change of virtual wealth are largely psychological. This is sometimes recognised in the statement that it is only the quantity of money in circulation that can affect prices, and that the part hoarded cannot exert any influence. But there is by no means any sharp difference. A manufacturer is always deciding from day to day the question whether to hoard or spend in his business, and precisely similar questions affect every individual purchaser.

There can be no dispute that the value of money is determined and can only be affected by the quantities of goods people in the aggregate voluntarily abstain from enjoying, and only indirectly by the quantities in the market for sale. But this view does not even pretend to answer the further question how the goods offered for sale affect people's *incomes* either real or monetary, except in so far as to suggest that habit and necessity will at any particular period prescribe some most convenient ratio between virtual wealth and income, which, if disturbed, will tend to come back to its original value.

Virtual Wealth and Incomes

We shall make no exhaustive attempt here to analyse virtual wealth, but shall treat it as a fact capable of measurement by the price-level. But it may be of help to trace further the consequences of individuals trying to increase or decrease their virtual wealth.

To simplify the issue, let us suppose the total quantity of money is unchanged, and consider a purchaser deciding that, in future, instead of keeping in the house, or the bank, money sufficient on the average for a month's housekeeping, he will keep only enough for a week. He consequently buys at once three weeks' supplies, and that is all he can do. If the shopkeepers took no action, all that would have occurred would have been that the buyer's individual virtual wealth had decreased, but that of other people had increased to the same extent, and there would be no change. But if the shopkeepers refused to retain the extra money, and passed it on, and even if everyone equally tried to reduce his virtual wealth, then it must not be rashly assumed that the virtual wealth of the community as a whole would have diminished.

We must remember the musical chair analogy. Individuals may balance the pleasures of the table against the moral and æsthetic satisfaction that is engendered by gloating over crisp exemplars of the art of engraving, but for the community it is a case of Hobson's choice. Someone has got to own all the money in the community, and not own the wealth it can buy, whether they want to or not. The speed or reluctance with which they pass it on, or grudgingly part with it, to others less or more clever or fortunate than themselves, does not necessarily affect the virtual wealth or the purchasing power of money.

Thus with the total money constant, the desire to pass off money more quickly than before, if general, means that people on the whole receive it more quickly than before. Their monetary incomes increase, but whether their real incomes increase or not depends upon whether the quickened demand operates to increase the supplies.

It has this tendency, for the retailer finding his stocks depleted will order more, thus transmitting the stimulus of demand, so that more goods are produced, more wages and profits earned, and the money comes round more quickly to purchase the increased production. But, in general, there would probably be some rise of price as well, and to this extent, a consequent *decrease* of the aggregate virtual wealth along with some *increase* of real incomes, caused by the desire of everyone to *diminish* their virtual wealth. Conversely a general desire to increase virtual wealth tends to increase it, but it also *diminishes* money incomes and to a smaller extent, probably, real incomes.

This point of view certainly brings out vividly the effect of everyone's desire to possess more money. The only way for everyone to possess more money is to increase the total quantity of money. If this is not done, the desire operates to *reduce* the national monetary income. Most people are beginning to realise that life itself is not a quantity but a rate, and that it is far more important to possess a big income than a large sum of money. If all people acted oppositely to their natural inclinations, and refused to retain any money a moment longer than they could help, the national monetary income would thereby be increased. Whilst the desire to possess more or less money cannot affect the total quantity of money, it can and does affect incomes in the opposite sense; the more freely the nation spends money the more money it has to spend, and the less freely it spends the less it has to spend. The universal desire to *possess* money is not to be confused with the desire for leisure and the disinclination to work, but is its exact opposite. People who possess money and desire to continue possessing it have to forgo spending it faster than they are receiving it. Those who will work only under the stimulus of an empty larder are trying to reduce their money, i.e. their virtual wealth, to a minimum. Under the system described, individuals would be free to keep as much or as little money precisely as they chose without interfering in the least with the circulation of money or the production of wealth. It would be possible to make the latter a maximum, so that neither labour nor capital was unemployed, however avaricious people were, and loth to pass on the money they received.

Hoarding and Mutual Credit

If the price-level, rather than the quantity of money, is kept constant, two of the main factors which affect the virtual wealth of a country, in opposite directions, are first, hoarding, which increases it, and secondly, mutual credit or lending, which diminishes it. Under a precious metal currency the first is an evil and the second a benefit, but under a stabilised paper currency the position is reversed. We have seen that the only part of the nation's credit different from an individual's power of running into debt is the virtual wealth. To increase the latter means that people voluntarily abstain to a greater extent than before, which enables, and indeed should compel, the nation to pay part of its expenses by the issue of new money. Hoarding as a practice increases the virtual wealth and enables the nation to that extent to run into debt without paying interest. Clearly when a miser's hoards are put back into circulation the virtual wealth is diminished to this extent. In the opposite category, the much vaunted financial expedients in the economising of money diminish the virtual wealth and the quantity of money corresponding with a given price-level.

It is instructive to consider a simplified example. If we take the case of an agriculturist and his annual crops, and suppose that, just before his harvest, he has no money and no wealth, finished and ready for sale. When the harvest is reaped he has, say, £H, when it is sold he has £H, and for a year this sum then steadily diminishes till at the next harvest it is zero again. Now bring in a merchant agreeing with the farmer to give one another mutual credit, so that just before the harvest the farmer instead of having no money owes the merchant £H/2. The merchant from the sale of last year's harvest would have £H, but as the farmer owes him £H/2, has only £H/2. The harvest when reaped is thus now sold by the farmer to the merchant for £H/2. Halfway through the year the farmer has exhausted his money, and the merchant has sold half the crop for £H/2, which he lends again to the farmer. In this way only half as much money is necessary as would have been required but for mutual credit. If, again, the farmer parts with his crop, half to repay a debt of £H/2, quarter for payment of £H/4, and gives the merchant credit for the remaining £H/4, clearly only one-fourth as much money as before is required. These mutual arrangements between individuals take the place of the precisely similar ones between the individual and the community, which the institution of money effects. It is one thing to regard as beneficent such methods of economising in the use of currency, when its provision entailed much waste of labour in the search for the precious metals, but quite another when, without any labour at all, people can be released from the necessity of contracting such mutual indebtedness and given the comfort of owing nothing to anybody by the right use of paper money. Bilgram (loc. cit.) estimates the sum total of debts on which interest must be paid as probably four times the amount of currency, including deposit currency, in use in the U.S.A., and that the yearly interest payments "absorb" more than a quarter of the whole currency. This is no doubt excellent from the creditors' standpoint, but there can be little doubt also that the debtors would prefer and be less fleeced under a system where the money was not so overworked.

An Analogy to the Governor of a Steam Engine

Fortunately it is entirely unnecessary to go further into all these complicated paradoxes. "We should be lost in endless calculations." It is as manifest an absurdity to try to calculate the precise effect of all the relevant circumstances upon the general price-level, as to calculate the effect on the speed of a steam engine of each unknown variation from moment to moment in the load, the lubrication, and the supply of steam. Nevertheless, the speed of a steam engine is regulated automatically with the utmost ease. The speed of the engine, which is the integrated and determinable result of every factor which operates in the working of the engine, itself, by means of a governor, opens or closes the throttle admitting steam, opening it should the speed fall off, and closing it should the speed increase.

On this analogy, the price is the integrated and determinable result of all the separate and indeterminable factors which affect the working of the industrial system and the virtual wealth of the community. It is measured by the index number which expresses the cost of living in monetary units. A governor of price-levels would increase the currency in circulation gradually as the industrial machine was given a larger and larger load, just as the governor of a steam engine under the same conditions would gradually increase the quantity of steam admitted from the boiler.

When the maximum amount of wealth the industrial system can produce is being produced, just as when the maximum amount of steam the boiler can furnish is being used, a larger demand will raise prices in the one case and reduce the speed in the other.

A Reply to some Misunderstandings

We must, in contemplating the proposed system, shake off some of the illusions induced by the experiences of the operation of the old system. It is undeniable that wealth could be increased, and that millions of workers, much unemployed land and capital are waiting financial permission to increase production. It is undeniable that science has increased, and still is increasing, the factor of human efficiency in producing wealth. It is undeniable that an increase in the quantity of money in circulation without a corresponding increase in the rate of wealth-production does increase prices. But the experience that it is practically impossible to reduce prices by contracting the currency, without at the same time contracting production and ruining those engaged in industry, is derived from our haphazard system.

By hypothesis, on the new system prices *are* kept constant, so far as any variation of them is detectable by its effect on index number. Skilled statisticians would detect the tendency to rise or fall before the public became aware of it in their marketing, just as the governor of a steam engine detects the tendency for the speed to increase or diminish before it can be ascertained by the eye or otherwise than by a very delicate instrument. The reasons why a contraction of the currency does not, in fact, reduce prices do not operate when prices are maintained constant by an automatic regulation of the currency by index number. Industry is ruined not by the constancy of prices, but by their fall, by stocks becoming unsaleable except below cost. A contraction of the currency to check an upward tendency of prices would ruin nobody, though after the upward tendency has occurred, the contraction is powerless to bring them down again without imposing still graver evils.

Hence, although there is every reason to suppose, so long at least as science and invention continue to develop, that the task of the statisticians advising as to the volume of currency the nation required, would be at first, and for a long time, the easy task of advising the issue of more money, should the necessity arise for them to advise a contraction of the currency, there is no reason to anticipate the evil effects that now attend the contraction of the currency *after* prices have already greatly risen.

In an age of scientific expansion and powerful incentives towards "saving," a time of rising prices, under a free monetary system, implies a time of war, civil commotion, pestilence or famine, whereby the revenue of wealth falls off, not, as at present, a time of boom and speculation, due to the quantity of money being arbitrarily increased. Of course to the speculator and profiteer, although probably not to the solid business man, if any such remain, the system will naturally appear to work the wrong way. So far from a time of rising prices being regarded as a calamity to be avoided at all costs, it will be regarded as a time of expansive prosperity. Mr. Hartley Withers, discussing the writer's proposals, makes this illuminating comment.[54] After approving of the plan of issuing the new money required to maintain the constancy of prices, of State Debt, as "a simple and inexpensive operation," he proceeds:

> "But when it is the other way about, and debt is issued so as to contract currency at a time of rising prices, the process seems likely to be both expensive and unpopular. No use could be made by the Government of the currency received from subscribers to the new loan; it would have to be destroyed to carry out the scheme, and so the operation would be dead loss; at a time of expansive prosperity implied by the circumstances, the Government would probably have to pay a handsome rate to get its loan out, and it would have to lay this sacrifice on the shoulders of the taxpayer, knowing that thereby, if the measure succeeded, it would be checking the rise of prices that makes the business world so happy."

It is a curious commentary upon the writer's thesis that what is wrong with the ruling classes of the world is that they begin by mistaking debt for wealth, and end by regarding scarcity as expansive prosperity. At the same time the passage illustrates the almost incredible state of fog in the minds of those supposed to be financial experts when matters of national rather than of individual finance are under consideration. To redeem National Debt is an act of financial rectitude, provided for by honest Chancellors of the Exchequer by the Sinking Fund, into which any excess of money extracted by taxation automatically flows. But to destroy Treasury notes extracted by the same process is "dead loss." It makes one wonder whether those who are responsible for the Nation's finances realise that National securities and money are both wealth from the standpoint of the individual owner and both debt from the standpoint of the community. The only difference is that the one is a deferred debt, not repayable on demand, and the other a debt repayable in wealth on demand.

---

[54] *Bankers and Credit*, p. 244.

CHAPTER XI

THE RIDDLE OF THE SPHINX

A Symbolism for representing Economic Transactions

We have gradually drawn in the threads of our analysis of the nature of money and wealth to the point where it is necessary to try to obtain a mental picture of the economic system as a whole and how it works. What is now required is a simple and informative symbolism or shorthand to represent sufficiently accurately the industrial system and the chief economic processes of production, exchange, and consumption.

Those unfamiliar with the mathematical sciences may be unaware how powerful a weapon of research a correct and informative symbolism is. With regard to the simple operations of arithmetic, without our systems of figuring, a life-time's study would hardly be too much. Before the days of the Arabic numerals – which were really invented by the Hindus – with its system of nine figures and a zero, the operations of multiplication and division used to be performed by an elaborate system of empirical rules upon a calculating frame known as the "abacus." The most proficient professional calculators after a life-time at the work could not attain to the standard reached under the modern system by a school-boy or girl of ten Something of the same state of things applies in economics.

For lack of simple means of expressing the operations of industry and commerce, chiefly so as to keep on record the totality of the important facts, during the changes of ownership of which they essentially consist, even elementary consequences, such as arise, for example, from the continuous circulation of money, are apt to be unforeseen until they occur. The difficulty is not reduced but rather increased by the fact that almost everyone knows and understands one aspect of the system quite thoroughly. It is necessary rather to see the whole at one glance. The first step is to represent the changes of ownership that occur in barter. This may be done as shown in Fig. 2. Thick broken lines are used to indicate the flow of wealth with the arrow pointing from production to consumption. Barter would then be represented as in the figure, where two such streams of wealth are shown meeting at a mart, A, in which the individual owner of one kind of wealth detaches himself from it and attaches himself to the other kind of wealth. The paths of the owners arriving at the mart with one kind and going off with another kind of wealth are thus shown by thin lines beside the streams of wealth.

The institution of money enables exchange of ownership to take place with only one kind of wealth, whereas barter demands that two kinds should meet at the same place and the same time. To represent money unbroken thick lines will be used, the arrows indicating the direction in which the money is circulating. This is shown in Fig. 3, which represents the owner of the money, or buyer, detaching himself at the mart, A, from the money and attaching himself to the wealth, and the owner of the wealth, or seller, attaching himself to the money and detaching himself from the wealth.

Money lines are necessarily, in the final result, closed paths, the same money *circulating* and not, like the wealth, flowing continuously on.

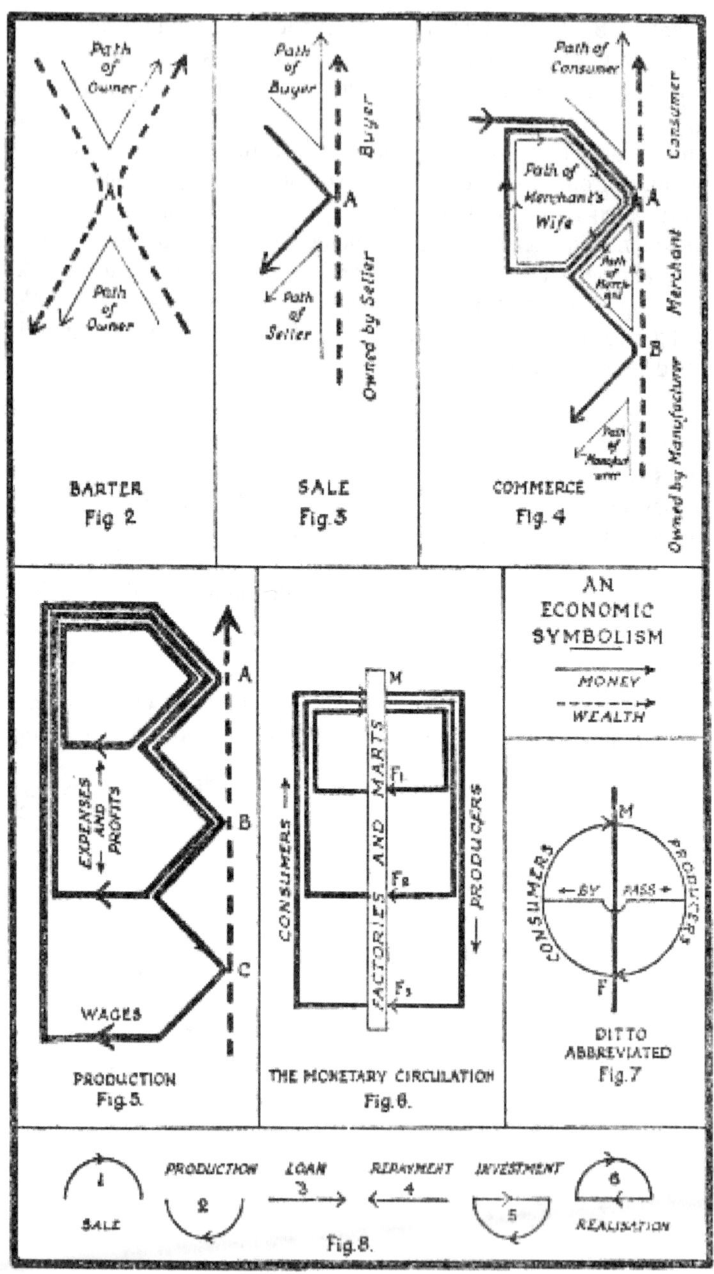
Path of Owner
A
Path of Owner
BARTER
Fig 2
Path of Buyer
Buyer
A
Path of Seller
Owned by Seller
SALE
Fig.3
Path of Consumer
Consumer
Path of Merchant's Wife
A
Path of Merchant
Merchant
B
Path of Manufacturer
Owned by Manufacturer
COMMERCE
Fig. 4
A
EXPENSES AND PROFITS
B
C
WAGES
PRODUCTION
Fig.5.
M
FACTORIES AND MARTS
F_1
F_2
F_3
CONSUMERS
PRODUCERS
THE MONETARY CIRCULATION
Fig.6.
AN ECONOMIC SYMBOLISM
MONEY
WEALTH
M
CONSUMERS
BY PASS
PRODUCERS
F
DITTO ABBREVIATED
Fig.7
1
SALE
PRODUCTION
2
LOAN
3
REPAYMENT
4
INVESTMENT
5
6
REALISATION
Fig.8.

The next diagram (Fig. 4) represents commerce, in which the buyer of wealth for consumption, or consumer, buys through a middleman or merchant, and the producer of wealth for money sells through the same middleman. The path of the wealth is continuous, but it now flows through two marts, A and B, where it is met by the money stream. After the first meeting, A, the money stream bifurcates. The money arrives at the retail mart A in the pocket of the consumer, and leaves in the pocket of the middleman. Part only goes on to the wholesale mart B and buys wealth from the producer. Another part, representing the merchant's expenses and profits, doubles back at once to the consumers' mart A. The *business* path of the merchant is a closed one travelling with wealth and without money and then with money and without wealth in an endless round, inside the productive system. It is difficult to represent the merchant himself in two places at once, but we may overcome the difficulty by supposing that it is his wife and family who trot off to the consumers' mart at A again with the profits earned, in order to purchase the necessaries of life. The whole monetary system is a system of similar closed paths interlocking with the flow of wealth. But the further repetition of the processes of exchange, and of a queue of middlemen travelling in closed curves, down the wealth stream with wealth and down the money stream with money, would add nothing new to the representation of the process beyond what is depicted in Fig. 4.

It will serve our purpose sufficiently well to represent the production of wealth in exactly the same way as occurring in a factory, C (Fig. 5), where a stream of money owned by the manufacturer is paid out as wages and originates the flow of wealth out of the raw materials and natural energies of the globe. We have already given (Chapter VI) an electrical analogy of the process, but for present purposes this extremely simple diagrammatic representation is sufficient. We distinguish money *inside* the production system in the ownership of merchants and producers in the streams flowing from A to B to C, from that *outside* the system in the hands of consumers in the streams that all converge at A, the consumers' mart. Naturally there may be any number of marts or factories, or combinations of the two, in which wealth is taken in from a previous factory and an additional process performed on it before it is passed on to the next. If now, understanding the symbolism, we simplify further by leaving out the wealth stream altogether, we shall arrive at something like Fig. 6, representing the monetary circulation only, in which on the left of the diagram the money is in the hands of consumers outside the system and on the right in the hands of producers and merchants inside the system. It is simply a series of closed circuits, all flowing together through the consumers' mart M into the productive system and out of the productive system through a number of wholesale marts and factories, as indicated in the diagram by F, in an endless round. Still further familiarity with the symbolism will cause a still further simplification to something like Fig. 7, where the closed circle represents the clockwise circulation of money, divided by the vertical line into two sides, the consumers' and producers' sides, and connected by a horizontal "by-pass" for transferring money from one side to the other.

The System in Equilibrium

We will first consider such a system of production operating in a steady or "equilibrium" state under a constant price-level, so that monetary quantities form a true measure of average wealth quantities. That is to say, we suppose that there is established a certain unchanging distribution of the money inside and outside the system, and a certain unchanging quantity of wealth in all stages of manufacture from start to finish in the system, and a certain unchanging quantity of still unconsumed wealth in the possession of the consumers. We do not mean to say that the money or the wealth are stagnant. An equilibrium condition is simply one for which, if we took two instantaneous photographs at different times, they would show the same result.

Though production and consumption are going on at full speed all the time, they reach the point at which they balance, and though the circulation of money is going on all the time, at any instant as much flows into any part of the circuits as flows out.

Then we need not postulate anything at all about what this equilibrium condition may be. We are solely concerned with *the effects of changes from that condition* reckoned as the datum-line, or starting-point. We are dealing, at this stage, solely with the monetary system as a closed circulation, and, until the implications of this are clear, many further questions, which usually are the only ones considered, cannot be considered at all. Our studies are at first entirely independent of the question as to how the wealth and money are distributed, as between wages, salaries, profits and interest. Even if we leave these questions entirely alone, and accept the distribution, whatever it may be, as a fact, without asking whether prices are fair or exorbitant and services paid for real or imaginary, we have still a good deal left to understand about the working of the monetary system.

At first, for simplicity, we shall also take no account of the equally important question whether permanent or perishable wealth is being produced, but will rather assume that, as is at the moment true, the community has both unemployed labour and capital to bring into productive operation. That is, we shall assume that fluid or consumable wealth, which actually does flow out of the system at the consumers' mart, is being produced, in contradistinction to capital or fixed wealth, which remains in the industrial system and never comes out at all. Or, on the analogy to a water system, we shall at first assume the mains to be capable of distributing a larger volume of water without enlargement. The relative share of the product secured by the workers as wages, by the employer or merchant as profits, and by the moneylenders as interest, may be neglected. The effect on the system is independent of whether the money arriving at the consumers' mart comes as wages, profits or interest. In many cases, when points dealing merely with the general principles that must be observed for the money to circulate the flow of wealth, all three may be combined as "price." With such simplification, it obviously does not matter whether a manufacturer is borrowing money or not, so long as it is genuinely borrowed and not created. It is sufficient to represent his profits as divided between himself and his creditor, if he is carrying on his business on borrowed money.

"Price" is distributed as well as extracted

The next point is that, since we are making no assumptions whatever as to how the elements of cost are made up, there is no distinction whatever between cost price, sale price, wholesale price, retail price, and so on. Every £1 that leaves the circuit at F does so as wages, salaries, profits, interest, or other payments for services, real or imaginary. At a constant price-level on the average it puts into the system £l, and needs the passage of £1 at M to take it out again. At most we commit an error in the sequence of events thereby. Thus, if we consider some quantity £X that has been put into the system – and for which £X has been paid out as wages and salaries at F – to be spoiled or destroyed within the system and never to come out at all, it is made good by a corresponding diminution of the manufacturers' or merchants' subsequent profits. If we suppose that there occurs, because of some speculative cause, a rise in the sale prices of certain goods in the system – and on a constant price-level a lowering in consequence of the price of the other things – more profits than otherwise flow out of the system in that case and less in others. We are, in fact, defining cost not merely as price paid by the consumer to take out wealth from the system, but equally as price paid to the producer for putting it in. In the long run, if there is no change of the quantity of money or in the state of the system, every passage of money at M is balanced by an equal passage at F. The one is the measure of the wealth taken out and the other of that put into the system.

If the price-level does not vary, then not only is the monetary value of the stocks of fluid manufactured and partly manufactured wealth in the system, in an equilibrium condition, constant, but also the actual average quantities of wealth are also constant.

How to increase Production

We are now entering upon a series of inquiries which never before seem to have been properly investigated, but which are vital, once we have the courage of our convictions that in a modern industrialised state in a scientific era the production of wealth for consumption is physically almost indefinitely extensible. We wish to find out precisely how a given level or volume of production can be changed to a higher level. We make the necessary stipulation that the price-level shall remain constant during the operation and that there shall be no fictitious lending. The increases in the total quantity of money are to be made by the nation in accordance with the price-level as the indicator. Clearly the easiest way of rebutting the assertions that bank credit and fictitious loans, if issued for production and not for consumption, do not raise prices, is first to find the conditions under which prices are not changed in changing from one level of production to another.

So little do the professional economists ever seem to have envisaged the continuous circulation of money that puerile and fanciful distinctions are made as to the effects of putting money into the system at different points of the circuit and with different psychological intentions, in general to stimulate either "production" or "consumption." These usually amount to no more than this, that in the first case new wealth is produced against the new money and therefore prices cannot rise, whereas in the second the new money encourages consumption and therefore prices must rise.

When we stipulate, as the first essential, that prices shall remain constant, irrespective of the changes of the flow of money and of goods, we shall find our system *most extraordinarily obstinate*. It requires about the same amount of patience and intelligence as the solution of a cross-word puzzle or an acrostic to find the solution of the problems we are to put to it. In the very condensed forms shown, the diagrams (Figs. 6 and 7) are capable of yielding much information. The reader is advised to draw them out on large-scale paper, and with a few different coloured counters or different kinds of matches, representing wealth and money, to try for himself the effect of any proposed scheme for rehabilitating industry. Much less would then be left for still unexplored authority to pronounce upon *ex cathedra*.

Here are some useful principles that will be found to emerge as the result of such trials.

The Six Possible Operations

Six different types of operation are possible.

Two, consumption and production, which alter the wealth and money *in*[55] the system in opposite directions, leaving their sum total unchanged.

Two, simple transferences of money from consumers to producers, or vice versa, which leave the wealth in the system unchanged.

Two, combinations of the above which increase and decrease the wealth in the system, leaving the money unchanged.

These are set forth and symbolised in Fig. 8:

(1) Sale for consumption, in which the wealth in the system is decreased and the money increased | for £.

[55] For the meaning of "in the system" see earlier.

(2) Production for wages, etc., in which the wealth in the system is increased and the money decreased | for £.

The combination of (1) and (2) to equal extents leaves both the wealth and the money in the system unchanged.

(3) The sinking of money in industry, preparatory to increasing production.

(4) Withdrawal of money from industry, after ceasing from production.

(S) Combination of (3) and (2), whereby the wealth in the system is increased and the money unchanged.

(6) Combination of (1) and (4), whereby the wealth in the system is decreased and the money unchanged.

Operations (1) and (2)—in which wealth and money exchange £ for | leaving the sum total, Wealth + Money, completely unaffected – can effect only temporary fluctuations or oscillations without lasting effect upon the equilibrium conditions of the system. The rest, which permanently increase or decrease the volume of production, are in sharp contradistinction, and are the operations important to our inquiry.

For let us suppose, with constant price-level, production is speeded up beyond the normal. A glut of goods and shortage of money occurs in the industrial system.

Again, an increase of consumption leads to a shortage of money among consumers.

To speed up both equally there must be a more copious circulation of money than before, and this means either more money *and* more wealth in process of manufacture or an actual shortening of the time required for production, which is a natural period, not an arbitrary one, *and* a shortening of the time taken for the money to circulate once round the system, which again is a very conservative period.

That is to say, not only in the production of wealth, but also in the circulation of money, the times and quantities are severally of importance. The physical facts are not sufficiently expressed merely by their ratio. It may be correct to speak of the production of wheat as so many bushels a second, but we must not so lose sight of the fact that the natural period in which to express the quantity produced is, in this country at least, one year. So for every kind of wealth there is a natural period of production which cannot be curtailed, however much it may be extended. In the circulation of money we have also not merely a rate of flow in which £1 a day is identical with £365 a year.[56] Especially where the money passes out of the industrial system into the consumers' pockets we have a succession of jumps – *pecunia facit saltum.* Profits are distributed quarterly, half-yearly or yearly; wages weekly, fortnightly or monthly; and so on. If we tried to make a system in equilibrium work at double rate, not only would there necessarily result a permanent deficit of finished wealth for sale,[57] but everyone in receipt of monetary income would have to be paid on the average as much as before twice as often as before. Otherwise there would be a shortage of money.

The Necessary Quantity of Money

Let us go back to the consideration of a system in stable equilibrium and suppose that all consumption and purchase at M for consumption is suddenly stopped, but production allowed to go on until all the money in the industrial system is drained out through F. Then all the money is outside the system. Again, suppose the opposite – consumption and production stopped, but purchase for consumption going on at M until all the money is drained out of the consumers' pockets into the industrial system. Then all the money is inside the system. Neither operation affects the sum total of money + wealth, either (1) in the industrial system, or (2) outside of it. The imaginary operations merely serve to separate wealth and money and to put all the one on one side and all the other on the other. In an ideal system, probably, the quantity of money should be equal to that of the finished wealth. If with the last halfpenny drained out of the consumers' pockets there is any finished wealth at all in the industrial system, there is no

---

[56] The "velocity of circulation," or rapidity of turnover, in the quantity theory of money – which is simply the average number of times the total money *changes hands* in a year – seems to have no important significance whatever. A more natural period would be the average period of complete circulation back to the starting-point.

[57] Proved earlier.

money to buy it, and therefore the system is overstocked. If with all the money in the consumers' pockets there is more or less finished wealth than this to be purchased in the industrial system, either the excess of wealth or of money cannot be exchanged, or, if exchange were effected, constancy of prices could not be maintained.

These considerations give us an idea of the correct quantity of money in a simple state of things where money and wealth always change hands £ for |. This quantity should be equal to the total stocks of finished wealth in and outside the system – those awaiting sale in the consumers' mart plus those already bought and not consumed. We may call it £*Q* or |*Q*. It is affected, in practice, by hoarding and the granting of mutual credit in opposite directions. But the money must bear some definite ratio to the wealth. For simplicity at first we shall neglect these factors. In such a simple system the quantity of money inside the system is equal to the quantity of still unconsumed wealth outside the system and the quantity of finished wealth inside the system is equal to the quantity of money outside the system. So that if consumers have £*X*, they will have | $(Q-X)$ unconsumed, and the producers will have £$(Q-X)$ and |*X* ready for sale. *Q* being constant, *X*, as we have seen, may fluctuate without seriously affecting the system.

The Effect of Increasing Money

We will first try to see in a broad way the effect of merely increasing the quantity of money in the system, neglecting the *minutiae* concerning the way the new money is issued and the particular point in the circulation at which it is introduced. The point is fundamental, and it is very essential to understand clearly what, with an unchanging price-level, would actually happen. We will simplify the process of production by distinguishing finished wealth ready for sale and unfinished or semi-manufactured wealth, and we will call the average time required from start to finish for the wealth being produced *T* weeks. We will suppose that, through a doubling of the money, a system in equilibrium doubles its production and consumption. If it were producing |*A* and spending £*A* per week on consumption before, it now produces and consumes |2*A* per week. The first week puts in an *additional* |*A* of *unfinished* wealth and takes out the same quantity of *finished* wealth. After *T* weeks its stocks of finished wealth are |*AT* *below* the former equilibrium level, whilst its stocks of unfinished wealth are |*AT* *above* it. Assuming these necessary finished stocks exist, it might be thought that the danger of shortage had been avoided, as from now on, after the $(T + 1)$ th week, one |A additional finished wealth weekly appears for sale.

But that is not so. For, *ever* after, stocks of finished wealth remains |*AT* below the former equilibrium value and stocks of unfinished wealth |*AT* above it, whereas the new equilibrium of production and consumption requires that finished stocks should be *doubled*. The community, in fact, must permanently put up with less stocks of wealth for consumption than it had before increasing consumption, and these can never be made up so long as we confine our operation to types (1) and (2), the simple exchange of wealth and money.

The Need of Abstinence or Saving

We may now consider how the stocks of money and wealth in the production system are increased and diminished. The normal circulation of money leaves them, as we have seen, unaffected, for each £1 passing in and |1 passing out at M, £1 passes out and |1 passes in at F. To increase them the flow of money must be by-passed, as it were, from outside to inside the system without passing through the consumers' mart. This money then flows in without taking out any wealth, and flows out putting in wealth, whereby the stocks increase.

This process we have already symbolised by 

This process we have already symbolised by various ways, all alike, however, in requiring *genuine abstinence from consumption.* Someone on the way to the mart to purchase supplies must be induced to lend his money to the industrialist and abstain from his customary consumption to that extent. More simply still, the industrialist himself may forgo profits, and, instead of distributing them, put them back into his business with the same result. In either case the manufacturer increases his production, takes on more workers and diminishes unemployment by passing out the money loaned as wages, etc., so putting the equivalent of wealth into the system.

If neither the lending public nor the producers can be induced to abstain from consumption for such a purpose, they can be taxed. Hitherto, however, taxation never seems to have been designed for any purpose other than the payment of Government expenditure. This obviously is merely a transference of purchasing power from the pockets of one set of consumers to those of another, quite futile for our purpose. But if the proceeds of the tax were not used to defray Government expenses, but lent to the producers, it would effect the object arrived at. Again, a Government loan might be raised from the public in lieu of imposing taxation and the proceeds lent to the producers. But struggle with this puzzle how we may, there is no escape from the initial abstinence if a productive system is to be built up from a lower to a higher level of production. We shall later revert to the probable consequences of trying to avoid this initial abstinence. We are dealing with the effect produced on an equilibrium condition by arbitrarily altering one of the factors at a time. Abstinence from consumption alone is capable of increasing the stocks of wealth in the system. Similarly, if we "by-pass" the factory and transfer money to the consumer's pocket without passing through the productive system, quite obviously to this extent we drain the equivalent wealth out of the stocks in the industrial system.

This is abstinence from production. It has been symbolised by and normally results from a producer retiring from business.

The Problem solved

Now let us try to envisage the initial and final equilibrium states of the system in which production and consumption have been increased by some factor greater than unity – call it r. That is now $|rX$ are to be produced and consumed in the same time as $|X$ were. Clearly everything must be altered by the factor r. If before £Q sufficed, now we must have £rQ, and so £Q $(r - 1)$ of new money must be issued. Before consumers had £X and $|(Q - X)$ still unconsumed, producers £$(Q - X)$ and $|X$ for sale. Before, also there was some quantity – call it $|S$ – of semi-manufactured wealth in the system. Now these quantities must all be multiplied by r. We have postulated a system in which certain quantities came into a definite relation as the result of experience teaching each individual concerned the best ratio between money and wealth required for the conduct of his affairs, and clearly if we merely alter the scale it suffices, as a first approximation, to alter everything proportionally. It is rather a mis-statement of the truth to picture a physical glut of finished wealth awaiting customers. What actually happens is that each manufacturer knows the correct ratio between the volume of business and the stocks necessary to carry it on in the most efficient way, and will not depart far from that ratio. It would be a dead loss to him if he tried to carry too much stock and he ceases production should his stocks become excessive. So also he might, for a brief time, try to carry on in a boom with deficient stocks, but would in practice raise prices if he could not bring up his stocks to the required ratio for the efficient conduct of the business.

The task of accumulating an extra |Q $(r - 1)$ of finished stocks in the system is thus accomplished by those, normally consuming and entitled to consume, abstaining and transferring their powers of consumption to new workers, who put in as much as they take out. Merely hoarding the money would clearly be worse than useless. This, of course, is gradually accomplished, in a manner gone into in more detail later, until the stocks are built up from raw material to finished products, and the first of the latter are ready for sale. As fast as this occurs the new £ Q $(r - 1)$ required to distribute it must be printed and issued to the consuming public to maintain indefinitely the new volume of production and consumption at the higher level. The issue would normally be against Government expenditure, paid for in this way in lieu of by taxation. In practice, of course, the rate of issue and its exact amount would not depend on any theoretical or complex calculation, such as has here been essayed, but, as already explained, in accordance with the actual index number of price-level and as soon as the appearance of the greater volume of new wealth on the market justified the belief that a new issue could be made without causing the price-level to rise.

But we may as well complete the accounting in the simple case exemplified. Ultimately, of the £ Q $(r - 1)$ issued to the consumers, £$(Q - X)$ $(r - 1)$ will find its way permanently *into* the system in exchange for |$(Q - X)$ $(r - 1)$, and £ X $(r - 1)$ will remain in the consumers' hands. So that the stocks inside the system rise from £ X and £ S to £ rX, and £ rS, and from £$(X - Q)$ to £ r $(Q - X)$ in money, because these are the equilibrium conditions which will look after themselves. But what will not look after itself and has to be "managed" is (1) the initial genuine abstinence and transference of purchasing power from consumer to producer; (2) the issue of new money. The first without the second is an evil as great as the second without the first.

For it means that in spite of all the efforts and sacrifice involved the goods purchased cannot possibly be sold at constant price. The money for continuing the new scale of production no longer finds its way into the system as soon as the loans cease. The extra workers taken on to increase production are thrown out of work. The extra stocks accumulated have to be sold off, and, while this is being done, as much additional unemployment is caused as extra employment was furnished during their accumulation. So that now employment falls temporarily below even what it originally was, just as at first it rose temporarily above it. In fact, this elusive and yet supremely elementary riddle has probably been responsible for as great an amount of futile human effort and waste of life as all the more show tragedies of famine, pestilence and war put together.

The Relation between Abstinence and New Money

The most important correction that has to be introduced into the foregoing reasoning is to allow for the effects of hoarding and mutual credit, and it is very simple. Instead of there being required £Q to distribute |Q of finished stocks, we shall require some other quantity £KQ, where K is an unknown factor. It will only change slowly with the business and domestic habits of the people. Instead of the issue of £Q $(r - 1)$ of new money, £KQ $(r - 1)$ will be required. But these considerations do not in the least affect the necessity for abstinence from consumption to the full[58] extent of the increased stocks both of finished and semi-manufactured wealth. In practice one would, of course, be quite independent of the necessity for knowing beforehand the numerical values of the various quantities and factors involved. The price-level is the sole indicator required; but the unemployment figures and whether or not factories are working at full capacity are, of course, valuable guides on the general question.

On the ideal system suggested the money in the consumers' pocket – neglecting hoarding and mutual loans – should equal the quantity of finished wealth for sale. The increase of money called for must in any case be proportional to, if not equal to, the increase of finished stocks. The initial abstinence is definitely equal to the increase of total stocks, both finished and unfinished, necessary to build up the system to a higher level. This means that the new money issued can

[58] Part of this abstinence may be derived from the unwitting abstinence of money holders and not from conscious investment, as is about to be considered.

never repay more than a part – usually a small part – of the initial abstinence; at most the ratio of finished to total stocks of wealth.

Later we shall see that not only, as here, the accumulation of fluid capital, but in all cases of the accumulation of capital, indebtedness to individuals is incurred which can never be repaid and therefore must bear permanent interest.

A more detailed Illustration

Few people who have not tried to find a way of doing it will be prepared to credit the statement that it is absolutely impossible to increase the stocks of wealth in an industrial system and to build it up from a lower to a higher level of production without some form of initial abstinence or "saving" on the part either of consumers or producers. We have sufficiently outlined the general solution of the problem, but it may be instructive to consider one or two points in more detail. Suppose we consider the production of a commodity from start to finish in three successive factories or markets. The first manufacturer, dealing with the raw materials, will need the first loan to enable him to increase his output and pay more wages, etc. Suppose he receives a loan of £l_1, which he pays out as wages and profits, putting into the system $|l_1$ of new unfinished wealth. As soon as it is ready to pass to the second manufacturer, the latter will need a loan of £$l_1 + l_2$, £l_1 to buy the $|l_1$ from the first factory and £l_2 to pay out as wages, etc., for its conversion into £$l_1 + l_2$. The first manufacturer needs no further loan because, receiving £l_1 by sale of his product, he can repeat his increased output a second time. In the third period the third manufacturer will need a loan of £$l_1 + l_2 + l_3$, $|l_1 + l_2$ to buy the material from the second manufacturer and £l_3 for his costs in converting the material a further stage to $|l_1 + l_2 + l_3$. Of the £$l_1 + l_2$, the £l_2 enables the second manufacturer to convert a second batch of goods and the £l_1 the first manufacturer to produce a third batch.

The loans being supposed genuine, all of this time there is no depletion of the normal stocks of finished wealth. But by loans to the extent of £$3l_1 + 2l_2 + l_3$; $|l_1 + l_2 + l_3$ of additional wealth is now ready for sale, and two separate quantities of intermediates £$l_2 + l_1$ and £l_1 are on the way. The three manufacturers have increased their regular wage and other payments by £l_1, £l_2 and £l_3 respectively.

Let us suppose the loans now cease. The thrifty and the business fraternity have done their part, and the wealth is appearing in the consumers' mart for sale. How on earth can it be sold? If it is not sold, clearly then the extra payments £$l_1 + l_2 + l_3$ cannot be longer continued. Not only is it true that it can only be made, but it is as true that it can only be *sold* if these payments are continued. Consumption has hitherto not been increased by the accumulation, since the loans, if genuine, merely transfer to the new workers the finished goods, which the lenders themselves, otherwise, would have purchased and consumed. When the loans cease, consumption will not be increased, unless the new workers are continued. Since, before, the money in circulation sufficed to distribute the former flow of wealth, it is obvious that it must now be increased proportionally to distribute the increased flow, and this can most easily be put into circulation by remission of taxation and paying for Government expenditure with the new money issued. If no new money is issued to purchase the wealth for consumption the whole of the elaborate process is undone. The stocks cannot be sold, the extra wages, salaries, profits, dividends, etc., cannot be paid, the extra hands taken on must be again dismissed to resume their unemployment, and class hatred based upon the assurance that the ruling classes of the country either do not understand the elements of their business or else are deliberately attempting to enslave the workers is the natural outcome.

The Case of Existing Glut

If in the last example there was a sufficient glut of finished wealth in the market initially, only then could the initial abstinence be dispensed with and the new money issued at once as loans to industry. Suppose for the sake of an illustration such unsaleable finished stocks amounted to |M1. New money to a sufficient amount is printed and gradually issued, so as to leave the stocks of wealth above the requirements of the former scale of production and capable of maintaining the permanently increased level of production.

New money once put into the system goes on circulating, of course, for ever after, apart from accidental loss or destruction of the money. But it puts in at each circulation as much wealth as it takes out, always provided that the existing organisation is capable, without new capital expenditure, of handling the increased output and that sufficient unemployed workers exist. On the assumption made, by *one* such issue the wheels of industry might be set whirling merrily, but the medicine must not be repeated. Whereas by sufficient initial abstinence, precedent to the issue of the new money, the building up of industry can be definitely continued. The consumption of consumers, like the circulation of money, goes on for ever, and cannot be met out of continuous new issues. This is, therefore, a totally different proposition from that of a National Dividend, which could only be a possibility in a communalistic, not in an individualistic society. The circumstances that would make such an occasional issue of new money feasible would, of course, never arise if the money were national and regularly issued in lieu of taxation to maintain prices constant as the national output of wealth increased.

Thus the argument about the folly of saving society by any scheme of "tinkering with the currency," because a relatively small amount of money is sufficient to circulate an indefinitely large amount of wealth, is in reality double-edged. Society indeed could be saved just because of this. The amount of abstinence required, precedent to this small issue, is also almost equally trivial, at any rate where unemployed labour and capital exist in abundance. It would be preposterous to suppose that the ordinary business acumen of the industrial world would not supply out of profits the necessary stocks of materials if markets for them were assured by the proper issue of national money.

It has been necessary to insist uncompromisingly on the need of *initial* abstinence, but this must not be confounded with the chronic abstinence and "work more and consume less" slogan of the usurer. Precisely as with the issue of new money, the abstinence is needed only once. Granted unemployed labour and capital, abstinence at most to the extent of the fluid stocks of wealth in the system would *double* everyone's power of consumption on the average for *ever afterwards.*

How it would look to a Banker

We have just considered the one case in which an issue of new money could create permanent prosperity without initial abstinence, namely, when there is a glut of unsaleable finished stocks in the market. But if we examine the essential condition that has brought about this state of affairs we shall find that it is due to abstinence and nothing else, enforced and involuntary it is true, but none the less abstinence.

Individual owners have sunk their property or earnings in industry if stocks have accumulated, and have come to the end of their resources. These individuals usually are the producers themselves, and the investment intended to be temporary has become unrealisable. The goods are there, belonging to them and awaiting sale, but they cannot be sold.

Before we hastily conclude that the power of the banks to create money and lend it to industry is justified by this instance, it is well to ask precisely whether these are the conditions under which bank credits would, in fact, be extended or curtailed.

Industry is glutted with unsaleable goods. There was a market during the time in which the manufacturers payments, of wages, etc., out of their own resources to produce the accumulation maintained a market. The producers transferred their claims on the market to the new workers who put in the accumulation. But now they are at the end of their limited resources and their capital is all tied up in manufactured goods, the process of accumulation stops, and with it the demand on the market for goods from those formerly engaged in creating that accumulation. The bottom drops out of the market. Swollen and depreciating stocks must be sold when there are no buyers. It is at this psychological moment that the industrialist must approach the banker for the new money to enable industry to carry on. He can point to the fact that production has vastly exceeded consumption, that there has, in banking phraseology, been a great speculative boom, that there is no market whatever for the things he produces and which he could continue indefinitely to produce if he could sell them, and then humbly ask for credits to facilitate production! The banker would think him mad. He would say, "Is it not obvious to you that your production has already outrun markets, and that until the glut of stocks is disposed of credits must be curtailed, not extended?" So production is forced down now as much below normal as during the initial period of accumulation it was above normal. The accumulations are taken out by the elaborate process of transferring purchasing power, from wherever the remaining money of the country happens to be at the moment, by taxation to maintain the unemployed and carry on somehow, and then, as soon as the effects of the initial abstinence have been completely dissipated, that is the psychological moment when the banker will inflate.

The Consequence of Fictitious Abstinence

The consequences have already been sufficiently indicated. Stocks of finished wealth are depleted and stocks of intermediates only are increased up to the new level to maintain the boom. There is a shortage of wealth for sale and an increase in the money to buy it at one and the same time. Rise of price is inevitable under these conditions. But it must not be supposed that the rise of retail prices will, by causing each £l at the consumers' mart to take out a lesser absolute quantity of finished wealth, thereby increase the stocks. Not at all. Profits are merely increased. If there is a rise of 10 per cent in the price-level, each £1 takes out only 10/11ths of the unit of goods that was before worth £1, but of the £1, £1/11th is extra profit, and comes round again at once taking out the rest. The price of an article is sometimes defined as what it will fetch. It is undeniable that it is not only what it does fetch out of the consumers' pocket, but also what it puts into the producers' pocket. But the producer is also a consumer, and that part above the cost to the vendor, the profit, is regarded by him as his private property in his capacity of consumer. The rest has already been paid, or will be paid, to the other people engaged in production, each of whom treats it in turn as private property to be expended in the consumers' mart.

The symbolism becomes more elusive if the price-level varies, but this does not entirely vitiate the usefulness of this method of regarding the problem. Indeed it is here again only in so far as these unearned profits are put back in the business that either the quantities or monetary values of the stocks of finished wealth can rise.

At first there is merely an alteration in the distribution between the consumer and the vendor, also a consumer. What the one loses the other gets. But as the rise of price is transmitted through the industrial system to the factory and begins to affect wages and payments for services as well as profits, then the absolute quantity of wealth put into the system by the payment of £1 is reduced. The stocks of wealth in the system, till then unaltered in quantity by the rise of price, now begin to decrease in quantity. They go on decreasing in quantity – and rising in monetary value per unit of quantity – until the increased amount of money in circulation pays only for the same quantity of production as before the increase – except in so far as, by refraining from distributing excess profits, the producers themselves or other genuine investors may be adding to the stocks of wealth in the system.

The existence of wealth is evidence that someone has produced and has not yet consumed it. The existing wealth is the excess of production over consumption and decay from the beginning of time. The whole of it – neglecting that part in fixed communal capital, such as harbours, roads and the like – has individual owners who have abstained to this extent from consumption. Beyond this, abstinence equal in value to the total money of the country is exercised by the owners of money, who voluntarily, but for the most part unwittingly, abstain not only from consuming but also from owning.

It would lead too far into the morass of economic uncertainty further to go into the question of the consequences of a changing price-level and all that it entails. But the general nature of the effect of a rise of prices may be indicated. Apart altogether from any *increase* in the level of prosperity before even the former level can be *regained*, after the rise of price has occurred losses equivalent to the excess profits made during the rise must be contributed by someone. Naturally this is resisted strenuously by all those engaged in production, employer and employed alike, and this accounts for the difficulty of reducing the price-level after it has risen. It must suffice if it has been shown that the mere issue of new money, whether by the State, the banks, or by counterfeiting, though it temporarily stimulates production and consumption, yet by depleting stores of finished wealth leads to rise of prices and, except in so far as it is counteracted by real investment supplying the missing stores, ends in depressing the system below its former level of real production at an inflated price.

What hitherto has limited Production and Consumption

But, once more, we may ask the oft-repeated question, What under the system in vogue during last century limited the expansion of wealth production? – this time to answer it. The rise of prices is the expression of the shortage of finished goods. It leads naturally to the attempt to supply these by import from abroad. There are no goods ready to export in return. In other words, the rise of prices makes that unprofitable. But there is the one finished form of wealth which is artificially kept at constant money-price, namely gold, and the country therefore is drained of its gold to pay for the excess of imports.[59] Automatically this rendered the position of the banker insecure and his bank liable to be broken by a call for legal tender, before the War and the moratorium, at least, if no longer now. So credits are called in, money is destroyed and the volume of production reduced to a limit safe to the banker but insufficient to support the nation. As we have seen already, in so far as there was a simultaneous inflation of the currency in all countries, so that gold did not tend to flow from one to another, there has occurred a permanent rise of the price-level in all countries and the restriction of the currency does not then come automatically. But the banker's financial interests are predominantly those of the creditor class. He toils not, neither does he spin, but lives on interest. Thus a rise of prices, which cannot be avoided so long as no one gives up the money he creates to lend, is a very unwelcome consequence. Receiving fixed monetary interest payments, the bond-holder and the purely creditor class in general see their real incomes diminished proportionally to the rise of prices. On the other hand, if industry is ruined their claims are *the first* to be settled. Hence the currency is restricted and the attempt made to force down prices, even though there is no risk of insolvency to the banks, by reason of the fact that the mechanism is completely controlled by those who have little to lose and much to gain by this disastrous policy.

The Only Way of avoiding Initial Abstinence

It is interesting to note also, in another direction, how incompatible the banker's psychology is with the physical factors of wealth production. It is clear that, for a given price-level and for any given rate of production and consumption of wealth, the more money there is in the country the less rapidly it must circulate. If it took the same time to circulate once round the system as, on the average, to produce wealth, the quantity of money could be the same as the total stocks of finished and semi-manufactured wealth, and no other abstinence would be required than the voluntary non-interest-bearing abstinence of the owners of money. The money could be issued "against

---

[59] A whole library has been written on this theme, treated as a cause rather than an effect.

the goods" in the industrial system, as is sometimes urged. Instead, the whole *raison d'être* of banking, derived from the time when the precious metals were the only currency, is to "economise" in the quantity of money necessary and to increase its velocity of circulation to the greatest possible extent, so that it may never remain "barren" and "idle," but shall be put over and over again to "productive use."

Whereas, if the circulation could only be slowed down to conform with the natural time of production of wealth, it could be issued proportionally to this increase of production without raising prices at all. Itself it would pay for the abstinence required to increase stocks.

Who Gains and Who Pays?

With the production of wealth essentially a finished science, it is an insult to our intelligence to regard it as, like the weather, beyond the wit of mortals to control or understand. There should be an end of the fevered alternation of the trade cycle. It should give place to uniform prosperity, whereby famines and droughts are reduced to their real local world significance and the whole world can co-operate with mutual advantage. There are plenty of people, dowered with exceptional gifts, to whom this sort of thing would not appeal. But they are the gainers and not the sufferers under the present chaos. It is the consumer that pays for all the brilliant gambling and speculation as well as for all the fundamental ignorance and incompetence that make the individualistic system what it is. When democracy has grasped that, nowadays, the production of wealth is really an affair of scientific engineering, and not primarily one of how to make pieces of paper bring in interest, and that it is not only idle but highly dangerous for science to expand its wealth unless the currency is proportionately expended for use, it will have learned something which, altogether matter-of-fact, lies about as near to the root of economic freedom as it is at present possible to get. It is certainly a good deal nearer to it than the partisan creeds of politics, whether the older issues of individualism and socialism, or the curious hybrids being developed in Russia and Italy. So far we have not progressed in these matters much beyond the Irishman's idea of feeding his pig, fattening it up one day and starving it the next to get streaky bacon. The pig died, and our streaky civilisation of the fat and the lean is in extremity as dire.

CHAPTER XII

ACCUMULATION VERSUS DISTRIBUTION

The Accumulation of Capital

In the preceding study of the question how to foster production and abolish unemployment we emphasised the key part played in the problem of price by initial abstinence from consumption until the goods being produced are ready for consumption. The case was limited to the accumulation of the necessary stocks of fluid wealth in the system on the assumption that unemployed labour and capital were available. But identical considerations govern equally the accumulation of fixed capital. We may imagine that the flow of wealth proceeds in solid walled arteries, and may distinguish between fluid wealth and fixed wealth – by the former term meaning that part which actually flows out of the system and appears in the consumers' mart for sale, and by the latter, the organs of production themselves, which have to be put into the system by processes identical with those for fluid wealth, but which never comes out or can come out for consumption. It is really more correct to consider in this category of fixed wealth that proportion of fluid wealth which is necessary to fill the arteries, for though it is always passing on, there is necessarily always a certain quantity in the system, which cannot be reduced without permanently reducing the output. True, there is a difference if we contemplate a continuance of the past alternations of the level of prices and production, but there would be none with a reasonably stable system. There is no sense in going to all the effort and trouble involved in building up the system with the intention later of pulling it down again. Whereas, if we deal with the accumulation of fixed capital, not only does it never come out of the system at the consumers' mart, but it never can come out. Sooner or later it comes to the end of its useful life within the system itself.

In general terms, the *only* possible way to increase the stocks of wealth in the system, whether precedent to producing a larger output or to accumulate capital in the first instance, is to by-pass money past the consumers' mart so that it passes through the productive system twice in its circulation instead of once. This puts into the system twice the value of wealth which it takes out. But it creates debts to the individuals who give up their purchasing power, and, however we struggle with the problem, we have to arrive at the conclusion that *these debts can never really be repaid*.

It is an undeniable postulate that all the wealth put into the system, reckoned in terms of the costs of production, not only does not but cannot come out.

Like Money, Capital is Individual Wealth and Communal Debt

Certain kinds of wealth, it is true, may serve different purposes, and may be the fixed capital in one industry and the raw material of fluid wealth in another. To a very unimportant extent a community might "live on its hump" like a camel, depleting its capital accumulation for consumption. But this is exceptional. No primitive community would reckon upon eating its ploughs if short of bread. The financial mentality of modern man prevents these elementary considerations from being properly appreciated. Production and distribution being regulated by money tickets, no proper distinction is made between ploughs and bread, because both equally exchange for money. The economist has failed to enlighten him as to the two totally distinct categories of wealth. Modern man is therefore apt to think that he can consume the same whether what is produced is consumable or not! He can do so only if he can exchange the one form of wealth for the other by foreign trade.

Irrespective of whether the equivalent of wealth put into the system is, or is not, ever to come out of the system, all costs incurred must be abstracted from the pockets of the consumer, either at or *en route* to the consumers' mart. If this is done at the consumers' mart, as much wealth is taken out of the system as is put in again when the money circulates out of the productive system. The amount abstracted from the consumer is necessarily greater than the amount he receives, very greatly so if capital, not exchangeable for consumable wealth, is being accumulated, but invariably so to make good waste and depreciation.

This is not merely a trite statement that the consumer pays more than cost price for his goods, because it must be remembered, in this method of approaching the subject, that all profits are considered part of costs as much as wages and nothing is hypothecated as to whether the costs are reasonable or extortionate, necessary or avoidable. It means that money must always be by-passed into the system without passing the consumers' mart, whereby more wealth is put in than is taken out.

Thus, in the case of waste, if a batch of goods worth £ *X* in total costs is spoiled in the making, profits are reduced £ *X*, and instead of this money finding its way into the consumers' mart it is put back in the system at the points required to cause the production of *X* anew. The same is true of new capital extensions financed out of profits. New enterprises and large extensions are financed out of fresh loans, and if these are genuine loans the operation is of the same nature and can be briefly described as the by-passing of the consumers' mart.

All such operations involve the creation of debts to individuals. Some, as in the making good of waste and depreciation, are treated at once as bad debts. They are written off and forgotten about as they are incurred and do not bear interest. Others, as in financing capital extensions out of profits, involve the creation of no new formal debts, but bear interest in enhanced payments on already existing ones. But new loans involve the creation of new debt charges, and of these it is as true as of the debts written off as they occur for waste and depreciation, that they can never be repaid. The ownership of these debts changes hands precisely as for consumable wealth. Interest is a payment for the use of capital, but is in no sense a *repayment*, the debt being unaffected in amount by the amount already paid. Repayment in the sense of reconverting the capital into consumable wealth is in all but exceptional instances impossible, and in the end these debts must be written down and written off as the wealth rots in the system.

At first sight nothing could seem easier, having permanently increased the revenue, than to pay back those to whom we are indebted for the initial saving with some of the wealth that is being produced.

But it is forgotten that the wealth produced has individual owners, who may exchange the goods they produce for the ownership of the accumulated capital. But this merely transfers the debt, it does not repay it. True, nationalisation, in which the capital is redeemed by taxation or other form of general levy, would vest the ownership in the whole community. But even that is really a transference of the ownership of the debt from individuals to the community and not repayment in wealth.

The Doubtful Heritage of Science

The consequences of this insufficiently appreciated point are seen in the conditions under which any so fortunate as to be born in a scientific era must now enter the world. It is estimated that capital to the extent of £1,000 and probably more has to be accumulated to provide the newcomer, when adult, with the necessary equipment for him to labour effectively and with a house in which it is possible to rear a family. At 5 per cent interest, these aspirants for the privilege of being the heirs of all the ages must pay at least £50 a year out of the produce of their labour in perpetuity, a doubtful heritage assuredly. But it is one of the deeper futilities of individualistic economics that it does not provide a means for the redemption of these debts, which are not to be escaped if the community is to develop its revenue of wealth and expand its population.

The Futility of Taxation

Taxation, death duties and the like, as will be obvious if the effect is worked out on the diagram, normally merely transfers ownership from one set of people to another, and only alters the particular individuals who arrive at the consumers' mart with money. Except in the rare event of being levied to provide loans to industry, as, for example, when £M3 of public money was loaned at 3 per cent against the construction of the *Lusitania* and *Mauretania*, it does not by-pass the consumers' mart. On the contrary, by reducing the amount of surplus money in the hands of consumers, it may prevent them from investing it.

The State finds that, for its continued existence, it is vital to lessen the weight of the dead hand of the past, so that its citizens may not be reduced to helots under the burden of debt into which they are born. The canons of an individualistic society, which will not allow it to own revenue-producing enterprises, and have confined its powers of taxation to providing for its expenditure upon services out of which a monetary profit cannot be made, render it impotent. It may slash as savagely as it pleases at the individual capitalist, but supertaxes and death duties merely transfer his property to other individuals. In so far as the debts, unlike the National Debt, represent wealth permanently immobilised in the arteries of the productive system, they defy repudiation and that facile remedy of the statesman, the depreciation of the currency. Taxation on these lines merely transfers the ownership from the original holders to a new set and results in substituting for one aristocratic devil seven plebeian ones.

The State, owning no revenue-producing enterprise, cannot, if the value of money is not to be depreciated, subsidise an industry, endow motherhood, grant pensions to widows, assist universities and hospitals, or grant everyone a National Dividend save directly out of the pockets of the taxpayers in the community. Apart from its Virtual Wealth, its much appealed to credit is simply its power of running into debt. In this it is certainly the superior of any individual or corporation, but merely because it can tax its citizens to provide for the interest. Even the gigantic credit of the State is now, surely, nearly *spent*.

But, without owning the industries or even the banks or the land, the State could, if it controlled the issue of currency and every form of credit in which new money is created, go a long way to putting its house in order, and could strike effectively at monopolies in every form. It could give economic freedom to its citizens in so far as to ensure to everyone the right to earn a living.

We are approaching here certain questions raised by Major Douglas and the school of Social Credit Reformers.[60] It must be said at once that, although there are obvious points of resemblance between many of the points of view set forth in this book and those of the Douglas School, especially as regards the diagnosis of the industrial

---

[60] Compare *Economic Democracy and Credit Power and Democracy*, C. H. Douglas; *The Community's Credit*, C. Marshall Hattersley; *The Flaw in the Price System*, P. W. Martin, and other recent works; and the weekly review, *The New Age*, which is the organ of the movement.

deadlock and the existence of fundamental errors in national as distinct from individual accountancy, the resemblance ends there.

The Agricultural Position of this Country

There is no disagreement between us as to the physical possibility of abolishing poverty and unemployment completely by catering for and engineering, as distinct from financing, a vastly increased scale of living of the masses no less than of the few, and that one of the keys to the problem is in issuing effective demand, i.e. money, in order to distribute for use and consumption the almost indefinitely extensible revenue capable of being produced in a scientific age. In this respect, although agricultural produce is in a different category from manufactured articles and capital, even for the former there seems no good reason to doubt that supply will follow and long keep pace with demand, and that it is only effective demand that is lacking. This is of course not yet true for this country as an isolated community in the present state of agriculture. The most that experts in agricultural economics seem prepared to concede is that the country could supply on an economic basis about one-half the food it consumes. The following extracts from *Food Production in War*, by T. H. Middleton, are germane to this question.

> P. 320, footnote: "One million Calories approximately equals a year's supply of energy for one person; the numerals may therefore be read as persons provided with food."
> P. 322: "The net gain which the country secured from the produce of the 1918 harvest was not less than 4,050,000 million Calories.
> "... The average food supply of the United Kingdom in 1909–1913 provided 49,430,000 million Calories, and the total product of the home soil was 16,872,000 million Calories. The gain in the output of home-grown food in 1918 was therefore about 24 per cent. In other words, whereas the country began the War with supplies provided by its own soil which would have sufficed for 125 days out of the 365, in the year in which the Armistice was signed it had secured a harvest that would have sufficed for 155 days out of the 365. The crops were grown and the stocks fed under conditions that were altogether abnormal; but the land's extra produce was equivalent to the supply of 30 days' food for the nation living its normal life.

> "It should be noted that the extra month's food supply which the 1918 harvest represented falls far short of the total quantity of human food that the 1918 harvest could have furnished if the prolongation of the War had compelled us to stretch our resources to the uttermost. As was stated at the time, if we had reserved for live-stock the pre-War oat crop, but closely milled all other grain and used it for bread, and if we had made the full use of potatoes that a hungry nation might make, we could from our cereals and potatoes have provided a quantity of food equivalent to forty weeks' consumption of bread-stuffs, and by slaughtering our live-stock the additional foods required by the population in this period would have been procurable. But, fortunately for us, no such drastic methods were necessary."
>
> Discussing the question whether this country could feed its entire population, this author concludes that, from the purely agricultural point of view, there would be no special difficulty, meaning that the people were fed by a Food Controller as a farmer feeds his stock; but dismisses the suggestion as absurd if it means a practicable proposition under the existing economic system that the people would consent to and pay for.
>
> "But between the 34 per cent of our food requirements supplied by our land in 1909–1913 and 100 per cent there is a wide margin, and if the vanished hand of the Food Controller could be restored and he compelled us to satisfy from 40 to 50 per cent of our total needs from our own land, it might be no bad thing."

But the peculiar position of this country, in which agriculture, instead of being carefully fostered, has been allowed to decay, must not be taken as settling this question. It is merely the obverse of the opposite situation abroad. In the newer countries we hear of corn and other forms of food, after too abundant harvests, being used as the cheapest fuel, of farmers being ruined by an over-production of crops and stocks, and forced to restrict production severely to maintain an economic livelihood, that the output of rubber similarly is being limited to keep up prices to the level at which it pays the producer to continue production, and so on – all horrible actual practical examples of the fatal effect of a falling price-level in restricting production. The problem, if there is one, is one of exchange, not production. This country must be able to make the equivalent of other kinds of wealth to offer in return to the newer countries where food production is still in excess of consumption.

That is to say, if home production in general were liberated from the stranglehold of finance the whole problem could be solved. At some remote future, if population outruns the improvements of agricultural efficiency by new scientific advances, no doubt a real problem would arise. But that time, at the worst, is still far off.

Analysis of the Douglas Scheme of Social Credit Reform

But as regards concrete proposals to be adopted to bring about the new era and, still more important, as regards the theoretical and physical interpretation of the working of an economic system, the Douglas School is, for the most part, not merely in divergence with but in point-blank contradiction to the conclusions here set forth.

Here the primary mistake, to which the wrecking of the system has been traced, is the passing, with the development of modern banking, of the prerogative of the issue of currency from the nation to private hands for usury as a mode of livelihood, and the fatal dislocation consequent upon money being destroyed when production outruns markets and issued when demand outruns supply. It is claimed that beyond a definite amount of wealth, called the Virtual Wealth, which the owners of money voluntarily abstain from owning – the monetary value of which is measured by the money in circulation and which is a function of the number of the population and their economic prosperity – the "National Credit" is indistinguishable from that of an individual, being simply a power of running into debt and paying interest out of the taxes. Salvation, if society is to remain individualistic, must come by enforcing initial *genuine* abstinence from individuals equal to the growth of the cost-value of the whole industrial mechanism as it is expanded, less only the relatively trivial part represented by the increase of Virtual Wealth as measured by the total money circulating.

The Douglas School appear to look for salvation in the precisely opposite direction. They look to the National Credit as a means of distributing new purchasing power, and, so far from recognising the necessity of any initial abstinence, even go so far as to stipulate that these national issues shall be new money and *not* out of past savings. They claim that since only a small part of the costs of industry are distributed as payments to consumers, goods must be sold below cost price to make up the difference. Or, alternatively, National Dividends should be paid out of the National Credit to everyone irrespective of their participation in production – much as the subsidies are now paid, but out of taxation, to the unemployed. Basing their stand on the undeniable proposition that industry exists to produce goods in the largest possible quantity and in the most expeditious and efficient manner rather than to make work for unnecessary and often highly inefficient and unwilling workers, and that industry could, if allowed, produce more than sufficient for everyone, they set their face against taxation and, in general, the limitation of large incomes to provide for those in need as entirely unnecessary and politically, if not ethically, mistaken.

They look to the State to dispense money rather than to take it away. They appear vaguely to contemplate so bringing about a state of things in which wealth was restored to its proper importance in the economic life, for the use and maintenance of life, rather than, in Ruskin's phrase, the "power over the lives and labours of others." Everyone having their physical wants abundantly supplied, the wealthy could neither consume so much as to cause any inconvenience to the rest nor could they unduly increase their consumption by employing a retinue of hired personal servants and attendants to minister to their wants, since no one would be compelled by reason of actual economic want to work for them. If they needed servants they would have to pay them liberally and treat them properly. Similarly in industry there would be no need of economic compulsion to get the work done. Machinery and growing intelligence would make of industry a profession, sought by those desiring to devote themselves to its service and shunned by the degraded and servile, who even now do more harm than good.

This will probably be recognised as a not unsympathetic, if imperfect, exposition of the principles and aspirations of this very interesting new school of economic thought. Much more will be heard of it. It possesses vision and may one day become a real driving force in politics. It has already brought back into being some of the original passion and enthusiasm of the earlier reformers, before the sterilising and paralysing influence of mercantile economics side-tracked the leaders of the progressive movement into devious paths and insincere denunciation "about it and about," the while their followers "evermore came out by the same door wherein they went."

Those who agree with the essential conclusions arrived at in this book will find no compromise possible on certain fundamental principles relating to the physical nature of money, credit and capital. Beyond this the school neglecting altogether the facts of the existing ownership of wealth, do not honestly face the real obstacles to its more abundant distribution. Further, the view that all the costs of production are not distributed already, as payments for services real or imaginary, as well as recovered from the consumer, seems of the nature of a misunderstanding. In the same category is the argument that because all wealth produced is not distributed to, but is paid for by, the consumer, it is physically possible to make up the deficit out of the national credit. The Douglas scheme seems somewhat prematurely to assume the existence of a communal rather than an individualistic State, in which there are no debts, no rights of property and no private ownership of capital, and in which all the existing paraphernalia of wealth production is to be regarded in all singlemindedness as having been accumulated with the primary object of production rather than with that of being hired out for production. This work is, by contrast, confined to less ambitious themes, and may be regarded as an attempt to find out the best that the individualistic state of society can offer if it were intelligently administered.

The Risk of Discrediting the New Economics

These relatively mild and practical proposals will not satisfy an extreme "New Economist." He will say with force: You admit the continuous displacement of human labour by machinery and every form of labour-saving device, which, if it has not yet gone so far in agriculture as in engineering trades, has for that reason the further yet to go. You admit, therefore, that with increasing potential production the titles to consume will find their way into fewer and fewer hands. How do you propose to meet this fundamental difficulty, or how does what you have proposed meet it?

The only answer that can be made to this is that the situation ultimately anticipated is still very far from having arisen, and that if we do not understand how the existing system works and wherein it fails we are likely to make it worse rather than better. Those who desire the immediate payment to everyone of a National Dividend – and women especially are attracted by this form of the Douglas scheme as a way of escape from the position of economic dependence upon the other sex – should face frankly the question where it is to come from and who is to give it up.

For even science cannot create wealth with the same facility as it is possible to create debts. Taxation is one source; unlimited credit, or running into debt indefinitely, is another; depreciating the value of the currency progressively, a third; while expropriation, the public ownership of all sources of revenue and the abolition of private property altogether, with common ownership of the national revenue, are others; and all of them have their avowed or secret advocates. But the idea that the nation is in possession of a mysterious talisman called credit which, when industry is unable to pay for the initiation of fresh production, can supply it with all that is needed without anyone giving up anything at all, and that this national credit consists of the accumulated result of all the past centuries of past effort, when the whole trouble is that these accumulations are owned by private individuals, is to push the confusion between debt and wealth to lengths that would have surprised even the author of *The Theory of Credit*.

On the other hand, even for modern science, the cleaning of the Augean stable of an industrialised nation is no light task. There would be very few, for a long time to come, unable to find in useful occupations the titles to consume if the nation seriously set itself to the task. There are millions requiring a largely increased supply of necessaries and ordinary commodities – not to mention the capital accumulations in increased stocks. We need also houses to live in, whole cities of slums must be rebuilt and poverty-stricken areas must be resuscitated, railways modernised and roads made, super-power stations created at the coal-fields to distribute to every corner of the country electric power, and there are increasing demands to be met for higher education, both of the young and the adult, and universities will have to be built to provide for the growing army of seekers after knowledge. All these projects involve production far in excess of consumption – hard work and abstinence for everybody. It would indeed be a matter for astonishment if, for a long time to come, in this country there were any prospect of dispensing with the services of any useful and willing member of the community. By then at least, if the suggestions made in this book were adopted, the nation would be already in possession of a large part of its capital by the process of redemption to be outlined, and could begin to consider seriously the question of a National Dividend. As things are at present that would be both premature and impracticable, and its colossal failure by discrediting the new economics would set back progress for a generation.

At the same time it is not necessary to follow the mistakes of the orthodox economists due to their ignorance of the modern science of production and their devotion to doctrines which, however applicable in the time of Adam Smith and Ricardo are to-day, with the growth of physical and biological science, very considerably out of date. Even in agriculture it is not possible to look at the problem solely "with the eye of the farmer." There is such a thing as "Power-Farming," a theme on which Mr. Henry Ford waxes eloquent in his book, *My Life and Work* (Heinemann, 1923). Mr. Ford, looking at agriculture with the eye of the engineer, concludes: "We shall have as great a development in farming during the next twenty years as we have had in manufacturing during the last twenty." Even in this country the change that has come over the subject is already very marked.

CHAPTER XIII

CAPITAL REDEMPTION

The Production of Capital involves Less Consumption

Those who agree with the physical as distinct from the metaphysical conception of the nature of wealth will need to spend little time on proposals to make up to the consumer, by means of consumers' credits, the part of the price or cost of the goods in the consumers' mart due to the accumulation of capital goods which are not distributed to the consumer. If people devote their time and energy to producing capital goods, there may be questions to solve as to the rightful owner of the capital goods accumulated, but there can be none whatever about there being less goods of a consumable character to be consumed. The proposal to reduce prices below cost by means of consumers' credits is, physically, like trying to liquefy the mains of a water-supply system to provide more water to the consumers – why pay for the laying of the mains as well as for the water, but to whom none of the mains are delivered with the water.

In an individualistic community the community owns little or nothing of a wealth-producing nature. In a community in which the production of wealth was socialised and the community owned the organs of production and the wealth produced from start to finish of manufacture, national dividends and consumers' credits would be a practical proposition. But as things are at present they merely would mean an increase in the National Debt, only reducible by further taxation covering not only the principal but also the interest.

On the other hand, if we socialise or nationalise production, the difficulty is not solved, as it is impossible to socialise consumption, which is essentially an individual affair. Money or some alternative device would still be necessary to distribute the product and to accord among individuals the title of ownership of the goods produced. Without an equitable and rational monetary system the millennium would be just as far off under Socialism as ever. We have, therefore, first to inquire whether the monetary system here proposed would operate justly in this question of the effect on the value of real wages of the diversion of part of the efforts of the community from the production of consumable goods to that of capital.

The Effect on Real Wages

We may contrast two modes of working the system. It may be worked so as to maintain its capital organs of production in full use in accordance with its needs but without increasing them. Then the quantity of consumable goods distributed is the maximum possible than can be permanently maintained, and the average scale of living is the maximum possible. Or we may suppose that the same system is worked to devote a large part of its whole effort, not to the production of things that can be consumed in actual living, but of those which can only be of use in the productive mechanism itself. The quantity of goods in the consumers' mart is then less than before and the average scale of living is proportionately reduced. Since Labour under an individualistic system is powerless to choose between the kind of work that yields the wealth it needs for consumption and that which does not, it is necessary to be satisfied that, under the system proposed, the real value of its wages is not affected by this consideration. Under the present system, in which prices rise before wages and can only be reduced by reducing wages, it clearly is. The future abundance of wealth will depend much upon whether fresh capital is being accumulated or not, and we have already examined the laws regulating these matters and the point at which further capital accumulation reduces rather than increases the average gentility of the community. But no one can possibly now maintain that it depends much on the ownership of the capital accumulated. The efficiency of an enterprise is not dependent on the names of its shareholders. If capital is being produced for export in exchange for consumables, the case is the same as if consumables were being produced at home. If they are exported for nothing immediate in return, that is exchanged for claims on the future wealth of other countries receiving them, of the nature of interest payments, the effort in producing them contributes nothing to the country's distributable wealth nor to its future power of producing wealth. But they form a fund realisable, as in time of war, to liquidate debts incurred by importation of goods.

If this question is examined thoroughly, it will be found that the real wages of labour are unaffected if prices are maintained constant. In brief, fictitious loans being ruled out, capital can only be accumulated by genuine abstinence on the part of individuals entitled to consume. Their decision to produce capital goods instead of consumables is at the expense of their own consumption and not at the expense of the community in general. The injustice, if there is one, is of another kind, if the choice rests entirely with individuals with money to invest.

The Depreciation of Capital and the Shifting of the Burden on to the Public

It is often argued that the capitalist is not such a fool as to invest money in capital beyond the extent to which it can be used and produce a revenue. The fact is that if he has more money than he wishes to spend he must do so, and his decision whether to spend or "save" is more dictated by his own circumstances than by the consideration whether more capital is required by the nation or not. If there is more than enough, though the rate of interest may be temporarily lowered, the price of goods is not necessarily lowered. If there is twice as much capital as is necessary, the consumer might be far better off by paying a higher rate for the use of half the amount than a lower rate for the use of all at half its proper capacity. But competition is a passing phase, and is more and more replaced by combination keeping up the rate of interest. An excess of capital unwanted in peace production, in time of war would find an outlet for its unused capacity. So arises the incentive towards militarism and aggression in international politics, in order to secure markets, or alternatively, as serving the same object, to fight about them.

The interests of property are among the most powerful of all political forces, and, faced with loss, the owners of property will move heaven and earth to invent a means to shift the burden upon the shoulders of the public. The era of competition gives rise to one of combination, to be followed in ripe old age by nationalisation.

Inevitably with the lapse of time and growth of scientific knowledge capital depreciates and gets out of date. If the amount sunk in it is large enough to form a powerful political interest, the burden is more and more shifted to the community. By political action an old and inefficient means of conducting an industry or service may be prolonged long after it should be, because of the great loss that would otherwise fall upon those who have invested their money in the capital. So that it is altogether too naïve a view of the real world to regard the investor as acting on his own risk and entirely bearing the loss when the capital accumulated is too much or is rendered obsolete by scientific progress. It is necessary here to substitute for the false idea of the spontaneous increment of capital the true one of its continuous decrement, and to provide a method for the continuous redemption of capital out of revenue.

The Origin of Interest on Capital

Some of the considerations dealt with in this chapter are germane to the perennial question of the origin of interest, meaning the hire-payment for the use of organs of production in production rather than monetary interest, much of which arises merely by the artificial restriction of the medium of exchange. The conventional theory that it is a reward of abstinence need not long detain us. A man who abstains from consumption might reasonably expect to be able to consume what he has abstained from consuming, but there is no *à priori* reason why he should expect so to be able to consume more. With very few exceptions – that of vintage wines may be admitted – wealth, as is well known, depreciates with keeping. Interest is not the real inducement to save so much as the oncoming of old age and the necessity of providing for dependents, in the first instance, leading later to the special needs of a hereditary leisured class and its obvious inability to survive as a class, with continuous genealogy, without some such convenient institution. One may logically subscribe to the doctrine of the necessity of the existence of a leisured class in troubled times to keep alive the torch of culture and learning. As times become less troubled the desire to make its survival less of an anomaly may even act to keep alive all sorts of civil, religious, and racial antipathies better decently buried. But to pretend to look forward to the day when the whole world will constitute itself such a leisured class and live for ever after upon interest is to betray the elementary ignorance of the laws of nature which it was originally the professed *raison d'être* of the leisured class to correct.

Inevitability of Interest in an Individualistic Community

On the view of the nature of wealth here expounded there is no mystery whatever about the origin of interest upon capital in private ownership. History tells us that capital has always been able to exact interest payment for its use, and it is important to know whether, like gravitation, it is an inevitable phenomenon, or whether, with the growth of a true science of national economics, it would disappear, like the interest on money in so far as it may be due to an artificial shortage and monopoly of the medium of exchange. The answer is that, in an individualistic society, interest upon privately owned capital is inevitable; because, powerful and little in need of incitement by the reward of abstinence as the human passion to acquire and save is, the very last thing any individual would devote his savings to would be the organs of production, other than those he required himself, if there were no interest payment for their use. Capital we have put in the second category as one of the forms of permanent wealth – Wealth II as it was styled – and it is already in certain respects fully consumed. The energy employed in producing it has already run to waste, and, unavoidable and necessary as its use is for production, itself it is good neither to eat nor to possess, nor can it be transformed into other varieties of wealth. So that if the initial expenditure incurred in making and accumulating it is not recouped in the form of interest, as a hire-charge for its use, it cannot be recouped at all. The debt charge created by its production cannot be repaid apart from some such physical miracle as the conversion of a plough into bread. It is one of the major difficulties of the subject that there seems no obvious method of equating the sum-total of hours of past labour, expended on its production, against the expenditure of present effort necessary to make it productive. In other words, there is no simple ethical principle to which to appeal to determine the just rate of interest. In practice the rate of interest, like the price of an article, is fixed by "what it will fetch," and in these matters ignorance and misconception play as large a part as purely physical considerations.

But it is interesting to note in passing the banker's attitude towards a sum of money in terms of that of the rate of interest, as set forth by MacLeod, though it is a point of view with purely mathematical rather than physical justification. Assuming a continuous growth of money with the lapse of time, the capital sum may be regarded as the sum total of all future interest payments over an infinity of time, discounted to their present-day value. But this is necessarily true *whatever the rate of interest may be,* and therefore the view is of no help in our present quest.[61]

The Scientific Argument against the Unregulated Continuous Private Ownership of Capital

On the energetic view of wealth, the argument against the unregulated continuous private ownership of the organs of production, save such as are worked by the owners themselves, is in practice as great as against permitting "the uninterrupted powers of usury." It enables the individual member of the community and the heirs to do what is a physical impossibility for the community as a whole to do, namely, to live indefinitely upon the fruits of a definite amount of effort by a process of permanent economic servitude of other individuals. This book holds no brief either for individualism or socialism, and is concerned merely to find the chief cause of modern unrest and the simplest methods of correcting and removing them. Next to an honest monetary system, the need for the continuous redemption of revenue-producing capital out of income appears to be the most important step towards reform. The State also should exercise a general control over the question as to the due balance to be preserved between the production of goods for use and consumption and the accumulation of fresh capital, as it did during the War.

The Deeper Futilities of Individualistic Economics

These, it is to be feared to the general reader, painfully minute inquiries will have been well spent if they serve to tear the veil from the deeper futilities of the individualistic system of economics that have hitherto prevented any general material progress towards economic freedom. Not only is it true of money, but it is equally true of capital

[61] In mathematical symbols, MacLeod's theory is $C = \int_{t=0}^{t=\infty} iC\,\varepsilon^{-it}\,.\,dt$ where *C* is the capital and *i* the fractional rate of interest per annum. Then *i C. dt* is the interest accruing in the element of time *dt* (years). The present value of the element that accrues at the future time *t* years is *i C.* s^{-it}. *dt,* and the capital is the sum of the present values of all such elements from now to infinity.

that it is communal indebtedness as much as individual wealth, implying as much poverty on the one side as riches on the other. That is not the case for wealth in the sense of the actual consumable and perishable goods which nourish and maintain life. But whereas in the case of money, rightly understood, the debt never need be repaid and is wholly beneficial to everyone concerned, the debt in the case of capital, however much is paid, never can be repaid, and, in a world employing ever more and more capital per worker, has to be regarded as a growing burden upon the propertyless. If this sort of civilisation is to continue to function at all, the purposes for which taxation is levied must be radically extended and used no longer solely for the purpose of defraying current Government expenditure, but also for fostering and building up industry and for the redemption of capital indebtedness.

The State must begin to exert, as the trustees of the propertyless, the same foresight and acumen as the individual does for himself. Whereas the present sudden passion for the nationalisation of industries, like the railways and coal-mines, in the most unexpected quarters, is suggestive of the desire to saddle the community with what are no longer financially lucrative propositions.

A Scheme of Compound Capital Redemption

The following practical suggestion is designed to meet the situation as an alternative to the nationalisation of industries *en bloc*, the financing of which means merely addition to the National Debt. The income-tax levied on unearned incomes should be earmarked as a tax for the redemption of capital and its purchase by the community, and not as a source of revenue out of which to defray the costs of government. It can be readily calculated that if an unearned income-tax of 4s. in the £ were used to purchase the capital, and the interest accruing from previous purchases were devoted to the same purpose, the whole of the capital would be so purchased and pass to the ownership of the community in a period of time twice that required for the interest payments to equal the capital – that is to say, in forty years for a security paying 5 per cent, in fifty years for one paying 4 per cent, and so on.

Under such a scheme the taxpayer could be given the option of an income-tax-free security terminating at the appropriate period, or of paying income-tax upon it from year to year as now. In the latter event the Government brokers would purchase the equivalent of similar securities in the open market. In the former event, although no change would be called for so far as the shareholder was concerned until the security terminated, naturally the part ownership of the State in the concern would be recognised by representation upon the governing body of shareholders.

This case may be termed "compound redemption," where the interest upon past purchases as well as present taxation is employed in the redemption.

Simple Redemption

It is obvious that this method could be applied only to revenue producing securities. In the case of simple debt, like the National Debt, the interest is itself derived from taxation, and it would probably be too much to expect the public to go on providing it after the debt had been redeemed. In this case what may be termed simple redemption would apply, in which only the taxation is available for redemption, and the debts as acquired would be destroyed. It can be calculated that for one-half of the debt to be redeemed about seventy years would be necessary, and the times for other proportions are given in the Appendix in tabular form below.

Naturally here, as the debt diminishes, the rate of redemption diminishes in like ratio, whereas in the case of compound redemption the rate of redemption increases as redemption is effected. This brings out vividly and in quantitative fashion the advantages of compound over simple redemption, and the precise measure of the disservice to the State done by an economics founded on the interests of a leisured class, denying to the State the right of productive ownership.

The sole change involved in these proposals is the ear-marking of tax on unearned income for capital redemption and the provision of the expenses of government from other sources. What these would be have already been indicated.

A reasonably honest national money system would, as shown, already effect a large direct saving to the taxpayer, and the greatly enhanced national prosperity that would result from selling goods as well as being able to produce them would make the task of a future Chancellor of the Exchequer comparatively easy.

If this were practical, a not unimportant advantage would arise from the steady market produced for all securities by the continuous redemption annually of 1 or more per cent of the total. Investors would invest their savings far more cheerfully if their securities could be sold without risk of unnecessary loss through the limited nature of the market they command and with something of the readiness of a Postal Order or a War Savings Certificate. The Government would be always buying, and if the market value of the stock appreciated so would the value of the publicly owned part appreciate. The system appears to realise the widely felt necessity of making the payment of interest, like the span of human life, terminable rather than perpetual. This occurs after the return of twice the principal, free of tax, on all classes of productive security, about one-fourth of the redemption being effected by taxation and three-fourths by purchase out of the interest of the part already redeemed (or alternatively by interest on deferred taxation), with a tax of 4s. in the £.

In an Appendix the mathematics of these processes and some tables in connection with them have been worked out.

MATHEMATICAL APPENDIX

MATHEMATICAL PRESENTATION OF COMPOUND REDEMPTION.

If i is the fractional rate of interest per annum, p the proportion taken by taxation, and G is the fraction acquired by the Government at any time t (years) from the start, we have

$$dG/dt = ip\,(1 - G) + iG$$

in which the first term represents the redemption by present taxation, and the second that by the interest on the capital already redeemed. The solution of this is

$$t = \frac{1}{i(1-p)} \log_{?} \left\{ 1 + G\left(\frac{1}{p} - 1\right) \right\} \text{ or } G = \frac{p}{1-p}\left(\varepsilon^{it(1-p)} - 1\right)$$

$1/i$ is the period of years in which the investment returns the principal as interest, and may be replaced by the symbol P. If the tax is 4s. in the £, $p = 0{\cdot}2$, and the expression becomes

$$t = 2.875P\,\{\log_{10}(1+4G)\}$$

So that if G is 1, $t = 2{\cdot}0125\,P$, or for a 5 per cent investment, 40·25 years. In the following table the time for a variety of values of G are given:

G	0·1	0·2	0·3	0·4	0·5	0·6	0·7	0·8	0·9	1·0
t/P	0·42	0·725	0·98	1·19	1·37	1·53	1·66	1·8	1·91	2·0125
t	8·4	14·5	19·6	23·8	27·4	30·5	33·2	35	38·2	4·25 years

The figures in the last column refer to a 5 per cent security, with income-tax at 4s. in the £.

For the case of complete redemption ($G = 1$) the expression is

$$\frac{t}{P} = \frac{1}{1-p} \log_{?} \left(\frac{1}{p}\right)$$

and in the following table is given the time of complete redemption for various rates of taxation, in terms of the period *P*. This represents also the total return to the investor of the tax-free terminable investment in terms of the original principal.

Tax	6s.	5s.	4s.	3s.	2s.	1s. in the £
t/P	1·73	1·84	2·01	2·23	2·25	3·29

It is of interest also to deduce the expressions showing the proportions redeemed respectively out of taxation and out of the interest upon the part already redeemed. We will denote by G_r the first, and by G_1, the second, i.e. $G = G_r + G_1$.

We then have

$$\frac{dG_r}{dt} = ip\left(1 - G\right) \text{ and } \frac{dG_1}{dt} = iG$$

Putting in the value previously found for *G* and integrating gives

$$G_2 = \frac{p}{1-p}\left[\frac{p}{1-p}\left(1 - \varepsilon^{it(1-p)}\right) + it\right]$$

$$G_1 = \frac{p}{1-p}\left[\frac{1}{1-p}\left(\varepsilon^{it(1-p)} - 1\right) - it\right]$$

For the particular case, where the whole of the capital is redeemed, i.e. $G = 1$, denoting by *T* and *I* the parts in this case redeemed by taxation and interest respectively, we get

$$T = \frac{1}{1-p}\left[\left(\frac{p}{1-p}\log_{?}\frac{1}{p}\right) - p\right]$$

$$I = \frac{1}{1-p}\left[1 - \left(\frac{p}{1-p}\log_{?}\frac{1}{p}\right)\right]$$

If *p* is given the value 0·2 (4s. in the £), we get for *T* 0·254 and for *I* 0·746, i.e. for this case, about one-fourth is redeemed by taxation and three-fourths by interest payments on the part already redeemed. The values for other rates of taxation are given in the table:

Tax	6s.	5s.	4s.	3s.	2s.	1s. in the £
I	0·69	0·72	0·746	0·735	0·827	0·89
T	0·31	0·28	0·254	0·215	0·173	0·11

MATHEMATICAL PRESENTATION OF SIMPLE REDEMPTION

Here $dG/dt = ip(1 - G)$ and $t = -\{1/(ip)\}log_e(1 - G)$

If $i = 0.05$ and $p = 0.2$, $t = -230log_{10}(1 - G)$

With these values of *i* and *p* we obtain:

G	0·1	0·2	0·3	0·4	0·5	0·6	0·7	0·8	0·9	0·99
t	10·5	22·2	35·7	51	69·5	92	121	161	230	460 years

CHAPTER XIV

INTERNATIONAL RELATIONS

The Elements of Foreign Trade

It is now generally understood and admitted, as a result of the War, that the position into which this country has drifted is becoming increasingly precarious in its excessive dependence upon foreign trade for the maintenance of its food supply. It seems inevitable that, as the world fills up and new countries develop, they will more and more tend to consume the food and raw materials which they produce and more and more make their own factory products. So that from a double cause our present mode of living, in which we have allowed agriculture in this country to decay and concentrated upon the manufacture of articles which are becoming increasingly difficult to sell abroad, cannot indefinitely continue. Apart, however, from the danger of war, the problem is not a pressing one.

This question bulks so largely in the minds of many people that they almost refuse, with unconscious naïvety, to consider the question of internal reform at all. They seem to ascribe to the irrational and haphazard system some mysterious and unspecified advantage for the conduct of foreign trade which would be jeopardised by the nationalisation of money and the stabilisation of the currency. But unless these are going to make foreign trade and the exchange of manufacture for food more haphazard and difficult than at present, there is no case against internal reform. One does not in real life refuse to consider a cure for a disease because it is not a universal panacea.

Most people are beginning to realise, also as the result of the experience of the War, that foreign trade, like reparations, is not really a question of money at all.

Foreign trade being essentially barter, money appears in all its nakedness as a simple acknowledgment of the debt of the community issuing it, repayable on demand in wealth only within that realm and quite unobscured by the principle of virtual wealth which gives it such importance in its own country. A foreigner may want a supply of our money for use *here*, just as we may want a supply of his to use *there*, but a supply of our money there or of his money here is merely the acknowledgment of a debt payable on demand in wealth, but in a distant place and realm, of no practical advantage to anyone. It is idle to send a supply of money abroad to pay for goods.

It all has to come back again before it is of use as purchasing power. A small, but not uninstructive, illustration of the principle is when a foreign correspondent encloses a stamped envelope for a reply!

corn — tractors — platinum

BRITAIN ←—— AUSTRALIA ←—— U.S.A. ←—— RUSSIA

↓ ——————— herrings ——————— ↑

The Trade Balance

The bulk of foreign trade is really carried on by the buyers and sellers in each country separately settling amongst themselves, leaving only any outstanding balance to be settled. Such trade balances are conveniently discharged by shipping gold from one country to the other. Thus a British buyer of foreign goods pays his account not directly to the foreign seller, but to the British seller of goods to foreign buyers, through suitable agents that carry on this class of business. The same is true of other countries, and the technical details need not further detain us. By suitable international agencies it is similarly arranged that the outstanding balances need not be settled as between one country and another, but only as between each and the rest of the world put together. Thus, if we want corn from Australia, Australia tractors from the United States, the United States platinum from Russia, and Russia herrings from us, equal values of each may be and are bartered without any need for money at all.

It is not, therefore, the balance of trade between two countries that has to be maintained, but the balance as between any one country and the whole of the rest of the world together.

These are the realities of foreign trade, and the part played by money in it is apparent rather than real. If, as in all countries having international currencies on a gold basis, gold is given a fixed exchangeability in terms of money, the relative values of the currencies cannot vary very much with time, i.e. the foreign exchanges of these countries are stable. If gold were not sent to correct the trade balance, the exchanges would vary over wide limits, because, then, the goods entering pay for the goods leaving, whatever the relative proportion may be. If imports exceed exports the exchange goes against the country, until further importation into it is unprofitable both for the home importer from and the foreign exporter to the country with the relatively depreciated currency.

The International Aspect of Wealth and Debt

The function of gold in maintaining automatically, by its inflow and outflow, the value of money in terms of gold constant and preserving stability of the foreign exchanges among all the countries on a gold basis, without any other automatic regulation of the quantity of money in circulation, has already been fully dealt with. It does so correct the balance of foreign trade, but if currency were stabilised upon index number, the function of gold in foreign trade would be reduced to that of simple barter and could be open to no objection whatever. Even now, the foreign trader using gold for international payments, uses it simply as a commodity, and is quite innocent of any responsibility for the complex and often disastrous chain of consequences it entails in the business world by "concertina-ing" credit. The statesman shifts his responsibility for the currency on to the banker, and the banker in turn shifts the odium for his errors on to the importer.

The proverb of the devil among the tailors often suggests the true origin of many controversies, and this applies to one aspect at least not only of modern international conflicts for markets, but also of the internal Free Trade *versus* Protection controversies in all countries. It is easy to see that, when the export of gold is used as a means, not only of settling trade balances, but also as a means for contracting credit and checking "the rise of prices that makes the business world so happy," it must appear that the interests of export trade and import trade are diametrically opposed. The one is used to damage the other. But a moment's reflection on the theme that foreign trade is barter and that the best way to increase exports is to increase imports and vice versa, ought to suggest that the interests of both importers and exporters are identical.

The Fundamental Nature of the Problem

However, these questions really raise fundamental and, at present, almost entirely insoluble issues. We are brought up by them to ask whether men live to work or work to live. Canada produces a superabundance of food-stuffs. The shoe industry claims it could shoe Great Britain for the year by a few days' work at our factories. What more natural than to suggest an exchange of footwear for food? In practice we find the Canadian boot industries pressing for a tariff to preserve their home market from our imports, just as our farmers seek protection from foreign corn. If we contemplate free and unrestricted barter between the countries it is the Canadian farmer who would get the boots and our bootmakers the wheat, but the Canadian bootmaker and the British farmer would not benefit, in so far as there is a real plethora of both wheat and boot-producing capacity. Whereas what each and all need, in that case, is leisure, to work less whilst consuming more, and to devote an increasing part of their lives to other pursuits than the earning of a livelihood and the amassing of "wealth." There is, in the end, no other solution to the problems raised by the fecundity of science. The increasing number of people, who now actually do contribute little or nothing that is essential to the production of wealth and derive their claims to participate from permission to allow it to proceed rather from any positive contribution, that could not be better provided without them, as well as, at the other end of the scale, the increasing number who derive a pittance from the public purse, all tell the same story of the prodigal abundance that cannot be disguised even by all the waste and senseless conflicts that attend the present system.

When one contemplates a country like the United States, which it has been computed could easily supply almost the entire wants of the whole world without over-exerting herself, a country which has few real wants which it could not as well supply within its own territory, and therefore with little use for imports, but an almost infinite capacity for exports, the problem looks frankly insoluble.

Edged Tools

For it must be remembered, in international as in national economics, capital debts are not really repayable, and imply "power over the lives and labours" of other countries, though, no doubt, the object is no more sinister than for the case of home "saving." Export trade, when a nation has no equivalent wants to be supplied by imports, is for "invisible imports" in the way of interest upon capital debts, and may be, and usually is, fostered by lending the debtor nation the money to pay, which means forgoing payment in return for continued future interest payments. Thus, for a time, the home industries are "protected" against competition from imports, but one trembles to think of what the day of reckoning will really mean as between great and powerful nations, one anxious to repay and the other unable to allow repayment.

The phrase *caveat emptor* has a singularly sinister international application. "Let the buyer beware" of importing upon credit and insist that imports shall be balanced by exports, or run the risk of bartering an inheritance for a mess of pottage.

This country during the earlier part of last century exported far more than it imported, and acquired large holdings in foreign investments, which yielded an annual revenue, enabling it, towards the end of the century, to receive far more than it exported, without an adverse trade-balance. The War reduced very much these holdings abroad, and the trade-balance for 1925 has been estimated to be only £M28 in our favour, after allowing for the income of our remaining foreign investments. In the century preceding the War our exports, which at first were nearly double the value of our imports, increased only twice, whereas the imports increased seven times. But both have been dwarfed into relative insignificance by the swollen figures of national expenditure since the War.

Mr. Withers,[62] quoting an address by Mr. McKenna in October 1922, who said:

> "For over two centuries British capital has been lent to other countries. Year by year England produced more than she either consumed herself or could exchange for the products of other nations, and she could not obtain a market for the surplus unless she gave the purchaser a long credit. Foreign loans and foreign issues of all kinds were taken up in England, and the proceeds were spent in paying for the surplus production" – proceeds to argue that the payment of reparations from Germany should be sought in the same way.

---

[62] *Bankers and Credit*, Hartley Withers, 1924.

> "Germany, gifted with great natural resources and with unrivalled powers of work and applications, [ought] to produce a very considerable exportable surplus if she made the necessary effort and the necessary diversion of her productive power."

By "peaceful penetration" in Italy, Mexico, Brazil and other places where she is apt to be regarded as a menace to our trade and financial supremacy, she could, it is suggested, acquire investments and hand them over to her creditors. Surely, most people will agree that this is playing with edged tools, and that it is hardly worth while sowing the seeds of a new war to pay for the last one, and to depress our own industries by doing so.

Economic Freedom VERSUS Servitude

So in the international field no less than in our internal affairs we have to make up our minds whether it is wealth or debt that we really desire, whether to use the otherwise embarrassing riches of the age to promote economic freedom or servitude among nations as well as among individuals. International rivalries and antagonisms would be more intelligible if there were any longer a real economic, as distinct from chrematistic, foundation for them. In times when population was always tending to outrun food supply, before the effective occupation of the whole world, together with intensive modes of cultivation, had reduced the law of diminishing returns in agriculture to its proper local significance, growing nations were for ever being faced with the alternative of war or starvation. But now it is all the other way. The struggle is not for wealth, but to dispose of it advantageously to its owners, to convert present wealth into a claim upon future wealth, to sell it if possible, but, if not, to lend it so as to be able to derive from the debtor a permanent tribute of interest in the future. Old wars of conquest were often for similar ends, but universal conscription and the militarisation of whole nations, as a consequence of their being able to produce more wealth than they can consume, exchange, or even lend, is quite a new and curious phenomenon in history.

The struggle is only nominally between nations, and, by the survival of deep-seated herd-instinct, is directed along these traditional channels. It is, in reality, between the debtors and creditors of all nations in common, and no solution whether of social or international conflict is possible until debts are made terminable and a proportion of the interest payments upon them devoted as a sinking fund to their redemption. That it is entirely within the jurisdiction of each nation to determine for itself, for its own nationals and for its foreign investors alike, and, if there is no preferential discrimination against the foreigner, no just cause of international quarrel could thereby arise. The property of a private citizen or corporation, invested in a foreign country, is amenable to the laws of that country as regards taxation.

But international debts, of the kind which the War has left in its wake, are a far more serious menace to the peace of the world. They are not repayable, except by injuring the debtor class of the creditor nation, its workers, its industries and its trade, and they are not transferable among individuals as are private indebtednesses.

They are like stale waters, conserved during drought, after the rains have come and the rivers have resumed their normal flow, as unhealthy as they are unnecessary.

The Practical Problem

To come back to practical affairs from these general reflections, since no nation is justified in interfering with the internal affairs of others, it is only possible to consider the problem of foreign trade as it concerns any single nation. Whilst recognising that it is a part of a wider debtor-creditor problem, it is, so far as concerns the private investor at least, not different in this to the internal problem. The investor to the extent of his holdings in a foreign country is, in effect, a citizen of that country, and would be subject to the same provisions if such were made, for the redemption of capital, as the nationals of that country.

It is certain that in an individualistic society, as in a communal one, it is idle to produce or to try to produce things that are not in demand. In an individualistic society the onus is on those who, by reason of changing conditions, are no longer capable of earning a livelihood by their former occupation, to change their occupation. In Chapter III it was pointed out that this was, under modern conditions, a far less serious change than formerly, provided always that a sufficiency of other profitable employment for all the workers is secured. It may be necessary to recognise exceptional cases and tide over periods of too rapid readjustments, but, in general, we cannot escape the conclusion that exchange between nations should be free and unrestricted, and that it is desirable that each country should specialise in providing the classes of goods best suited to its natural resources and aptitudes.

By stabilising the currency upon index number we do not fix any particular prices, but only the general average, so that if some goods are in greater or lesser demand than others their price will rise or fall *relatively* to the others until the tendency is checked by increased or decreased supply, exactly as now, except that gold would be no longer an exception to this rule. No gold whatever need be used for internal currency, but it would still find, as a commodity, precisely the same use as now for correcting foreign trade balances.

The Function of Gold

Each country receives from abroad goods of the same value as it sends abroad. It is of the nature of the case that these must balance over long enough periods, except in so far as the debts may be converted into long-period investments not repayable on demand. The difference over short periods, the so-called favourable or unfavourable trade-balance, can never be large, and gold as a commodity serves excellently to redress such differences. All countries, even those not on a gold basis, will readily accept gold as a convenient and satisfactory form of temporary payment. If gold were demonetised and reduced to the rank of a simple commodity, the available stock of it in a country would furnish a precise indication of its trade-balance.

It is widely recognised that the present anomalous position of gold is a menace to international relationships. America has by the War secured the greater part of the world's supply, and if it were let out into circulation again it would play havoc with the existing monetary systems. On the other hand it could be honoured for international currency as now, but on a commodity basis, and be used to stabilise the exchanges in so far as temporary violent fluctuations are concerned, leaving them to find their own level gradually according to the monetary standards and currency systems adopted in the various countries.

Since there is every reason to anticipate that gold will, from now on, steadily depreciate in value in any case, the more rapidly the less use of it is made for currency and the more quickly and widely it is demonetised, and since all nations have been hoarding it or trying to do so under the mistaken impression that they were thereby "saving," it would seem to be a suitable case for the League of Nations to come to some equitable and friendly convention as to the future disposal of it.

They might agree upon the ratio in which the stocks should normally be held in the future in various countries as a national reserve for stabilising the exchanges and avoiding unnecessary and harmful fluctuations. But it is to be hoped they will not hand over the destinies of the world to the care of three or four of the most powerful banks to decide what it pleases them best is to be done from time to time, and institute a fraudulent gold standard, the value of the metal being just what those interested please to make it by arranging how much or how little of it is to be let out for currency. It is one thing for a nation to consent to play its due part in finding some use for and preventing too rapid depreciation of redundant gold and to take upon its shoulders the risk of loss by consenting to maintain for a time a limited quantity as a special reserve. But it is quite another question to perpetuate the stranglehold which a few people of anti-social instincts and mentality have, by cornering and controlling money, secured over the life and activities of industrialised and commercial nations.

The standard of value should be fixed beyond the possibility of being tampered with by anyone, however well-meaning and benevolent. But gold at its market value, whatever that might be, could still serve a useful purpose in stabilising international currencies and conferring upon foreign trade some of the benefits that would accrue from an internal invariable monetary unit.

A Suggestion for the Statistical Regulation of the Trade Balance

The question of foreign trade, which necessarily causes some apparently arbitrary restriction on the freedom of individuals, is a difficult one. One may trace always, in the accounts of acute commercial crises in the past, the feeling of indignation and irritation engendered by "unpatriotic" foreign speculators draining the country of its gold supply when most needed at home. Individualistic economics has never fairly met the fundamental difficulty of balancing imports and exports, when each is entirely unregulated and left to the private enterprise of individuals. If we wish to secure the maximum amount of stability and freedom of trade within our borders, it is obviously very undesirable to leave it exposed to violently intermittent competition from abroad according to the state of foreign exchanges. Questions, such as Protection *versus* Free Trade and the taxing of imports or subsidising of exports, ought by common consent to be removed altogether from the political sphere and left to statistical regulation of the same nature as that which has been proposed for the regulation of the quantity of money.

We have seen that if gold were demonetised for internal currency and used solely as a commodity for rectifying trade-balances, and stabilising the exchange, the available stock of it in the country would serve as a precise barometer of its international trade position. If these taxes were only imposed when the gold barometer showed them to be generally necessary, and to an extent that was necessary to maintain the stock of gold within definite limits, these questions might be removed from the battleground of partisan politics, and the chief objection to them, in that they create "lobbying" and corruption, would be removed. Thus a country would decide that its gold reserve should not rise above a definite maximum nor fall below a definite minimum. If it did, a tax upon exports used to encourage imports, in the first event, and a tax upon imports used to encourage exports in the second, would seem to be an impartial and statistical method of maintaining the just balance.

A National Stabilised Currency would assist, not retard, Foreign Trade

The suggestions made for nationalising and stabilising the internal currency in no way interfere with the conduct of foreign trade, or make it more onerous. It would be difficult to point to a single advantage that would be conferred upon the internal commerce and industry of a country that would not be of equal importance and benefit to its foreign trade.

Our dangerous state of dependence upon our foreign trade to provide our food supply is itself very largely due to our private banking system, and its unwillingness or inability to grant sufficiently long-period credits on the security of future production, which are a necessity to agriculture, liable in the best of circumstances to temporary set-backs through a failure of the harvest. Bad as the lack of security and the perpetual changes in the trade outlook are for industry, they are worse for the farmer, concerned as he is with essentially long period processes. Unless he can be given reasonably stable conditions it would be folly on his part to spend years of unremunerative effort in developments which in their very nature can only yield a return at some relatively distant date.

Is there a Financial Conspiracy?

It is very widely believed that there has been something akin to an actual financial conspiracy to enslave the world.[63] The Westerner is not exactly the quickest in the uptake where the elusive principle of Virtual Wealth is concerned. It has escaped the purview of the professed theoretical economists, who seem to have remained entirely oblivious of the profound changes going on under their eyes in the very nature of money. Conspiracy or not, there can be little question that the power these discoveries have put into the hands of financiers will, if not controlled, enable them in their own time and choice effectively to conquer the world.

Hitherto in this field of high finance, the semi-Oriental, cradled in the battleground between East and West, has been supreme. Before the development of science, the flood of mystical half-truths that inundated the Western world from this quarter had effectually subjugated it intellectually. The Westerner, in trying to assimilate and digest this exotic spiritual diet, entirely lost – and, indeed, counted it well lost – any intellectual independence. He was fascinated and hypnotised by the iridescent bubble of beliefs blown around the world by the Hebraic hierarchy, and even now, long after the lancet of science has pricked the bubble and let in the light, the alleged doings of the chosen people thousands of years ago is still considered an essential part of everyone's education, whatever else of human story and achievement be omitted. It would be unwise to underrate the influence of a dominant force of this magnitude over people's lives in accounting for the inversion of science, and it explains a great deal, otherwise unintelligible, about the terrible Victorian era.

But conscious conspiracy or not, and whether one race rather than another is responsible, there can be no doubt of the fact that finance has already more than half enslaved the world and few, if any, individuals, corporations, or even nations can afford to displease the monetary power. In 1916 President Woodrow Wilson said:

---

[63] Compare, for example, *Protocols of the Learned Elders of Zion*, from the Russian of Nilus, translated by V. E. Marsden, The Britons Publishing Co., 1925.

> "A great industrial nation is controlled by its system of credit. Our system of credit is concentrated. The growth of the nation, therefore, and all our activities are in the hands of a few men… We have come to be one of the worst ruled, one of the most completely controlled and dominated Governments in the civilised world – no longer a Government by free opinion, no longer a Government by conviction and the vote of the majority, but a, Government by the opinion and duress of small groups of dominant men."

We have given up the belief in physical miracles, only to be ensnared by metaphysical ones. Until the apparent miracle of Virtual Wealth is understood and mastered by those who would essay to influence the destinies of nations they will continue to be like clay in the hands of the astute financier. It is a consequence of this miracle that science has endowed ghouls and become the King-maker of Cacus, offering men the choice of freedom to be worked and preyed upon or leisure to starve in the richest age the world has ever known, and to nations armaments and conscription to destroy one another in order to create national security and securities, so that pious posterity may eternally honour their sacrifice and never cease to pay tribute to the national debt.

In this situation one distrusts the ability of the League of Nations to hold its own and bring about real peace. Their suggestion that there should be a sort of gold standard, the value of which can be made much what it is considered best by the eminent bankers and financiers advising them, is a sinister and distressing move, for it frankly hands over the real control of the world to the monetary power. The suggestions in this work, needless to say, are at the poles apart from this, which sounds like a travesty of the dream of uniting the world under a more catholic religion – a revised version of the golden calf, with a garment "not golden but gilded," and under a standard "not of gold but of gain." It would be the final step, whether a conspiracy exists or not, in the enslavement of the whole world by one central financial power.

Whereas it is obvious that national safety lies in the precisely opposite direction, in each nation understanding and controlling completely its own financial mechanism and regaining the powers so unwittingly abdicated and lightly allowed to go by default. Only then is it to be expected that it will be used to the general good and that the richest of science will be used to promote wealth rather than debt.

The Real Conspiracy

Whether or not there is a conspiracy among the "chosen people" to re-establish by gold the dominance they were wont to derive from God – and the Biblical history (Exod. XXXII) recalls a strictly parallel attempt, frustrated by the energetic action of their chief legislator – it must be admitted that it would be a revenge on science for its iconoclastic tendencies, not without a certain sardonic humour, if we wake up one day and find instead of the ten commandments a single golden rule. These are conjectural possibilities, and, no doubt, as in the time of Moses, there are still Jews and Jews. Let us hope so, at least.

But of the existence of a real conspiracy – a conspiracy of silence – on all monetary problems, in the Press and on political platforms, among editors, publishers and economists, who more than any others ought to be alive and awake to their infinite importance – there can be no question whatever. It exists, and anyone who has tried to call attention to the evils of the present system will affirm it. Mr. H. G. Wells is reported to have said:

> "To write of currency is generally recognised as an objectionable, indeed almost an indecent, practice. Editors will implore the writer almost tearfully not to write about money, not because it is an uninteresting subject, but because it has always been a profoundly disturbing one."

It was indeed a revelation to the author, accustomed to think of the battle for liberty of thought in scientific matters as having been fought and won centuries ago at the time of Galileo and the Inquisition, to find that in economics, as distinct from physics, it has not yet been won at all. If he had been a biologist no doubt he would have put the date as late as the controversy between Huxley and the bishops. On the other hand, if he had been a pure mathematician, he might have smiled at the very idea of anyone having to fight at all about, say, the truth of the propositions of Euclid.

Which is to say, that liberty of thought is an evolutionary growth rather than a sudden birth, extending in order from the affairs of the intellect to those of the soul, and only finally, if ever, to the affairs of the pocket. It was not without its humorous aspect in this connection to find in the recent condemnations in this country of the campaign against the teaching of evolutionary doctrine in certain States of the American Union certain disquieting parallels drawn between it and the precisely similar attitude of our own liberal *savants* towards psychical research, the teaching of the methods of birth control, or, as might have been cited as an instance, towards the new doctrine of Physical Economics. Liberty of thought still much depends on the circumstances.

One may sympathise with the motive for preserving a decent concealment and obscurity from the public gaze of the inner mysteries of the subject of money, whilst condemning the danger and folly of it. If economics were really a science it would not need to protect itself from criticism by a conspiracy of silence. A responsible criticism would in any scientific subject be met with instant response, and not by the ostrich policy of burying the head in the sand in the hope that that will thereby choke the ears and throw dust in the eyes of the pursuer also.

Every proposal to reform the system is always met by powerful interests pretending that the reform proposed is the old heresy of economic salvation by creating money. Precisely, then, if when practised by the Government or the private counterfeiter, it is a quack remedy, why are the banks constituted the duly qualified practitioners of such quack remedies and relieved by their office from responsibility for the ruin they cause?

It may be that our publicists are silent for the same reason as a doctor is when he hesitates to inform his patient that he is suffering from a fatal malady that baffles all scientific inquiry. What, then, can they reply to this charge, that the patient is made and kept ill by administering drugs that all know to be harmful and fatal? It may be that the danger is not to the country, except, indeed, the danger or recovery from its present impotent and drained condition, but to our public servants and officials, who, unless an amnesty were granted them, might reasonably expect to find themselves impeached, if real political government came to be re-established. Lastly, it may be, and probably is, that our professed leaders and experts in these intricate matters are in a dense fog themselves, and, not knowing what else to say, go on repeating what they were taught in their youth at college as economic science. Whatever be the reason, if this attempt to hide from the public the real facts of the existing monetary system and to suppress all public criticism and common-sense arguments in favour of its reform is continued, the already very prevalent view of the existence of a treasonable conspiracy against the State by the leaders of Finance will not lack foundation. Conscious conspiracy or not, the danger is exactly the same. A corrupt monetary system strikes at the very life of the nation.

CHAPTER XV

SUMMARY OF PRACTICAL CONCLUSIONS

It may be of assistance to the reader to collect and summarise the chief practical conclusions arrived at, as distinct from the theoretical analysis upon which they are based.

(1) The production of Wealth, as distinct from Debt, obeys the physical laws of conservation and the exact reasoning of the physical sciences can be applied. Wealth cannot be produced without expenditure, and a continuous supply of wealth cannot be supplied as the result of any expenditure once for all, for it is a form of energy, or the product of its expenditure under intelligent direction. Its production demands a continuous supply of fresh energy and continuous human diligence, nowadays, rather than physical labour. The scale on which it can be produced is practically limited only by the state of technical knowledge of the time. There is no longer any valid physical justification for the continuance of poverty. The phenomenon of unemployment and destitution at one and the same time to-day is solely due to ignorance of the nature of wealth and the principles of economics, and to the confusions between wealth and debt which have hitherto bemused that subject, even among those who have essayed its scientific investigation and elucidation.

(2) There are two distinct categories of wealth which owe their value to the opposite qualities of perishability and permanence. Both are alike in the manner of their production. But in the formation of the first category of perishable wealth the energy required is stored up for use later by life when the wealth is consumed. It includes food, fuel, explosives, fertilisers and all materials the usefulness of which depends upon the change they suffer in use. They can only be used once, and they usually function as the energisers and actual supporters of life.

In the second category of permanent wealth the energy required to produce it is not stored in the product – or, if it is, it acts detrimentally to durability in use – but has already gone to waste in the process. It enables and facilitates life, but does not empower it. It saves further expenditure of life-time to an indefinite extent, but does not support life. The category includes all classes of permanent possessions, of all degrees of actual durability, but distinguished from the first category by the fact that their destruction is incidental to and not the reason for their usefulness, and is a dead loss. This category includes the whole of capital in the sense used in this book, namely, organs of production used in production.

(3) Capital, by saving to an indefinite extent the expenditure of human time in production, appears to afford a continuous revenue of wealth without further work, but the origin of the wealth produced is in the continued use of capital by human agents, not in the capital itself. There is no ethical principle to which to appeal, in order to equate the time spent in the accumulation against the continuous expenditure necessary to make it productive, or to determine the just division of the wealth produced as between the capitalist and the worker.

(4) Money is now a form of national debt, owned by the individual and owed by the community, exchangeable on demand for wealth by transference to another individual. Its value or purchasing power is not directly determined by any positive or existing quantity of wealth, but by the negative quantity, or deficit of wealth, the ownership and enjoyment of which is voluntarily abstained from without the payment of interest, by the owners of the money, to suit their individual business and domestic affairs and convenience. The aggregate of this deficit is called the Virtual Wealth of the community, and it measures the value of all the money owned by the community, which is forced by the necessity of exchanging its produce to act as though it possessed this amount of wealth more than it actually does possess. The Virtual Wealth of a community is not a physical but an imaginary negative wealth quantity. It does not obey the laws of conservation, but is of psychological origin. It increases with the number of the population and the national income and varies over long periods of time with the habits of the people and the way they conduct their business and domestic monetary affairs. It is only when the Virtual Wealth is constant that the general level of prices is directly, and the purchasing power of money inversely, proportional to the quantity of money in circulation.

(5) Banks create and destroy money arbitrarily and with no understanding of the laws that correlate its quantity with the national income. They have been allowed to regard themselves as the owners of the virtual wealth which the community does *not* possess, and to lend it and charge interest upon the loan as though it really existed and they possessed it. The wealth so acquired by the impecunious borrower is not given up by the lenders, who receive interest on the loan but give up nothing, but is given up by the whole community, who suffer in consequence the loss through a general reduction in the purchasing power of money.

(6) The banks have usurped the Prerogative of the Crown with regard to the issue of money, and corrupted the purpose of money from that of an exchange medium to that of an interest-bearing debt, but the real evil is that we now have a concertina instead of a currency. These powers have fallen to them in consequence of the invention and development of the cheque system, unforeseen before it became an established fact. It has been connived at by politicians of all parties, who have betrayed the people and without their knowledge or consent have abdicated the most important function of government and ceased to be the *de facto* rulers of the nation. The issue and withdrawal of money should be restored to the nation for the general good and should entirely cease from providing a source of livelihood to private corporations. Money should not bear interest because of its existence, but only when genuinely lent by an owner who gives it up to the borrower.

(7) The value of money should not depend on the quantity of a single commodity, such as gold, and the standard of value should have reference to the general average of goods consumed and used in living. That is to say, the index number of general price-level, or its reciprocal, the purchasing power of money, should be maintained constant by regulating the total quantity of money in circulation.

The index number should be continuously ascertained by a national statistical authority who would report its findings to the national authority charged with the issue of money, so that the issue may be regulated to maintain the standard of value constant, much as the National Physical Laboratory in this country is charged with the standardisation of weights and measures.

(8) When the quantity of money is constant, its value or purchasing power is proportional to the Virtual Wealth, and when its value or purchasing power is constant, the quantity of money is a measure of the Virtual Wealth. The issue of money should therefore be regulated by its purchasing power, so as to maintain the purchasing power constant, more being issued if the purchasing power tends to rise, or the index number to fall, and some withdrawn from circulation if the purchasing power tends to fall and the general price-level to rise, very much as the speed of a steam engine under varying load is automatically controlled by steam being admitted by the governor when the speed tends to fall, and shut off when it tends to rise.

The money issued should defray national expenditure in lieu of taxation, or redeem interest-bearing National Debt. The withdrawal and destruction of money should be by taxation or by raising a National loan.

(9) It is recognised that the invariable standard of value proposed is a debtor-creditor standard to facilitate long-term business engagements and remove the speculative element introduced into them by change in the value of money. But in an era of increasing human efficiency in wealth production a debtor-creditor standard of price is not necessarily a "just" price. But no social progress can be secure until the purchasing power of money is made invariable.

(10) To initiate the system some £2,000,000,000 of National interest-bearing Debt should be cancelled and the same sum of national money (non-interest-bearing National Debt) issued to replace the credit created by the banks. The taxpayer would thereby be relieved of the payment of £100,000,000 a year interest on purely fictitious loans. This annual interest is a payment by the taxpayer to bondholders for money lent to the State, and it is transferred under the existing system to the banks for their services in creating new money as bank credit and conferring it on bondholders against their bonds as collateral security. The taxes are thus paid to the bank for doing what the taxes were imposed to prevent being done, namely, the increase of the currency. Otherwise there would have been no reason for the State to borrow at interest if it had not wished to prevent the increase of the currency.

(11) The banks should by law be required to keep national money, £ for £ of their liabilities for customers' "deposits" in current account, and only be permitted to lend money genuinely deposited into their keeping by its owners, who give up the use of it for the stipulated period of the loan and receive receipts in legal form subject to stamp duties on a scale designed to make it relatively unprofitable to lend for finicking periods.

(12) The failure of the nations to use to the full, for the enrichment of life, the ample powers conferred upon them by the progress of scientific and technical knowledge is traced primarily to the private issue of money and the mistaken principles which govern it. Credits should be issued, not cancelled (that is, the money in circulation should be increased not decreased), when supplies outrun demand.

Genuine abstinence from consumption, or "saving," is the essential antecedent to any increase of money in circulation if the price-level is not to be raised.

(13) To raise any productive system from one scale of production to a higher scale without causing a change of price-level, and so to absorb unemployed labour and capital, demands an initial abstinence from consumption equal to the increased stocks of semi-manufactured and finished wealth in the system, followed by an issue of money of lesser amount proportional to, but normally less than, the value of the additional finished stocks. In practice the issue would be determined by the price-level as indicator, with the returns of unemployment and the condition of industry as guiding indications.

(14) If the issue of money precedes abstinence the stocks of finished wealth in the system are permanently depleted and cannot be restored. This raises prices and tends after a short period to reduce employment and production even below the original level, at a monetary valuation inflated in proportion to the increase of money.

The rise of prices drains the gold out of the country, so that credits are curtailed again and industrialists have to reduce production.

(15) If the abstinence is not followed by increase in the quantity of money the additional stocks accumulated cannot be sold without reducing production, and, in consequence, the employment of labour and capital to an extent as much below the original level as the original abstinence temporarily increased it above that level. A criticism in the light of these conclusions is offered of the aims and proposals of the Douglas school of Social Credit Reform.

(16) The building up of any industrial system, and, in general, the accumulation of permanent capital, involves liability for debts to individuals which can never be repaid, and must therefore bear interest until written off or redeemed. In an individualistic society, if the citizens are not to be reduced to helots under this increasing burden of capital indebtedness, taxation should be extended beyond the purpose of defraying Government expenditure to provide for the redemption of capital. The mathematical laws for the simple and compound redemption of capital debts are worked out. In this way the nation would come in on the ground-floor and not after industries cease to pay, as with current nationalisation proposals.

(17) Taxation, as hitherto confined to the purpose of defraying Government expenditure, is entirely futile as an instrument of permanent social amelioration, and should be used in conjunction with, or alternatively to, the issue of Government loans, for other specific purposes, such as the building up of a greater volume of production, the reconstruction of agriculture, the preservation of the due ratio between production for consumption and new capital production, and, in general, for more actively influencing the proper development of the country, on the information supplied by the national statistical authority.

(18) A national currency based on index number and the intelligent expansion of the industrial system to its full working capacity would promote foreign trade equally with home trade, and better enable the nation to obtain by import the food it needs in exchange for exports.

(19) It is suggested that the use of gold as a commodity for international transactions, to adjust the balance of trade between nations, should be extended.

The League of Nations should undertake, for the nations it includes, the determination of the proportion of the total stock of gold which each nation is to keep as a reserve, rather than attempt to set up a fraudulent gold standard, the value of which can be made to suit the purpose of a few powerful Central Banks by a policy of hastening or retarding its demonetisation at their will.

(20) Whilst primarily intended to remove the menace to international relations arising from the immense accumulations of redundant gold, and to permit of its complete demonetisation safely by any country desirous of adopting an invariable standard of value based on index number, the use of gold as national reserves would serve a valuable purpose in stabilising international price-level and damping out violent fluctuation of the foreign exchanges due to temporary alternations in the balance of trade. But it is not proposed to fix or "peg" these, but to let them find their own level according to the standards of value and systems of currency adopted in the various countries.

(21) The national reserve of gold, acting as a barometer indicating the ratio of imports to exports, should be maintained by suitable means between defined limits of variation. As a possible mean, it is suggested that, on information supplied by the national statistical authority, imports could be checked by duties and exports encouraged by bounties if the barometer fell, and vice versa if it rose.

(22) It is claimed that these suggested reforms, whilst they do not entirely meet the deeper economic causes of social unrest, are necessary steps if an individualistic society is to continue and the nation in the future is to be in a position to deal with a further displacement of men by machinery and the methods of mass production, and to distribute monetary titles to consume in proportion to the quantity of wealth capable of being produced, rather than to the number of workers employed in production.

Conclusion

The stinging-nettle of economics, boldly grasped, need no longer obstruct the path of the social reformer who would give peace and economic freedom to the world. Its power to sting resides only in silly confusions which the world has outgrown, and which, in a scientific and mechanical age, even a bright child might be trusted to see through. Never again should there be any fear of disinterested disagreement as to the nature and the solution of the paradox of poverty and riches.

These old confusions eradicated, from being a subject like astrology or alchemy, economics will become a science. Already the separation of its subject-matter into the physical – *wealth* – and the psychological – *debt* – brings with it the most astonishing simplification. There will, of course, be plenty of people who will argue that the psychological is as important as the physical. But few will have the hardihood to claim that the understanding of the psychological side can offset crude initial physical misconceptions between wealth and debt and the vulgar perpetual motion fallacy of the older economists. Such errors would have precisely the effect they have already produced in a world administered by and made up of supermen and angels.

Democracy so far has but seized the shadow and has yet to grasp the substance of sovereignty or be discredited for all time. Its first step must be to end the conspiracy of silence in its organs of publicity and instruction concerning the one prerogative of government which underlies and controls all effective political action, and to insist upon its monetary system being as public and open to criticism and conscious alteration as its political system.

With adequate knowledge of the physical realities that dominate the economic affairs of peoples, the road is clear for unlimited progress and the attainment of universal peace and prosperity. The evils that in the past have paralysed the very heart of nations lie patent and beyond concealment. So they pass beyond the power of further harm. Only that rarest kind of courage – intellectual fearlessness and honesty to face things as they are and not as they appear – is required to abolish poverty and economic degradation from our midst in less time than the War took to run its course. Whilst on the international horizon there dawns the hope that a rational solution may be found to the problem of modern war, and a better use be made of the prodigal gift of science than to destroy the surplus wealth and population in lighting for markets and the increase of national debts.

Were all the most powerful vested interests in the world solid and interlinked against the cause of humanity and freedom, were money, the lust of power and the distilled essence of all the superstitions that have ever swayed the minds of men, arrayed against the growth of knowledge, who need doubt the ultimate issue? The road is open for all men and women of good-will to drive onwards to their goal.

In the eight years that have elapsed since Peace, the clouds of darkness have again descended, and already people know in their hearts that it is only a matter of time before another war will come, greater and more terrible than the last in proportion as it is delayed. Not an iota of the fundamental economic causes which produced the last has been altered. The peace has abundantly sown the seeds of future inevitable national conflict. The vast potential productivity of the industrialised world, particularly in the engineering and chemical industries, must find an outlet. If that outlet is by financial folly denied it in the building up and reconstruction of the home-life of nations, it remains as a direct and powerful incentive to the fomenting of war.

If anyone doubts, let them visit, for example, a modern steel works – of which there are many in this country, each alone, it is estimated, capable of supplying the total national requirements in our present impoverished state. Even if he chanced on a day when the plant was in full operation, he would see only a man here and there doing almost nothing to speak of, where, only a generation ago, the place would have been alive with an army of almost naked workmen rushing about and shepherding the moving flow of incandescent steel. A few 15,000-h.p. motors, worked with the sunshine of the summers of the palæozoic era, have emancipated the human worker to leisure in the streets, to live on the dole and rear his family so against the day when the nation shall need them all again, and war, the consumer, shall turn all this potential wealth into national debt. Yet we affect to be shocked by the customs of the ancients, who exposed their superfluous young naked to the rigours of the winter's night, or sacrificed them with music and religious fervour on the altars of Moloch and Mammon.

The searchlight of the exact sciences can reach even into such dark and secret recesses of the human soul. From the dawn of civilisation the deep inborn herd-instinct towards the amassing of "wealth" has been in conflict with the physical impossibility of doing so. So arises "the principle of death," which Trotter[64] has recognised as embodied in the very structure and substance of all human constructive social effort. As with earlier civilisations, so, it would appear, with ours – it has swung laboriously up to its meaningless apogee only to lapse again into darkness, fated, like them, possibly, to leave no trace in human memory, or but the faint and dubious whisper of tradition.

The wheels of God grind small, but they grind exceeding slow. O future! we the dying salute thee! The course is set, the race is nearly run. Time, the destroyer, is on our heels. Our Youth is spent, and old and feeble are the puppet hands gold chooses to direct our destiny. Give us back, O powers of the light! but one more hour before the pendulum of night descends again. The lamp is lit, but its beam needs time to grow

64 *Instincts of the Herd in Peace and War*, W. Trotter, 1919, p. 241, "The Instability of Civilisation."

ere those to come can hope to grope their way. Slow down the sunset and upspeed the dawn, lest youth resurgent should arrive too late.

ON THE RECENT MASSACRE,

(After Milton.)

Avenge, O Lord, thy slaughtered sons, the Old
World shambles richening with their scattered bones;
Ev'n them who kept thy truth, the scoffer owns,
When all our fathers worshipped gods of gold.
The generous quest of youth and science sold,
The surplus changed for ever-bearing loans,
The wreck-strewn shores and devastated zones
Of war forget not; resurrect their mould.
The flower the fire has mown, the roots decay,
The dust and ashes of the harvest sow
In every cot and croft where still doth sway
The money tyrant, that from these may grow
A hundred-fold, who having learned thy way
Early may fly the Babylonian woe.

F. S.

Other titles

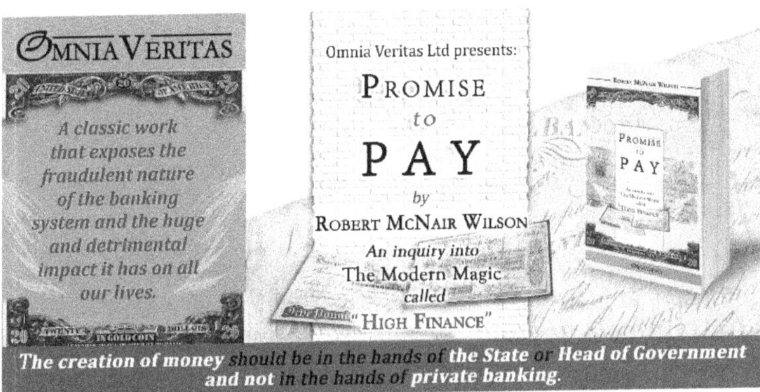

OMNIA VERITAS
"There was a class of persons who very well understood each other's interests, who very likely were related by racial and religious custom, and whose supra-nationalism transcended all city boundaries and borders of states."
Omnia Veritas Ltd presents:
The Babylonian Woe
by
DAVID ASTLE
"Yesterday it was a conspiracy against the men of a city, or a relatively small state; today a conspiracy against the whole world."
The Babylonian Woe
David Astle's masterpiece in a brand new edition!

OMNIA VERITAS
Omnia Veritas Ltd presents:
MYRON FAGAN
THE ILLUMINATI
AND THE
COUNCIL ON FOREIGN RELATIONS
The objective is to brainwash the people into accepting the phony peace bait to transform the United States into an enslaved unit of the United Nations' one-world government.
They have seized that power on orders from their masters of the great conspiracy

OMNIA VERITAS
A free press is the guardian genius of a just, honest, and humane democracy, as Lincoln put it:
"To sin by silence when they know they should protest, makes cowards of men."
Omnia Veritas Ltd presents:
THE LEGALIZED CRIME OF BANKING
by
SILAS WALTER ADAMS
"There is a great deal of difference between a moral wrong and a legal right"
A liberating and much acclaimed book on the Federal Reserve system!

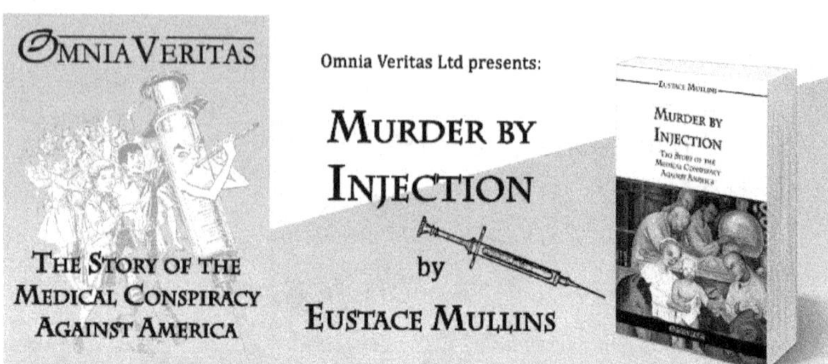
OMNIA VERITAS
Omnia Veritas Ltd presents:
MURDER BY INJECTION
by
EUSTACE MULLINS
THE STORY OF THE MEDICAL CONSPIRACY AGAINST AMERICA
MURDER BY INJECTION
The cynicism and malice of these conspirators is something beyond the imagination of most Americans.

OMNIA VERITAS
OMNIA VERITAS LTD PRESENTS:
MY LIFE IN CHRIST
BY
EUSTACE MULLINS
Christ did not wish to be followed by robots and sleepwalkers, He desired man to awaken, and to attain the full use of his earthly powers.
MY LIFE IN CHRIST
THIS is the story of my life in Christ

OMNIA VERITAS
Omnia Veritas Ltd presents:
NEW HISTORY OF THE JEWS
by
EUSTACE MULLINS
Throughout the history of civilization, one particular problem of mankind has remained constant.
NEW HISTORY OF THE JEWS
Only one people bas irritated its host nations in every part of the civilized world

OMNIA VERITAS
Omnia Veritas Ltd presents:
THE CURSE OF CANAAN
A demonology of history
by
EUSTACE MULLINS
Liberalism, more popularly known as secular humanism, can be traced in an unbroken line all the way back to the Biblical "Curse of Canaan."
Humanism is the logical result of the demonology of history

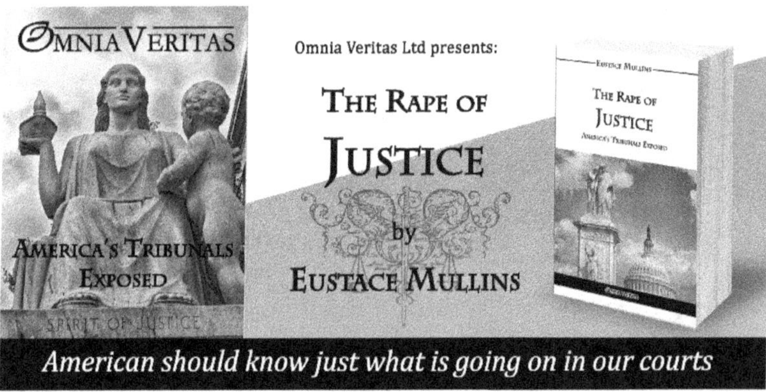
OMNIA VERITAS
Omnia Veritas Ltd presents:
THE RAPE OF JUSTICE
by
EUSTACE MULLINS
AMERICA'S TRIBUNALS EXPOSED
American should know just what is going on in our courts

OMNIA VERITAS
Omnia Veritas Ltd presents:
THE SECRETS OF THE FEDERAL RESERVE
by
EUSTACE MULLINS
UNITED STATES FEDERAL RESERVE SYSTEM
HERE ARE THE SIMPLE FACTS OF THE GREAT BETRAYAL
Will we continue to be enslaved by the Babylonian debt money system?

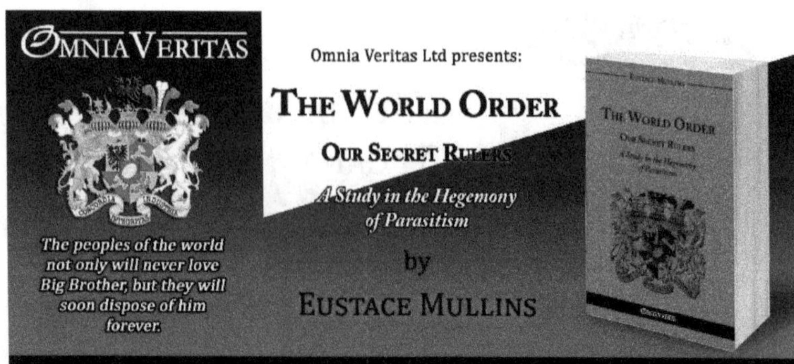
OMNIA VERITAS
Omnia Veritas Ltd presents:
THE WORLD ORDER
OUR SECRET RULERS
A Study in the Hegemony of Parasitism
by
EUSTACE MULLINS
The peoples of the world not only will never love Big Brother, but they will soon dispose of him forever.
The program of the World Order remains the same; Divide and Conquer

OMNIA VERITAS
Historians are finding less and less to celebrate about the Revolution...
Omnia Veritas Ltd presents:
THE FRENCH Revolution
A Study in Democracy
by
NESTA WEBSTER
An account of the bloody terror, the mob violence, and the overthrow of French religious tradition...
Hard political and historical facts compiled in this essential classic!

OMNIA VERITAS
"If we do not restore the Institution of Property we cannot escape restoring the Institution of Slavery; there is no third course."
Omnia Veritas Ltd presents:
The Servile State
by
HILAIRE BELLOC
Surprisingly compelling and enlightening, an indispensable of any serious economic study
Hilaire Belloc's classic in a new edition!

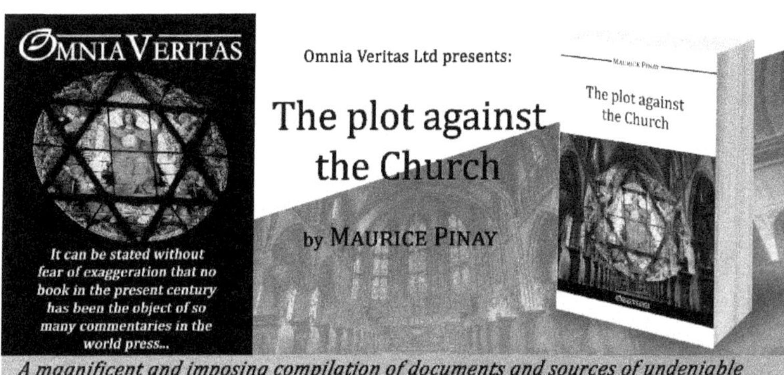
OMNIA VERITAS
Omnia Veritas Ltd presents:
The plot against the Church
by MAURICE PINAY
It can be stated without fear of exaggeration that no book in the present century has been the object of so many commentaries in the world press...
The plot against the Church
A magnificent and imposing compilation of documents and sources of undeniable importance and authenticity

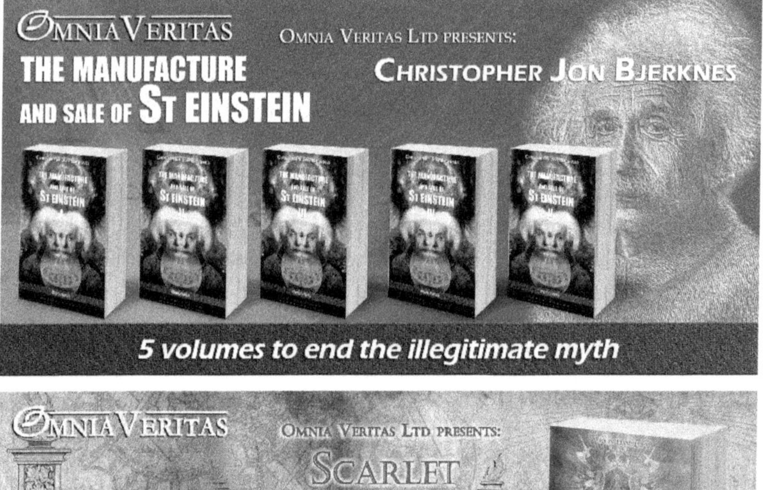
OMNIA VERITAS
OMNIA VERITAS LTD PRESENTS:
THE MANUFACTURE AND SALE OF ST EINSTEIN
CHRISTOPHER JON BJERKNES
5 volumes to end the illegitimate myth

OMNIA VERITAS
OMNIA VERITAS LTD PRESENTS:
SCARLET AND THE BEAST
My research has revealed that there are two separate and opposing powers in Freemasonry.
A HISTORY OF THE WAR BETWEEN ENGLISH AND FRENCH FREEMASONRY
One is Scarlet. The other, the Beast.

www.ingramcontent.com/pod-product-compliance
Lightning Source LLC
LaVergne TN
LVHW010052110826
845155LV00028B/307

* 9 7 8 1 9 1 3 8 9 0 5 3 7 *